CULTURAL LIFE IN NASHVILLE
1825-1860

THE OLD CAPITOL AT NASHVILLE
In 1854 this classical building, designed by the architect William Strickland, was symbolic of Nashville's maturing culture.

CULTURAL LIFE

in

NASHVILLE

on the Eve of the

Civil War

By F. GARVIN DAVENPORT
Professor of History, Transylvania College

Chapel Hill

THE UNIVERSITY OF NORTH CAROLINA PRESS

1941

COPYRIGHT, 1941, BY
THE UNIVERSITY OF NORTH CAROLINA PRESS

PRINTED IN THE UNITED STATES OF AMERICA BY THE SEEMAN PRINTERY,
DURHAM, N. C., AND BOUND BY L. H. JENKINS, INC., RICHMOND, VA.

To My Mother

PREFACE

THIS BRIEF STUDY does not pretend to be a complete social history of Nashville in the ante-bellum period. The word "culture" has been interpreted to mean intellectual and aesthetic attainment and this definition automatically restricted the author's subject. While the lower classes are not emphasized, the forces growing out of the general social background are given considerable attention in so far as they affect Nashville's march from a semi-frontier condition to a comparatively mature cultural status in 1860.

Educational institutions are always of fundamental importance in any culture. Consequently, the author has devoted much of his work to a study of Nashville schools and colleges. Special attention has been given to medical science because it had peculiar social and political connotations in addition to its more normal significance. Since Nashville was an important religious center a chapter has been devoted to religious leaders. Dramatics, opera, music, and minstrels have been given appropriate emphasis. A chapter on literary interests and literary contributions has been included. Finally, in the chapter entitled "Nashville Street Scenes," the author has attempted to present a bird's-eye view of the city and to bring out in relief the more important examples of architecture.

ACKNOWLEDGMENTS

The author is deeply indebted to a number of people who have given valuable assistance during the preparation of this study. My first debt is to Professor Frank Owsley of Vanderbilt University who directed the study as a whole. Without his encouragement it probably would not have been finished. Professor William C. Binkley of Vanderbilt has been very generous with suggestions and constructive criticisms and I wish to thank him, too, for his careful reading of the manuscript.

Many others have coöperated with me. I am especially grateful to Professor Randall Stewart of Brown University who contributed many valuable ideas which have been incorporated in the text and to the late Professor Marcus L. Hansen of the University of Illinois who frequently took time out from his own busy research schedule to give me some sound advice. Mrs. Frank Owsley gave me assistance on numerous occasions and I wish to thank her especially for making the Vanderbilt microfilm library and apparatus available for me. My former colleague at Transylvania, Dr. Blanche Henry Clark, now Dean of Women at Vanderbilt, gave me the benefit of her good judgment on several occasions. Mr. Porter Oakes of the *Nashville Banner* turned over valuable clues and important information, and Mrs. Brainard Cheney of Vanderbilt University Library was resourceful and helpful in a thousand different ways.

I wish to thank the following people for their services and coöperation: Mrs. Ruth Duncan and Miss Guyton Teague of the Peabody College Library; Mrs. John Trootwood Moore of the Tennessee State Library; Mrs. Marcell Workman and Mr. M. V. Lewis of the Nashville Carnegie Library; Mrs. Charles Norton and Miss Roemel Henry of Transylvania College Library; Dr. J. E. Windrow and Professor A. L. Crabb of Peabody College;

President Raymond F. McLain of Transylvania College; and my wife, Katye Lou Davenport, who assisted with the proofreading.

Finally, I wish to express my indebtedness to the following institutions: The Library of Congress, Library of the University of Texas, the Free Library of Philadelphia, Library of the Methodist Publishing House (Nashville), Library of the Tennessee State Historical Society, The American Baptist Historical Society, The Filson Club, the New Orleans Public Library, and the University of Kentucky Library. I wish to thank the Free Library of Philadelphia in particular for its photostatic service.

   Lexington, Ky.   F. G. D.
   February 26, 1941.

TABLE OF CONTENTS

CHAPTER	PAGE
Preface	vii
Acknowledgments	ix
I. Culture Versus Frontier, 1825-1850	1
II. Educational Opportunities, 1850-1860	32
III. Nashville Physicians and Medical Science	56
IV. Religious Leaders in Pulpit and Press	84
V. The Nashville Theater: Drama and Opera, 1850-1860	117
VI. The Nashville Theater: Concerts and Minstrels, 1850-1860	145
VII. Amateur Amusements: Benefits and Balls	160
VIII. Pens and Printers' Ink, 1850-1860	169
IX. Nashville Street Scenes, 1850-1860	199
Bibliography	211
Index	225

CULTURAL LIFE IN NASHVILLE
1825-1860

CHAPTER I

CULTURE VERSUS FRONTIER
1825-1850

IN 1850 NASHVILLE was on the threshold of a decade of accomplishment. Everywhere there were signs indicative of energy, of improvement, of progress. New homes, new hotels, new public buildings graced the streets. The new theater was completed and opened to the patrons of the dramatic art. For the first time in its history the city was organizing a public school system and plans were being made to construct new buildings to take the place of the dilapidated structure which housed the University of Nashville. After several postponements and false starts, a medical school was being organized as a department of the university. The private schools of the city were eager to serve all those who would grant them patronage, and the time-honored Nashville Female Academy was described as being in a "flourishing condition."

The botanical gardens of the Nashville Horticultural Society were manifestations of general public interest in scientific progress. The gardens were stocked with choice fruit trees and the greenhouses contained numerous specimens of plants and flowers. The arrangement of shrubs, evergreens, and winding walks converted the grounds into an attractive park. Rustic seats and the gardener's Elizabethan cottage created an air of hospitality and romance that was not overlooked by the younger set.[1]

The city was well supplied with newspapers and since 1848 had been receiving news by telegraph over a line that connected Nashville with Louisville and the eastern seaboard.[2] Various weekly and monthly journals, some with a subscription list of

[1] *The Naturalist and Journal of Natural History, Agriculture, Education and Literature* (Nashville, 1846-1850), I (1846), 85-86.

[2] Nashville *Republican Banner*, March 6, 1848; *Southern Business Directory and General Commercial Advertiser*, I (Charleston, 1854), 53; Thomas Lou Nichols, M.D., *Forty Years of American Life, 1821-1861* (New York, 1937), 198.

ten or twelve thousand, were sent from Nashville's publishing houses to the people of Tennessee and the Southwest. The new capitol building was a symbol of Nashville's political importance in the state. The fact that Nashville was chosen as the meeting place of the States' Rights Convention in 1850 was indicative of the city's importance in the South and the Southwest.

And yet in 1850 Nashville was still a semi-rural city which harbored much that was reminiscent of the frontier tradition.[3] The spirit of the times engendered much unwarrantable pretension. The tendency to boast and to exaggerate was characteristic of nineteenth-century America in general, but it was peculiarly characteristic of the West. It was inevitable that Nashville, born of the wilderness and nurtured in infancy and adolescence by pioneers and the sons of pioneers, should receive as part of its inheritance a certain amount of frontier philosophy and frontier psychology. From time to time in the past, the frontier spirit, in various manifestations, had been a hindrance to educational and cultural progress in Tennessee. But in spite of the slow and hesitating cultural development of Nashville before 1850, in the last decade of the ante-bellum period it seems that the city was favorably known wherever literature and science were cultivated.

This fame was not due to the achievements of the fifties alone. The foundation for this intellectual development had been laid in the preceding decades, and it was due in no small degree to the ideals and the labors of the educator, Philip Lindsley (1786-1855), and the scientist, Gerard Troost (1776-1850). These two men, the former the president of the University of Nashville from 1824 to 1850, and the latter professor of chemistry and mineralogy at the same institution from 1827 to 1850, and state geologist from 1832 to 1850, drew the attention of the educational and scientific world to Tennessee and to Nashville. A few years after the death of both Lindsley and Troost, Dr. W. K. Bowling, a prominent

[3] The population of Nashville in 1850 was 10,165. There were 2,028 slaves and 511 free colored people. South Nashville had a population of 1,353, of which 313 were slaves and 16 free colored. The population of Memphis was 8,841, of Knoxville, 2,076, of Murfreesboro, 1,917. *Seventh Census of the United States* (Washington, 1853), 575.

Nashville physician, asserted that "The great Lindsley and Troost ... in making this seat of learning immortal, left the impress of their own mighty intellects upon their generation and coming posterity will feel and respond to its awakening influence."[4] This is unstinted and perhaps exaggerated praise, but the quotation emphasizes the point that Nashvillians in the fifties recognized their debt to Lindsley and Troost who had, without question, made worth-while contributions to Nashville's cultural life.

Philip Lindsley, the son of Isaac and Phebe Lindsley, was born near Morristown, New Jersey, on December 21, 1786. It seems that he received most of his primary education at home, although he was in sporadic attendance at boarding schools and a grammar school at New Vernon. In later life he admitted that his mother was incomparably his best teacher. Young Lindsley did not have to be coaxed to study. Although he showed a healthy interest in youthful sports, such activities never interfered with his reading or with his lessons. It was not unusual for him to ride ten miles on horseback to borrow books of history or biography. As his parents were strongly attached to Presbyterianism, it was only natural that the Bible and other religious literature found a prominent place in his education. He knew the Lord's Prayer before he could read, and he was well acquainted with the Bible before he was twelve.[5]

In 1799 Lindsley entered Robert Finley's new academy at Basking Ridge, New Jersey. This academy became known as one of the best in the country and it is quite evident that Finley made a deep and lasting impression on Philip Lindsley, who regarded him in later years as a model educator.[6]

Lindsley left Finley's school in 1802 and entered the College of New Jersey (later Princeton) as a junior and graduated with

[4] *The Nashville Journal of Medicine and Surgery* (Nashville, 1851-1861), XI (1856), 167.
[5] L. J. Halsey (ed.), *The Works of Philip Lindsley, D.D.*, 3 vols. (Philadelphia, 1866), I, 12-15; III, 10-27.
[6] *Ibid.*, III, 12; IV, 14; William B. Sprague (ed.), *Annals of the American Pulpit; or Commemorative Notices of Distinguished American Clergymen of Various Denominations*, 8 vols. (New York, 1857-1869), IV, 465-466.

the A.B. degree in 1804. After teaching in James Stevenson's academy at Morristown and in Finley's school at Basking Ridge, he returned to Princeton in 1807 and received the A.M. degree in September of that year. The president of the college, Samuel Stanhope Smith (1750-1819), who admired Lindsley, persuaded him to remain at the college as junior tutor of Greek and Latin and to study theology. For the next seventeen years he was closely connected with Princeton.[7]

The period of Lindsley's residence at Princeton, from his acceptance of the tutorship in 1807 to his resignation and removal to Nashville in 1824, was important in relation to his subsequent career as an educator. In 1810 he was licensed to preach by the Presbytery of New Brunswick. In 1812 he was promoted to a senior tutorship at Princeton and the next year he became professor of languages. He was also college librarian during most of this seventeen-year period, a position for which he was well adapted because of his love for books. In 1817 he was ordained by the Presbytery of New Brunswick and in the same year he was elected vice-president of the college. From 1822 to 1823 he was acting president and could have been president had he so desired. This honor, however, he declined, as he did similar offers from Transylvania University, Ohio University, and at first, Cumberland College.[8]

Why did he finally yield to the importunities of Cumberland College? Probably because he saw possibilities in the Southwest which were not disclosed to less farsighted men. Probably, too, because the educational needs of the Southwest challenged his ambitions and his ingenuity. Be that as it may, Lindsley visited Nashville in 1824, and when he returned to Princeton he had made his decision. He was ready to cast his lot with the struggling institution beyond the mountains. While still at Princeton

[7] *Idem.*
[8] Halsey (ed.), *Works of Philip Lindsley*, III, 16; I, 12-13; Philip Lindsley to Rev. William B. Sprague, Nashville, February 2, 1848 (MS in Peabody College Library). Transylvania University offered Lindsley $1,800 a year and $300 "to aid him in his removal to Kentucky." Minutes of the Board of Trustees of Transylvania University, April 18, 1817 (MS in Transylvania College Library).

(July, 1824), he began his duties as president of Cumberland College by issuing an appeal for funds to help relieve the financial embarrassment of the western college. But although his plea was eloquent and his reasoning sound, the fact that Cumberland College was "to be a Christian, but not a sectarian institution" made it impossible for him to appeal directly to the supporters of any one church. Consequently, the donations were disappointing.[9]

It was the day before Christmas, 1824, when Philip Lindsley, together with his family, arrived in Nashville. There was a sharp contrast between this immature village on the Cumberland and the Princeton environment to which the Lindsleys were accustomed. Even so, this town of the Southwest which was to be their new home, in spite of its primitive aspects, must have appeared as a veritable oasis to the travelers after their tortuous journey over the mountains.

In spite of the crudities, or perhaps because of them, Nashville in the twenties was a picturesque town and the natural beauty of its setting perhaps compensated in part for the material and cultural refinements which it lacked. In 1823—and in all probability the scene had changed little by 1825—there were only about five hundred buildings in the town. Less than a dozen boasted a third floor, and even some of the larger two-story dwellings were constructed of logs. There were at least seventy-three log houses within the corporate limits and on the college grounds, which at that time were outside the town limits.[10]

Exactly how Lindsley reacted to this new environment is difficult to say. Being a newcomer to Nashville, he was probably diplomatic enough to refrain from stating openly his opinions of the town and of Tennessee. However, within a few years he published in the Nashville papers anonymous essays which reflected in an exaggerated and humorous manner the true thoughts in his mind.

Over the pseudonym "An Old Field Pedagogue" Lindsley de-

[9] *Nashville Whig*, February 21, 1825; Halsey (ed.), *Works of Philip Lindsley*, I, 88.
[10] *Nashville Whig*, February 21, 1825; Nashville in 1823 (MS in Tennessee Historical Society Collection).

clared that nothing in Tennessee ever reached perfection. There were no good fruits or garden vegetables and meat of high quality was scarce. The same was true of fish, butter, cheese, and pumpkin pies. In general there was "nothing but cotton, tobacco, corn, whiskey, Negroes and swine, and these not worth the growing."[11] Obviously, Lindsley was not too well pleased with Tennessee food products. Continuing in this satirical mood, he declared that everything "degenerates in Tennessee. Doctors are made by guess . . . lawyers by magic . . . parsons by inspiration . . . legislators by grog . . . merchants by Mammon . . . farmers by necessity . . . editors and schoolmasters by St. Nicholas. . . ."[12]

Lindsley found the population of Nashville and Tennessee mobile and restless. This was characteristic of frontier and semi-frontier regions, and Tennessee was no exception. Nashville was subjected, probably more or less willingly, to the charlatanry and knavery of migratory entertainers. Jugglers, animal trainers, rope-walkers, fiddlers, fire-eaters, lecturers, to say nothing of panaceists of all types, visited Nashville, fooled the people and with what cash they were able to obtain left town as quickly as possible.[13]

Beggars, false and bona fide, were seen frequently on the streets and it was not unusual for them to stop at the homes of the well-to-do citizens to ask for work or to beg for alms. The false beggars were the greatest nuisance. These men posed as alienated or orphaned Turks, Russians, Germans, Italians, or Spaniards, and they carried duly certified papers telling their tale of woe. Within a period of three years Lindsley was visited by two hundred and fifty-nine "shipwrecked Germans, Spaniards, and Portuguese" and other beggars of all sorts.[14] These characters indicated by signs that they could not speak English and inevitably presented forged credentials in English which spoke

[11] Halsey (ed.), *Works of Philip Lindsley*, III, 629.
[12] *Idem.*
[13] *Ibid.*, 630; *National Banner and Nashville Whig*, May 25, 1831; *National Banner and Nashville Daily Advertiser*, May 7, 1833.
[14] Halsey (ed.), *Works of Philip Lindsley*, III, 611.

and lied for them. Some beggars were content to be American citizens, especially if they had fought in the War of 1812 or in some Indian rebellion. Lindsley was impressed by two crippled soldiers who paid him a visit. According to their story, they had fought with Jackson at New Orleans and "had been dying ever since."[15]

Lindsley discovered that some of the habits of the western gentlemen were as crude as those of beggars. The common practice of spitting tobacco juice over the floor was offensive to him. "The habit of spitting acquired and rendered unavoidable by the practice of chewing tobacco," he declared, "is so offensive to all well-bred people as to exact some surprise that *gentlemen* should continue it."[16] Nashville chewing tobacco enthusiasts were as likely to spit on the floor of the church as they were on the floor of the saloon. Lindsley himself had an unfortunate experience in church one Sunday. While the congregation was standing during prayers, a well-dressed young man leaned over and spat tobacco juice into Lindsley's pew in such amounts "as fairly to put all devotion out of countenance."[17] His embarrassment was profound, but he forced himself to remain, although impatiently, until the service was over.

While Nashville, in many respects, was still a backwoods town, it was able to boast of certain appendages of a more advanced civilization. A reading room was opened in 1825 "for the accommodation of the newsmonger, lounger, and stranger" as well as for those citizens who were studiously inclined. This establishment was maintained by subscription and contained many of the principal papers of the United States, to say nothing of various literary works.[18]

Good drinking water was scarce, but soda water shops had made their appearance and were serving carbonated sarsaparilla to thirsty Nashvillians who were either too youthful or too abstemious to drink the more potent beverages sold in the barroom

[15] *Ibid.*, 612.
[16] *Ibid.*, 623.
[17] *Ibid.*, 624.
[18] *Nashville Whig*, February 28, 1825.

of the Jackson Hotel. This hostelry was probably more accommodating than comfortable. At least, it was very reasonable, room and board being $12.50 a month.[19]

The medical profession was quite well represented in Nashville even at this early date, but doubtless some of the so-called "physicians" were merely quacks. However, some of the practitioners in Nashville and Middle Tennessee had received professional training at Transylvania University, the University of Maryland, and the University of Pennsylvania.[20] In March, 1825, five Nashville physicians were appointed by the Mayor to constitute a board of health. This body had no real authority, no definite aims, and apparently accomplished nothing. It was a step in the right direction, but Nashville was destined to wait until after the Civil War for its first permanently organized board of health and sanitation.

Even in this early period Nashville had a museum of "natural and artificial curiosities."[21] Indeed, the citizens in general, according to Timothy Flint in his *History and Geology of the Mississippi Valley,*[22] showed "an encouraging interest in the advancement of science." The fine arts, too, were represented in a pale sort of way by traveling artists who exhibited oil paintings in hastily improvised studios, such as a vacant room over a feed store. Most surprising of all, the drama had been introduced to Nashville before 1820, and an amateur theatrical club had been organized before 1825.[23] In 1826 a new theater, incidentally Nashville's third since 1819, was erected at a cost of $20,000.[24] Such an institution seems almost incongruous, but Nashville was

[19] *Ibid.,* February 21, May 7, 21, 1825.

[20] A few of these, such as Lunsford Pitt Yandell, were to rise high in their profession. Yandell became editor of the *Transylvania Journal of Medicine and the Associate Sciences* and in 1837 was instrumental in founding the Louisville Medical Institute. He practiced in Murfreesboro from 1826 to 1830 and in Nashville from 1830 to 1831.

[21] *Nashville Whig and Banner,* June 22, 1826.

[22] Timothy Flint, *The History and Geology of the Mississippi Valley, to Which Is Appended a Condensed Physical Geography of the Atlantic United States, and the Whole American Continent* (Cincinnati, 1832), 339.

[23] Douglas L. Hunt, "The Nashville Theater, 1830-1840," in Birmingham-Southern College *Bulletin* (Birmingham), XXVIII (1935), no. 3, pp. 3-8.

[24] *Ibid.,* 13; *National Banner and Nashville Whig,* October 11, 1826.

a town of strange contrasts. If at first thought oil paintings, museums of natural history, and grease paint seem anachronous in a town still partly composed of log cabins, it must be remembered that Nashville was the most important town in Tennessee, and hence a logical place for speculators and promoters of all types to exercise their genius. Furthermore, many of the citizens were half starved for entertainment, and they turned to the theater as a happy escape from the drabness of life in a rural town. The crassness of the histrionics and the uncomfortableness of the auditoriums did not daunt these pleasure seekers.

In 1825 Nashville did not have a public school system, and was not to have one for a quarter of a century. However, various private schools were in existence, and the Nashville Female Academy had been in operation for eight years.[25] During the session of 1825 this institution enrolled one hundred students, and advertised that its stock was being sold on the installment plan.[26] Cumberland College was Nashville's bid for fame in the realms of higher education. When Lindsley became president in 1824, the institution was eighteen years old, but had made little headway against the evils of illiteracy and frontier prejudices.

Lindsley's education, experience, and ambitions fitted him for the task of building a university in the Southwest. In some respects, this proved more difficult than expected. He soon discovered that Tennesseans were more interested in the dinner bell, a horse race, or a cock fight than in the activities of a literary institution. Many of the people of Nashville were rising above the frontier level, but the frontier tradition lingered on, especially out in the rural districts, and it was necessary for Lindsley to grapple with it time and again.

To explain the ramifications of the frontier mind is far from simple. To attempt to explain any movement or any idea prevalent in the public mind of the frontier in terms of one or two obvious causes is to misunderstand frontier psychology. Each movement, each idea, each hatred was based upon a multiplicity

[25] *Ibid.*, June 25, 1825. [26] *Ibid.*, March 7, July 9, 1825.

of interrelated causes. Prominent among these were ignorance, false pride, and unrelenting prejudice. In a new country self-preservation and the desire for bare physical necessities exercised a primary influence. Vigor of constitution and brute strength were more valuable to the frontiersman than literature, history, or science. This idea, born in the minds of the first generation of a frontier people, became the inheritance of succeeding generations, and frequently became a tradition that was difficult for the subsequent cultural forces to overcome. Of course, when Lindsley moved to Nashville in 1824 the raw frontier had disappeared. But Tennessee was still "The West," its society was fundamentally rural, and certain characteristics of the frontier remained. These characteristics were intricately interwoven with the frontier tradition. When analyzed, this tradition presents three features of importance to this study. They are exalted individualism, religious intolerance and bigotry, and a general suspicion of all eastern educators. It was such a tradition that proved to be an obstacle to Lindsley's ambitions.

It was typical of Lindsley that from the very beginning of his presidency of Cumberland College he set his aims and his ambitions on the highest plane, although he realized that he might never live to see his plans become actualities. "Let us aim at perfection," he said,[27] and this became his motto. In his inaugural address in 1825 and in subsequent lectures, he made public his plans for what he termed "The grand experiment." He wished to build a university that would rank with the best universities in Europe. Provision was to be made for instruction in all the sciences, in philosophy, and in literature. In 1829 he asserted that "Nashville is the only place where a medical school would even be thought of; and physicians know full well that such is the fact. If Tennessee then is to have such a school, it *must* be established in Nashville."[28] Two decades later this prophecy came true.

[27] Halsey (ed.), *The Works of Philip Lindsley*, I, 106.
[28] *Ibid.*, 167-168; John Wooldridge (ed.), *History of Nashville, Tennessee* (Nashville, 1890), 387.

The announcement of Lindsley's plans brought three immediate results. The first was favorable comment in the Nashville press. The *Nashville Whig* declared that "The college which has been again brought into active operation by the incessant exertion of patriotic citizens, now presents a subject of deepest interest and anxious solicitude to all those who wish to see Tennessee assume her proper intellectual rank among her sister states."[29]

Secondly, the Lindsley administration drew up a new set of regulations, known as the Laws of Cumberland College. According to these laws, which were enacted by the Board of Trustees in November, 1825, candidates for admission into the freshman class were obliged to be familiar with Greek and Latin grammar, with Caesar's Commentaries, Cicero's orations, Virgil, and the Greek testament. English grammar, arithmetic, and geography were also named as prerequisites to college work.[30] An unusual requirement pertained to dueling. No person was admitted to the college who had ever fought a duel or who had ever taken part in a duel. If any student became involved in such an "affair of honor" after matriculation, he would be expelled immediately.[31]

It would seem from a study of these laws that the students at Cumberland College were allowed little freedom. The hours of study were from sunrise to breakfast, from nine o'clock until twelve in the forenoon, and from two until five in the afternoon. During the winter session, the period from eight in the evening to bedtime was likewise devoted to study. During the study hours the students were required to remain in their rooms unless they were called out to recite or by some urgent necessity. Students were especially requested to remain in their rooms after the ringing of the evening bell, unless their absence could be explained easily and justifiably to the members of the faculty. Furthermore, no student was permitted to leave the college

[29] *Nashville Whig*, June 25, 1825.
[30] *Laws of Cumberland College* (Nashville, 1825), 7.
[31] *Ibid.*, 16-17.

grounds on Sunday without permission. Each student was expected to attend church on Sunday and college chapel twice daily during the week.[32] Students who did not live in the college dormitory or with the faculty could reside only in approved boarding houses. Of course, this did not apply to those who lived at home. All dormitory students were required "to diet with the steward of the college."[33]

The third result of Lindsley's initial campaign to lay the foundations of a great university took the form of a legislative act. On November 27, 1826, the state legislature incorporated the officers and trustees of Cumberland College as the University of Nashville.[34] Thus Lindsley's visionary institution became at least a legal actuality, and by January 2, 1829, the *National Banner and Nashville Whig* was able to announce that "The cause of learning has advanced amongst us . . . with a steady, if not accelerated pace." As a matter of fact, the University of Nashville was struggling against great odds. The obstacles to success were associated with what may be termed the frontier tradition.

Any thesis that maintains that Tennessee civilization was always on a high cultural plane because of the intellectual qualities of some of the pioneer leaders, completely ignores the fact that these leaders were soon followed by undesirable characters in great numbers. It is true that a certain amount of intelligence and initiative was needed to blaze the trails, lay out the towns, and build the foundations of government, but no special qualifications were necessary in order to follow a trail that was wide open and peculiarly alluring. Consequently it was only natural that the leaders, "the huntingshirt gentry,"[35] were followed by the common herd which included shyster lawyers, fake preachers, ignorant farmers, counterfeiters, and fugitives from justice. To be sure, this element never constituted the entire population of

[32] *Ibid.*, 10, 14-15; Frederick Hall, *Letters from the East and from the West* (Washington, 1840), 154.
[33] *Laws of Cumberland College*, 12-13.
[34] Tennessee *Acts of a Local or Private Nature*, 1826, pp. 45-46.
[35] [Charles Fenno Hoffman], *A Winter in the West*, 2 vols. (New York, 1835), II, 219.

the frontier, but for many years it was an obstacle to enlightenment and was the cause of lamentation on the part of Philip Lindsley and other public men who had a sincere interest in promoting a more refined civilization.

In 1830, John Bell, Nashville lawyer and politician, found "the rude and fearful spectre of arts unduly prized, learning generally unappreciated, and every effort to create a thirst for science and a taste for general improvement paralyzed by the cold indifference of the better informed and by popular jealousy and suspicion."[36] According to Bell, even the best farmers of Tennessee, while living in plenty, had no desire for the advantages of cultivated society. The same was true, he declared, with respect to merchants, physicians, lawyers, and clergymen, "except such individuals of these respective classes as have been graciously supplied from the intellectual redundancy of our sister states."[37]

Bell's statements should be accepted cautiously as he was pleading the cause of education and no doubt his enthusiasm caused him to make questionable generalizations. The indifferent attitude was present, and it was an obstacle to educational progress, but Bell exaggerated the situation when he placed the emphasis on the professional classes, especially where Nashville itself was concerned. Granted that some of the professional men were indifferent to the university, it does not automatically follow that they were opposed to education. Perhaps they were too busy attending to their personal affairs, or perhaps they were opposed to Lindsley.

With respect to the common people, Bell was close to the truth. He realized that the minds of a frontier people were "in a forest state," and that it was necessary to clear away physical and mental encumbrances before a mature society could develop. He believed that Nashville in 1830 had passed this incipient stage, and that its citizens should take more interest in cultural and intellectual affairs. Of the same opinion was William G. Hunt,

[36] John Bell, *An Address Delivered at Nashville, October 5, 1830, Being the First Anniversary of the Alumni Society of the University of Nashville* (Nashville, 1830), 4.
[37] *Ibid.*, 5.

another lawyer. In an address to the literary societies of the University of Nashville in 1831, he declared that Nashville could no longer use frontier influences as an excuse for cultural inactivity.[38]

Both Bell and Hunt realized that Nashville lacked many of the finer elements of civilization. Both declared that frontier conditions had been the initial cause of this situation. But both overlooked what Nashville had actually accomplished and at the same time expected too much of the town. They were doomed to disappointment if they expected Nashville suddenly to cease its existence as a country town and become over night a highly polished community.

Lindsley, too, underestimated the frontier forces still in operation throughout the state. In order to understand these forces it is necessary to examine first of all the problem of the public lands. When Tennessee was authorized to appropriate the vacant lands within its boundary (1806), the federal government decreed that one hundred thousand acres be set aside for the support of two colleges, one to be located in East Tennessee, and one in West Tennessee. Congress desired these lands to be sold for not less than $2.00 per acre, thus creating an endowment of $100,000 for each college. Unfortunately, when the Tennessee legislature proceeded to execute these provisions, it was discovered that the only land on which the college claims could be located was a large tract south of the French Broad and Holston rivers. This tract was occupied by farmers to whom the state government had promised land titles at the rate of $1.00 per acre. Obviously, at the outset the potential educational fund was cut in half.[39]

This was only the beginning of the difficulty. The settlers in this region were viewed in the light of frontier heroes and consequently no persistent effort was made to collect from them the money they owed the government, part of which would have been used to endow the University of Nashville. Every attempt on the part of the legislature to collect this debt was frustrated by

[38] *National Banner and Nashville Whig*, April 22, 1831.
[39] Bell, *An Address Delivered at Nashville, October 5, 1830*, p. 8; *Annals of Congress*, 9th Congress, 1st Sess. (1805-1806), XV, 1264.

a powerful minority which represented the farmers who occupied the land in question. It was natural for these legislators to foster the interests of their constituents and it was natural for the farmers to think that they were simply fighting for the property which they had reclaimed from the wilderness. Because of their ignorance, many of these farmers did not really understand the situation and, consequently, they are not to be blamed because they jumped to the conclusion that the colleges were trying to force them from their land. They did not directly obstruct education, but prejudices were formed which were difficult to eradicate and which caused Lindsley to fear for the future of the rural people if they continued to deny their children an education.

"Were it in my power," he stated, "I would visit every farmer in Tennessee who is not already awake and endeavor to arouse him from his fatal lethargy . . . and urge him to reclaim his abandoned rights and his lost dignity by giving to his sons that measure [of education] which will qualify them to assert and to maintain their just superiority in the councils of the state and of the nation. . . . Educate your son in the best manner possible, because you expect him to be a *man,* not a *horse* or an *ox.*"[40]

But the rural people, and the townspeople too, clung to misconceptions which tended to thwart Lindsley's plans to diffuse knowledge throughout the state. There was an idea prevalent in the minds of Tennesseans that colleges and universities were beneficial only to the rich. This was a typical frontier attitude, intensified in Tennessee because of the difficulties which had occurred between the farmers, the universities, and the state legislature. Year after year Lindsley attempted to batter down this prejudice. It was absurd, he thought, to depreciate and to denounce colleges as being hostile to the interests of the poor and beneficial only to the wealthy. He maintained that the wealthy made sacrifices in order to build, endow, and maintain these institutions, and that the comparatively poor reaped the principal advantage.[41]

[40] Halsey (ed.), *Works of Philip Lindsley,* I, 225-226.
[41] *Ibid.,* 231.

In both urban and rural districts, Lindsley found himself face to face with frontier egotism and the frontier attitude of self-sufficiency. Of what use was education to these people who had wrested an empire from the wilderness? Lindsley attempted to point out to them their inferiority in every field of education. He warned them that vanity and incessant boasting was not the way to progress and enlightenment. Continuing on this subject, he asserted, "While we cherish this arrogant, superstitious, overweening self-sufficient spirit, we shall never seek nor desire improvement, because we fancy that the very acme of human excellence has been attained."[42] And he realized that even his adopted city was by no means free from this spirit.

It has been claimed that the frontier spirit was aflame with democracy and liberalism. There is some truth in the statement as applied to politics and statecraft, but considerable modification is necessary when it is applied to frontier religion. There were certain denominations, such as the Anti-Mission Baptists, which claimed to be the champions of American freedom; but actually, because of ignorance and bigotry, these sects were stumbling blocks in the path of progress and education. Although some of the pioneer preachers are to be admired for their rugged strength, it has to be admitted that the necessity of education was frequently ruled out of the picture and that bigotry and intolerance often reigned where the American Dream was supposed to be enthroned.

During the first three decades of the nineteenth century the most important denominations in Tennessee were the Presbyterians, the Methodists, and the Baptists. In the early years only the Presbyterians insisted on an educated clergy. It is not surprising, therefore, to find that the first group of college-trained men on the frontier were Presbyterians.[43] But although first on

---

[42] *Ibid.*, 243-244.
[43] William Warren Sweet, *Religion on the American Frontier*, II, *The Presbyterians, 1783-1840* (New York, 1936), 69 ff.; Donald G. Tewksbury, *The Founding of American Colleges and Universities before the Civil War with Particular Reference to the Religious Influences Bearing upon the College Movement* (New York, 1932), 91-103.

the scene, they were unable to maintain a paramount position as the frontier civilization expanded. This was due to several causes to be found within Presbyterianism itself. In the first place, each minister was allowed only two or, at the most, three congregations, with the result that Presbyterian cultural influence tended to be localized. In the second place, the inelastic Calvinistic doctrine came into conflict with frontier philosophy, while the Methodists, Baptists, and later the Disciples (Christians) found it comparatively easy to convert the frontiersmen. Finally, the Presbyterian church, in an attempt to adjust itself to frontier conditions during the period 1800-1840, was weakened by internal difficulties. So the Presbyterians, champions of education, were handicapped and in a sense fell a victim of their own intellectuality except in certain urban centers such as Nashville, and even here they were always a minority group.

Although Lindsley attempted to maintain a nonsectarian university in Nashville, the people were not likely to forget in this age of religious sensitiveness that he was a Presbyterian and hence a representative of the minority denomination. The majority of the people in Tennessee were either Baptists or Methodists and so for sectarian reasons alone it was only natural that suspicion should hover over the head of the President of the University of Nashville.

However, in this connection, sectarianism was only one difficulty that confronted Lindsley as he tried to build his university. Another obstacle was the anti-educational complex frequently in evidence among Methodists and Baptists. In this early period, the Methodists in general in Tennessee were not interested in education, although here and there appeared a preacher with a broader intellectual outlook.[44] The greatest factor in the spread of Methodism was the itinerant system. The Methodists did not wait for the people to come to their churches. They took their religion on tour and preached it at every village and crossroads.

[44] Peter Cartwright regarded educated ministers as "lettuce growing under the shade of a peach tree." W. P. Strickland (ed.), *Autobiography of Peter Cartwright, The Backwoods Preacher* (Cincinnati and New York, 1856), 80.

Frequently a single Methodist preacher traveled a circuit with twenty ports of call which might range from a frontier shack to the chambers of the state legislature. With such a system it was inevitable that they should outdistance their better educated Presbyterian rivals. The latter, with more permanent locations, were able to make local cultural contributions, but the communities that felt the influence of Presbyterian learning were few compared to those under the thumb of the more vigorous Methodist itinerant.[45]

It would seem that the Baptists on the frontier were prejudiced against education and especially prejudiced against an educated clergy. The most unprogressive sect among Tennessee Baptists was the Anti-Mission Baptists, mentioned above. They were opposed to academic and theological education and they denounced Sunday schools, Bible societies, and missionary organizations. It was their belief that preachers were called to the ministry by divine revelation and that any attempt on the part of the preacher to educate himself was sinful. The divine spirit chose the text for him and caused him to deliver the sermon based on it. To study a subject or make any preparation before delivering a sermon was considered an insult to the Lord. Everything was left to God and any attempt to assist Him by means of education or missionary organizations was presumptuous if not blasphemous. In 1846 there were 10,186 Anti-Mission Baptists in Tennessee. Only one other state, Georgia, had a larger number. Kentucky ranked third.[46] This is an indication that as late as 1846 the frontier influence was still strong in certain sections of Georgia, Tennessee, and Kentucky because Anti-Missionism, while it cannot be called the frontier synthesis, was definitely congruous with certain tenets of frontier philosophy. These frontier conditions that continued into the fifth decade of the

---

[45] The duties of a Tennessee itinerant preacher are presented in *The Life and Times of Rev. Carroll C. Mayhew* (Nashville, 1857); Sweet, *Religion on the American Frontier*, II, *The Presbyterians*, 69-70.

[46] Sweet, *Religion on the American Frontier*, I, *The Baptists* (New York, 1931), 66 n.

century, irrespective of eccentric and unprogressive religious denominations, tended to prevent liberal support for colleges.[47]

In view of the obstacles offered by frontier religion alone, Philip Lindsley had a very difficult task. Nashville, indeed, was becoming more and more a cultural oasis, but even the oasis seemed to suffer from intellectual droughts. There was always a certain amount of indifference to the condition of the university although the institution received its share of publicity in the press,[48] and Lindsley's addresses were usually published and widely circulated. Other factors, however, were working against Lindsley. As time went on and sectional feeling became more bitter the fact that he was an easterner was given considerable publicity and this eventually led to open criticism.

When Lindsley moved to Nashville in 1824, the slavery question was not a paramount racial or political issue, and sectional feelings, compared with the sentiments of the forties and fifties, were mild. Nevertheless, in 1825 the editor of the *Nashville Whig* asserted, "The disposition which is too general among the people of the south and west to keep alive a feeling of aversion, a spirit of hostility, toward our fellow citizens of the north, included under the general term of Yankees, is as much to be regretted as any other evil which now prevails. . . . This feeling originates in and is kept alive by prejudice."[49]

Lindsley, of course, was a "Yankee," and it is safe to assume that there were Tennesseans, even residents of Nashville, who were piqued because he had been chosen president of a Tennessee institution. By 1849 the personal opposition to him was becoming more pronounced. In October of that year a Nashville citizen sent an article to the press that indirectly blamed Lindsley for the shortcomings of the university. "If you expect a university ever to flourish in this city composed of the young men of the

[47] Tewksbury, *The Founding of American Colleges and Universities*, 24.
[48] *National Banner and Nashville Daily Advertiser*, March 16, 26, April 5, 6, 1833; *Nashville Whig*, October 24, 1843; *South Western Literary Journal and Monthly Review* (Nashville, 1844-1846?), I (1844), 175-176; advertisements and press notices in the various Nashville papers throughout the period.
[49] *Nashville Whig*, July 2, 1825.

south," declared this critic, "you must put a general at the head of them, a man who could win their affection and command their esteem and respect . . . select a president from the south or west, of sound active mind, a well balanced head, which will give him common sense about everything, a man of firmness, of urbanity, and a dash of chivalry in his composition. One who understands well the subject of our domestic institution of slavery, because the Southern States are the largest fields for patronage."[50]

Here may be seen the true basis for Lindsley's decision to resign the presidency of the university whose destiny he had guided for twenty-five years. Perhaps he had too much of the missionary spirit of the East, which was never welcome in either the South or the West unless skillfully handled. When Lindsley became president of the University of Nashville in 1824 his chances to fulfill his ambitions were favorable. But after 1831 the wheels of fate began to turn against him. No doubt he made a sincere attempt to adjust his philosophy to that of the pro-slavery South. Although the evidence on this point is scant, nevertheless it suggests that Lindsley's unpopularity in the late forties was due, if not to his attitude toward slavery, at least to his attitude on the question of sectionalism.

After years of persistent labor, Lindsley realized that he had expected too much of the people of Tennessee. He had aimed at perfection, but he secured only "a nucleus—a cornerstone." But it was in laying the foundation of the University of Nashville that Lindsley made one of his contributions to Tennessee civilization. Although the institution fell short of his ambitions, and toward the close of his presidency was described as having "a worm eaten appearance,"[51] nevertheless it became the cornerstone of the educational prominence of Nashville.

Lindsley himself was a pioneer in the sense that he attempted to bring to a backward section of the nation the fruits of education and enlightenment. After a quarter of a century of hard and often unappreciated labor, he left behind him in the minds

[50] *Daily Union*, October 23, 1849.   [51] *Daily Union*, October 19, 1849.

of some of his young associates a spirit of education noteworthy for its vitality and endurance. John Berrien Lindsley, because of the influence of his father and of Gerard Troost, was imbued with this spirit. The ambitions of Philip Lindsley were more fully realized in the career and contributions of his son.

While President Lindsley was campaigning in the cause of education, his professor of sciences, Dr. Gerard Troost, was attracting the attention of the scientific world by his work in ethnology, geology, paleontology, botany, and mineralogy. He excelled in the last, although he made valuable contributions in paleontology and geology. In Europe, he was best known for his contributions in natural history, as most of his discoveries in this field were announced in the scientific journals published in Paris.[52]

Gerard Troost was born in Bois-le-Duc, Holland, in 1776, the son of Everhard Joseph Troost and Anna Dornelia Troost. He was educated in the universities of Leyden and Amsterdam, and received special instruction from the French mineralogist René Just Hany (1743-1822) and the German geologist Abraham Gottlob Werner (1750-1817). After various experiences which ranged from teaching pharmacy in Amsterdam to serving in the Dutch army as health officer, Troost decided to live in the United States. He arrived in New York in 1810 and later moved to Philadelphia, where he married Margaret Tage in 1811. His first wife died in 1819. His second wife was Mrs. Mary O'Reilly of Philadelphia.

While in Philadelphia, Troost assisted in forming The American Academy of Natural Sciences (1812), and was president of that organization from 1812 to 1817. After experimenting with the manufacture of alum at Cape Sable, Maryland, in 1814, Troost returned to Philadelphia and became occupied with teaching, lecturing, and scientific investigations.[53]

[52] *The Western Journal of Medicine and Surgery* (Louisville, 1840-1855), VI (1846), 269-271; L. C. Glenn, "Gerard Troost," in *American Geologist* (Minneapolis, 1888-1905), XXXV (1905), 35-89.
[53] Henry Grady Rooker, "A Sketch of the Life and Work of Dr. Gerard Troost," in *Tennessee Historical Magazine* (Nashville, 1915-), Ser. II, Vol. III (1932), 3-19.

As his paramount interest was mineralogy, it was natural that he should be surprised to discover that little attention had been given to the crystalline forms of the minerals found in the United States. Many of these forms were not at all analogous with those described by European crystallographers. In several scientific articles, Troost offered a more accurate description of certain types of crystals which had been described only vaguely previous to his investigations in 1822, and in the case of the bevel-edged quartz crystals found at Lake George, New York, he presented an entirely new variety. Furthermore, he discovered some new varieties of pyroxene crystals, a new crystalline from of andalusite and laummite, and a new type of pearlstone. Also, he was the first to describe the yessite crystals found in Rhode Island.[54]

In 1825 or 1826 Troost decided to try Robert Owen's new system of living at New Harmony, Indiana. The amount of time he actually spent in New Harmony cannot be determined from the evidence at hand. However, between 1825 and 1827 he made a geological excursion into Missouri and made a preliminary study of calamine, cobalt, and lead in that region.[55] In 1827 he moved to Nashville and the next year he was appointed professor of geology, mineralogy, and chemistry in the University of Nashville. For the remainder of his life he was associated with Nashville and with Tennessee.

Shortly after his appointment at the University of Nashville, Troost began to make geological expeditions over Tennessee, and on October 16, 1831, he delivered an address before the state legislature on the natural resources of the state. The address con-

[54] Gerard Troost, "Description of Some New Crystalline Forms of Minerals of the United States," in *Journal of the Academy of Natural Science of Philadelphia* (Philadelphia, 1817-1842), II (1821), 55-58; "Description of a New Crystalline Form of Quartz," in *ibid.*, 212-214; "Account of the Pyroxene of the United States and Descriptions of Some New Varieties of the Yessite of Rhode Island, and Several Other American Minerals," in *ibid.*, 222-224; "Description of a New Form of the Andalusite," in *ibid.*, IV (1824), 122-123; "Description of a New Crystalline Form of Apophyllite, Laummite, and Amphibole, and of a Variety of Pearlstone," in *ibid.*, V (1825), 51-56.

[55] Gerard Troost, and Lessieur, "On Calamine, Cobalt and the Lead Ores of Missouri," in Silliman's *American Journal of Science and Arts* (New Haven, 1818-), XII (1829), 376-378.

tained a forceful plea for a scientific investigation into the geology and mineralogy of the region. According to the *National Banner and Nashville Whig,* "The views presented were profound, judicious, intelligent, and appropriate, and were illustrated with a clearness and strength that could scarcely fail to carry conviction to the mind of every hearer."[56] In a later issue, the same paper declared that Troost's address "attracted much attention in every part of our country and tended to bring Tennessee into notice abroad more perhaps than any circumstance that has occurred since the election of her distinguished citizen to the chief magistracy of the Union."[57]

Whatever the effect of the speech abroad might have been, it brought the desired result in Tennessee. On December 21, 1831, a geological survey was authorized and Troost was appointed state geologist, mineralogist, and assayer. He held this position, although at times precariously, until the office was temporarily abolished in 1850, a few months before his death.[58]

At a time when very little scientific work was being done west of the Appalachians, Troost made interesting and valuable contributions to mineralogy, paleontology, and geology. He made a careful examination of the coal beds of Tennessee, and was the first to locate definitely and to delineate the coal area. By analysis he came to the conclusion that Tennessee coal was superior in quality to the Kentucky coal then being used in Nashville (1835).[59]

Troost was the first to call attention to the excellent quality of Hawkins County marble, which was subsequently used exclusively for ornamental and building purposes. Had this been the only result of his work, the state would have been repaid for the expenditures incurred in the survey, but his contributions did not end here. He drew attention to the high-grade slate in southeastern Sevier County and to the zinc deposits in the eastern

[56] *National Banner and Nashville Whig,* October 21, 1831.
[57] *Ibid.,* December 7, 1831.
[58] Tennessee *Public Acts,* 1831, pp. 43-44.
[59] Gerard Troost, *Third Geological Report* (Nashville, 1835), 4-6.

section of the state. Troost had had experience with zinc ores before coming to Tennessee, and when he made his report on the zinc deposits he included a description of the various methods of reducing zinc and of manufacturing brass.[60]

In the thirties there were rumors that rich veins of gold had been discovered in the Ocoee district of Tennessee. After an examination of the region in the spring of 1837, Troost was very skeptical about the value of the gold deposits. In his fourth report to the legislature in 1837 he gave a humorous description of the methods employed by the prospectors in their search for the precious metal. The favorite method was the use of a divining rod, a forked twig of a hazel or peach tree, which was supposed to turn in the hand of the fortunate prospectors when they approached hidden gold. It was reported that by the use of the divining rod wedges of pure gold of forty pounds weight had been located, and deep shafts had been dug in order to get at them. But the diggings were always a little to the right or a little to the left of the wedges, and consequently they remained in the safe keeping of the hobgoblins which were supposed to haunt mines and to guard the precious metals of the earth.[61]

With respect to silver, Troost labored under the delusion that there were deposits of this metal along Calf-Killer Creek near Sparta. One day when watering his horse in the creek at Sparta he discovered an unusual specimen of ore that upon examination proved to be rich in silver. But this was all he ever found there, and in later years it was believed that some one had played a practical joke on him.[62]

As a paleontologist, Troost became interested in the fossils to be found in the Tennessee formations. In 1849 he prepared a list

[60] Gerard Troost, *Sixth Geological Report* (Nashville, 1841), 30-32; *Ninth Geological Report* (Nashville, 1848), 7-29; Troost, "Observations on the Zinc Ores of Franklin and Sterling, Sussex County, New Jersey," in *Journal of the Academy of Natural Science of Philadelphia*, IV (1824), 220-231; James M. Safford, *Geology of Tennessee* (Nashville, 1869), 487, 512; Safford, *A Geological Reconnoissance of the State of Tennessee* (Nashville, 1856), 74.

[61] Gerard Troost, *Fourth Geological Report* (Nashville, 1837), 26-27.

[62] Gerard Troost, *Fifth Geological Report* (Nashville, 1840), 43-44; Safford, *Geology of Tennessee*, 488 n.

of fossil crinoids in which thirty-one genera were mentioned, sixteen being considered new. Agassiz regarded Troost's study of the crinoids as highly important, and was "happy to be able to state that Professor Troost is preparing a monograph of all these crinoids, illustrated by 220 figures."[63]

Troost did write the monograph, in which he presented a description of one hundred and seven species of crinoids. He submitted this paper as an appendix to his tenth report, but the state refused to publish it. The politicians were more interested in exploiting coal fields and zinc deposits than they were in the geologic history of fossils. In 1908 a critical summary of the manuscript was submitted by Elvira Wood as a master's thesis at Columbia University. In this form Troost's contribution was published in Washington by the Government Printing Office in 1909.[64]

The work of the archeologist also had its fascination for the versatile Troost. About eleven miles southeast of Nashville in the bed of a shallow stream he discovered the bones of a mastodon. The head of the ancient beast protruded above the surface of the water and had been used for years by pedestrians as a stepping stone. In the vicinity of Nashville, Natchez, and in the Wabash Valley he discovered other remains. Some of these he identified as an extinct species of elephant, others as a more uncommon prehistoric animal which had been made known to the scientific world by Thomas Jefferson, and which was called, accordingly, Megalonyx Jeffersonii.[65]

Then too, Troost was interested in the prehistoric Indians who had inhabited the Tennessee and Mississippi Valleys. The mound builders puzzled him, as they did many an ethnologist. With

[63] *Proceedings of the American Association for the Advancement of Science* (Philadelphia, 1848-), II (1849), 63.
[64] Elvira Wood, *A Critical Summary of Troost's Unpublished Manuscript on the Crinoids of Tennessee* (Washington, 1909).
[65] Gerard Troost, "On the Localities in Tennessee in Which Bones of the Gigantic Mastodon and Megalonyx Jeffersonii Are Found," in *Transactions of the Geological Society of Pennsylvania* (Philadelphia, 1834-1835), I (1834), 139-146, 236-243; Troost, "An Account of Some Ancient Remains in Tennessee," in *Transactions of the American Ethnological Society* (New York, 1845-1853), I (1845), 355-365.

respect to certain skulls, bones, and trinkets found in Tennessee, Troost was quite certain that they belonged to a race of tropical origin. Strange idols were found in tropical shells, and some of the ancient utensils were made of a type of volcanic stone believed to exist only in South America.[66]

In addition to his varied interests in science, Troost was a man of many hobbies. For example, he was a collector of engravings, prints, and lithographs. Anything curious in natural history fascinated him, and he was known to give twenty dollars to any one who would bring him a curiosity, preferably alive, for his collection in his private room at home. This room was well stocked with snakes, turtles, birds, fishes, fossils, crystals, and Indian relics. Perhaps his best loved hobby was to study and collect reptiles. Featherstonhaugh, the English traveler and geologist, who was entertained by Troost in his Nashville home, was impressed by the curious pets which his host possessed. He believed that Troost was supremely happy when he was able to lounge in his rocking chair, talk about geology, and stroke the head of a large snake which was coiled around his neck.[67]

Troost, the scientist, was as much a pioneer in Tennessee as was Lindsley, the champion of education. And in spite of the fact that Troost, with his "childlike simplicity of manners"[68] and his congenial disposition, undoubtedly made friends more easily than Lindsley, nevertheless his work was not fully appreciated and his scientific attitude frequently clashed with the frontier mind both in the field and in the state legislature. But his profession and his ambitions, unlike those of Philip Lindsley, were not so dependent on public opinion. Ignorant farmers might call him a lunatic because he wandered around their fields hammering rocks but their opinion had no effect on his unquenchable scientific spirit. If farmers in Tennessee thought he was mentally unbalanced, or if certain clergymen thought he had no business

[66] *Idem.*
[67] George William Featherstonhaugh, *Excursion Through the Slave States, from Washington on the Potomac to the Frontier of Mexico*, 2 vols. (London, 1844), I, 194.
[68] Hall, *Letters from the East and from the West*, 158.

prying into the Lord's secrets, or if narrow-visioned politicians could see no need for a permanent state geologist, scientists in Nashville, Philadelphia, or Paris recognized his attainments and published them for all the world to see. Tennesseans, therefore, whether they wished it or not, became, with limitations, geology conscious. Certainly the University of Nashville had cause to be proud of her well-known scientist, and Troost's cultural background did much to improve the intellectual life of the city. Philip Lindsley's son, John Berrien Lindsley, for example, who was to be one of the most important educators in the state during the next generation, acquired much of his liberalism and aggressiveness through his association with Nashville's "professor of geology, mineralogy, and chemistry."

The social life in Nashville during the period under review (1825-1850) was a curious mixture of frontier customs and the more refined characteristics of a cultured people. The presence of the theater in the early twenties has already been noted.[69] The success of the theater in these early years may be attributed more to the novelty of the enterprise than to any consistent and sustained appreciation of the drama. It would be logical to expect an increased interest in theatricals during the thirties and forties, but as a matter of fact this was not the case. Abnormal conditions caused by the panic of 1837 and the Mexican War in the following decade tended to hurt the theater business not only in Nashville, but in the nation in general.[70] Then, too, the competition of the circus must not be overlooked.

The favor shown the circus and the neglect of the theater called forth editorial comment in the local press. On September 23, 1843, the *Nashville Whig* stated that "the theater and the circus are both open, but the latter is the favorite resort. While hundreds nightly crowd the circus, the representatives of Thalia

[69] Sol Smith, in his *Theatrical Management in the West and South* (New York, 1868), page 21 and *passim* makes some interesting comments on the early Nashville theater.
[70] Joseph Jefferson, *Autobiography* (New York, 1889), 45-52; N. M. Ludlow, *Dramatic Life as I Found It* (St. Louis, 1880), 206, 292, 380, 407.

and Melpomene perform . . . before some thirty or forty listless listeners . . . how has the drama fallen from its once high estate." By 1849 conditions were such that the *Daily Union* complained because Nashville was so deficient in places of amusement.[71] However, 1849 was an important year in the history of the theater in Nashville. It marked the end of an era of comparative indifference and the beginning of a period of active interest in dramatics. As the roaring forties gave way to the fabulous fifties, a new theater opened its doors to the Nashville public.[72]

There were other types of amusement during the thirties and forties that reflected the frontier influence. The barbecue and the bran dance will serve as good examples. The former was a feast held in the woods and was generally only for men. A trench was dug in the ground, a rod or two long, two or three feet wide, and two or three feet deep. The trench was filled with burning charcoal and then logs were placed across it. On the logs a whole hog or sheep or perhaps the quarter of a steer was placed and allowed to roast until Negro cooks decided that the meat was ready to serve. In addition to the meat there was plenty of wine and corn whiskey. If the occasion became too quiet a cannon might be discharged.[73]

The bran dance, which was distinctly a product of the frontier, was held in a section of the woods where the trees were not so close as to hinder the activities of the dancers. The ground was smoothed off and sprinkled with bran or sawdust to render it more elastic. Music was furnished by the fiddlers of the neighborhood. While bran dances and barbecues were originally given in the woods it is interesting to note that by the late forties they were being given at the Nashville race course.[74]

In spite of opposition from the churches, interest in dancing throughout the period was sufficient to support several dancing academies. In the thirties the popular steps included the cotillion, a series of round dances with intricate evolutions; the gavotte, a

[71] April 9, 1849.
[72] *Daily Union*, July 19, 1849.
[73] Hall, *Letters from the East and from the West*, 156.
[74] *Ibid.*, 106; Nashville *Republican Banner*, July 3, 1846.

Spanish importation; the allemandes, a fast German dance; hornpipes, which called for too much exertion to be popular in warm weather; the shawl, a type of square dance; and, of course, the waltz.[75]

During the thirties balls were given on every important holiday, including New Year's, Jackson Day, Washington's birthday, May Day, and the Fourth of July. So-called "cotillion parties" were given at frequent intervals in the hotels, in the dancing academies, or at the popular resort known as Vauxhall Gardens. Frequently dinners, banquets, or lunches were attended by the holiday celebrators before they made their appearance at the dance. The following advertisement found in the *National Banner and Nashville Whig* (December 16, 1831) is suggestive. "Christmas and New Year's Celebration. John T. Rawlins will furnish at the Nashville Western Boarding House, on Saturday the 31st instant, a hand-about for the ladies and a collation for the gentlemen, with a rich egg-nog, at $2.00 a head."

In the forties the cotillion parties gave way to quadrille parties and fancy costume balls. The latter were described as "brilliant" affairs where Margaret of Anjou, Rebecca the Jewess, Cinderella, ambassadors, sailors, and Santa Anna were impersonated by the beauties and the young blades of Nashville society. The food served at the balls and parties of the forties was more suggestive of refined society than the coarse fare of the early thirties. Nectar jelly, Russian cheese, French bonbons, nougats, cakes baked in fancy shapes, and ice cream pyramids were attractive both to the eye and to the appetite.[76]

It would seem that Nashville became a musical center as early as the thirties. According to the *Republican Banner* there was not a city in the United States of equal size that displayed as much interest in music as Nashville. While this was probably a slight exaggeration, it is true that organ, flute, violin, harp, and piano concerts were well attended, although minstrel melodies

---
[75] *Ibid.*, August 13, 1838.
[76] Nashville *Republican Banner*, January 5, 1846; January 26, 1848; October 4, 1848; *Tri-Weekly Nashville Union*, October 3, 1848; *Daily Union*, April 9, 1849.

were the most popular. In March, 1846, Wilhelmina Romberb, "the celebrated harpist from Europe," visited Nashville on her tour of the United States and composed a new march entitled "The Hermitage Grand March." This composition was dedicated to Mrs. Andrew Jackson, Jr.[77] In 1849, Nashville was favored with six grand opera concerts and a piano concert by Maurice Strakosch, "the pianist to the Emperor of Prussia."[78]

In the early thirties it was considered a mark of distinction for a town to have a lyceum or literary society. The Nashville Lyceum seems to have been most active in 1831, and it sponsored lectures on various topics ranging from philosophy to architecture. A decade later a series of popular lectures was given under the auspices of the Mechanics Library Association. These organizations were sponsored either by students or the better educated citizens.

The advertisements of the Nashville book stores indicate that the city offered a good market for literary works of all types. Listed among the more popular works were Gray's *Elegy*, Smith's *Wealth of Nations*, Mrs. Shelley's *Frankenstein, or the Modern Prometheus, The Koran*, Jane Austen's novels, Emerson's *Essays*, Prescott's *Ferdinand and Isabella*, Spark's *Life and Treason of Benedict Arnold, The Chronicle of the Cid*, and Bancroft's *History*. It seems that Bancroft's works were well received in Nashville. The editor of the Nashville *Daily Union*, after reading the third volume, asserted, "The author brings the history up to the boyhood of Washington and leaves the reader panting for that portion of the interesting story yet to be told."[79]

One way to sum up intellectual life in Nashville and Tennessee before 1850 would be to state that the people did not "pant" for learning and refinement, although many were beginning to realize the true value of education. The influence of the frontier mind as a negative force can hardly be overemphasized. Before 1850 there was not enough time for social and cultural processes

[77] Nashville *Republican Banner*, March 25, 1846.
[78] *Daily Union*, April 23, 1849.   [79] *Daily Union*, March 8, 1841.

to overcome all the obstacles, although Nashville made considerable progress. In the next decade this city developed cultural patterns of a high order and made contributions to education, science, and the art of living. Much of the credit for these accomplishments should go to such indefatigable representatives of education as Philip Lindsley and Gerard Troost who laid the foundations for a more refined social order.

CHAPTER II

EDUCATIONAL OPPORTUNITIES
1850-1860

WHATEVER FAME Nashville possessed as an educational center was due in large part to the Nashville Female Academy and the University of Nashville. Although these two institutions of learning were not perfect they were considered as "the parents of all others in the city, and as models . . . widely copied throughout the state."[1]

While this statement is fundamentally true, it cannot be applied to the University of Nashville as it existed in 1850. At that time the institution's plant was outmoded, its president was under criticism, and due to cholera there were no applications for admission. It was an opportune time for Philip Lindsley to withdraw gracefully from a position that was no longer pleasant. It was also an opportune time to reorganize the entire university and to construct new buildings. So Lindsley resigned and the institution was closed. The literary department of the university was reorganized under the leadership of Dr. John Berrien Lindsley.

It has already been noted that as early as 1829 Philip Lindsley thought that Nashville was ideally situated to become the seat of a medical college. He lamented the fact that there was no medical school in the city of his adoption, nor, for that matter, in the entire state. He wondered how long Tennessee would continue to send her youth to Philadelphia, Cincinnati, or Lexington to learn the healing art.[2] Over a decade later the desired medical school was still but a dream. "There is not a medical school in the state of Tennessee," declared the Columbia *Guar-*

---

[1] *Nashville City and Business Directory*, V (1860-1861), 26.
[2] Halsey (ed.), *Works of Philip Lindsley*, I, 169 ff.

dian; "will any reader or correspondent of the *Guardian* furnish us with a good reason why this state of things should be tolerated?"[3]

But the situation was tolerated for another decade and it was not until November 1, 1851, that the Medical School of the University of Nashville opened its doors to the public. The inaugural exercises were quite elaborate and were witnessed by the members of the legislature, who were received at the school by the trustees of the University of Nashville, the medical faculty, and the first class of medical students.[4]

No doubt one man in that inaugural assemblage experienced the pleasure that comes from a task well done. This was John Berrien Lindsley, professor of chemistry and pharmacy and dean of the new medical school. The medical school project as finally formulated had been conceived in his mind and it was due to his ability and determination that dreams and paper plans were finally converted into something more tangible.[5] The ambitions of Philip Lindsley were brought closer to realization in the accomplishments of his son.

John Berrien Lindsley and the men who coöperated with him were determined from the beginning to create an institution that would rank professionally not third or fourth but at the very top. The great obstacles in their path did not daunt them, but on the contrary seemed to inspire them to greater efforts. What did it matter that there were no lecture halls, no laboratory, no equipment? What did it matter that there was no dissecting material and no museums? All these things could be constructed, purchased, assembled. Nothing seemed impossible to these ambitious doctors. Not only were they able to create a medical

[3] *Guardian, A Family Magazine* (Columbia, Tennessee, 1841-1849?), I (1841), 121; see also Minutes of the University of Nashville, 1844 (MS in Peabody College Library).
[4] *Nashville Journal of Medicine and Surgery*, I (1851), 382.
[5] John Berrien Lindsley, Diary (MS in possession of Miss Louise G. Lindsley, Nashville. Typed copy in Peabody College Library; quoted in John Edwin Windrow, *John Berrien Lindsley* (Chapel Hill, 1938), 33, 36; Minutes of the University of Nashville, 1850 (MS in Peabody College Library).

school in a surprisingly short time but they were able to build one capable of holding its own with the best of the day.[6]

Local pride, perhaps a hint of sectionalism, made itself apparent at the opening of the new school. For example, it was pointed out to prospective medical students that the climate of Nashville was far superior to the cold and rigorous climate of Philadelphia or New York. Then, too, it was believed that life in the cities of the North would destroy the ideals of southern youth. The young medical students would be better situated in Nashville where checks might be placed upon the temptations to which they might otherwise succumb. Furthermore, it was claimed that the young ladies of Nashville and of the South in general were superior to any that the North had to offer. Consequently, as even the most serious medical student was urged to refresh himself occasionally with female society, it was best that he remain in Nashville where the women were inspirational, rather than run the risk of moral degeneration in northern cities where the homes of the best people would be closed to him.[7]

There were more substantial reasons for founding the medical school at Nashville. It was believed by its sponsors that climate and occupation, as well as social, religious, and political institutions of a people, tended to develop special forms of disease and to modify those which were common. Therefore, medicine should be taught in that region where it was to be practiced. The geographical location of the capital city was also in its favor. Situated in the center of Tennessee, it was easily accessible from all sections of the state and in 1851 Nashvillians were beginning to realize that their city was destined to be one of the railroad centers of the Trans-Alleghany region. The city was expanding rapidly in the fifties and the many public and private building projects were considered quite opportune by the medical faculty because where there was construction, accidents were bound to

---

[6] Philip M. Hamer (ed.), *The Centennial History of the Tennessee State Medical Association, 1830-1930* (Nashville, 1930), 51.

[7] C. K. Winston, "An Address, November 3, 1851," in *Addresses Delivered before the Medical Classes of the University of Nashville* (Nashville, 1851-1872), 16 ff.

occur and so the medical students would profit from first-hand observation of injured stone cutters, bricklayers, and mechanics.[8] This idea was expressed by Dr. C. K. Winston, of the medical faculty, when he declared "the rapid influx of population together with the casualties ensuing from an increase of machinery and rapidity of locomotion will afford ample materials for hospitals."[9]

By the fall of 1852 the new medical school was described as being "complete in all its fixtures, cabinets, and apparatus."[10] This statement, like many generalizations, perverted the truth to a certain extent and should be accepted with caution. The truth was that the school possessed at this time enough essential equipment to operate with a certain degree of efficiency, but not until Lindsley, Dr. Paul Eve, and other members of the faculty had made several "shopping" trips abroad were the museum, laboratory, and dissecting room equipped with apparatus in keeping with the lofty ideals and objectives of the directors.[11] With Troost's fine zoological collection as a foundation, the medical school was able to boast by 1858 of what was undoubtedly a valuable and serviceable anatomical museum. Difficulties arose in finding material for the dissecting room as it was unlawful to disinter bodies in Tennessee. However, there was no law against importation and the medical students soon found plenty of material on which to wield their knives. How the bodies and skeletons were obtained, where they came from, or to whom they belonged was considered no one's business.

The original plant of the medical school consisted of a "spacious building," 76 feet by 45½ feet. It was apparent almost from the beginning that this "spacious building" was not large enough and in the summer of 1854 two wings were completed and opened for use. According to the *Annual Announcement of the Medical Department* for 1854 the enlarged structure afforded

---

[8] *Idem; Nashville Journal of Medicine and Surgery*, X (1856), 357.
[9] Winston, "An Address, November 3, 1851," 17.
[10] *Nashville Journal of Medicine and Surgery*, III (1852), 258.
[11] *Ibid.*, VI (1854), 351; VIII (1855), 258; XI (1856), 84, 544. Lindsley made a trip abroad in 1852 and visited the most important medical centers. See his Diary, April 3, 15, 1852.

ample accommodations for lecture rooms, dissecting rooms, offices, a museum, library, and laboratory. There were two lecture halls, each one capable of seating an audience of 500 people. The anatomical rooms were equipped with skylights, thus assuring good ventilation and plenty of light. In 1854 gas lamps were installed and proved their value especially on gloomy winter days.[12]

The medical school established a clinic where the students witnessed operations. It also maintained a dispensary for charity patients. The patients who were not ill enough to be confined were termed "outdoor patients." Such persons came each day to the dispensary and were examined by the professors in charge in the presence of the students. Charity patients seriously ill with such diseases as typhoid fever or pneumonia were confined in what was termed the City Dispensary of the Medical Department of the University of Nashville. This infirmary was opened in May, 1855, and 175 cases were treated during the first six months at a total cost to the medical school of only $60. Out of the 175 cases treated there were seven fatalities, of which three were typhoid cases and four were tuberculosis cases.[13]

St. John's Hospital and the Tennessee State Hospital were opened to the students and faculty of the medical school. St. John's was operated by the Sisters of Charity who had been brought to Nashville from Ohio and Kentucky by Bishop Richard Miles, head of the Nashville Diocese of the Catholic Church. St. John's could accommodate only twenty to twenty-five patients at a time but it offered good service at a very low cost. Here the patient paid only $3 a week for his maintenance. There was no charge for medicine, nursing, medical attention, or surgical operations.[14] The state institution was a general hospital

---

[12] *Nashville Journal of Medicine and Surgery*, II (1852), 187; VI (1854), 351; VII (1854), 249; *Annual Announcement of the University of Nashville* (Nashville, 1851-1910), 1852, p. 9; 1854, p. 16.

[13] *Nashville Journal of Medicine and Surgery*, III (1852), 260; X (1856), 130-132.

[14] *Ibid.*, III (1852), 260; *The South-Western Monthly, a Journal Devoted to Literature and Science, Education, the Mechanic Arts and Agriculture* (Nashville, 1852), I (1852), 83-84.

and in 1856 the legislature, acting with the mayor and aldermen of Nashville, appointed the faculty of the medical school as a board of governors for a period of ten years. Thus with hospitals and clinics to supplement laboratory and lecture room, the medical student at the University of Nashville was able to see method and theory put into practice and to study at close range the course of various diseases.[15]

While plans for the new medical school were being discussed, the state legislature granted a charter for a law school, to be known as the Law Department of the University of Nashville. The faculty was to consist of not less than two nor more than five members. When the school finally opened, prematurely it would seem, in 1854, there were only two professors on its staff, and it was forced to close temporarily to complete its organization.[16]

The college year at the law school was divided into two sessions of sixteen weeks, and in order to complete the requirements for graduation the student was expected to remain through four sessions. In addition to his reading and his academic work,[17] the law student was expected to spend considerable time in the courts and at the sessions of the legislature. In this respect, the advantages of having the law school located in Nashville were obvious. In addition to the legislature, county, state, and circuit courts offered the students the chance to meet important members of the law profession and the opportunity to observe legal machinery in operation. Another asset which the Nashville law student did not overlook was the new state library which was to contain a valuable collection of law books by the close of the decade.[18]

During the years 1852 and 1853 the literary department of

[15] For a more detailed study of the medical school and medical science as it was known in the fifties, see Chapter III.
[16] Tennessee *Acts*, 1849-1850, pp. 533-534; *Annual Announcement of the University of Nashville*, 1854-1855, p. 15; Minutes of the University of Nashville (MS in Peabody College Library), March 9, 1855.
[17] The law student studied the works of about thirty authorities.
[18] *Nashville City and Business Directory*, V (1860-1861), 40-41; *Third Biennial Report upon the Library of the State* (Nashville, 1859), 146-149.

the University of Nashville was reorganized,[19] and a new building was constructed for the use of this department. However, the new literary department never functioned as an independent unit and was absorbed by the Western Military Institute, which was united with the University of Nashville in 1855.[20] So in reality during the decade of the fifties, the University of Nashville was composed of the medical school, the law department, and the combination liberal arts and military school known as the Military Institute.

There were two executive officers in charge of the military school, the superintendent and the commandant of cadets. The superintendent was responsible for the entire school. He was chief business manager as well as academic supervisor. The commandant of cadets had direct charge of the military exercises. He maintained a constant and strict supervision over the conduct of the cadets and drew up and enforced rules and orders pertaining to parades, inspections, drills, and discipline.[21]

Each professor in the institute was the head of his own department and was free to choose his own method of instruction, provided he maintained discipline at all times. Strict rules were applied to the instructors as well as the students. They were requested to keep a daily record of each student and to make a weekly report to the superintendent. It was necessary for each instructor to attend classes "with rigorous punctuality" and he could not detain a class or dismiss it ten minutes early without satisfactory reasons which had to be entered on his weekly report.[22]

There were many rules governing the life of the cadet. He could not drink liquor nor play cards. He could not chew tobacco during drill, and there were restrictions on smoking, although it was not absolutely prohibited. The cadet was forbidden to leave the grounds of the school without written permission.

---

[19] Tennessee *Acts of a Local or Private Nature*, 1851-1852, p. 595.
[20] Minutes of the University of Nashville, 1855 (MS in Peabody College Library).
[21] *Annual Announcement of the University of Nashville*, 1855-1856, p. 13.
[22] *Idem;* Windrow, *John Berrien Lindsley*, 51-52.

He was warned against forming combinations or engaging in mutinies. He was forbidden to write or draw pictures on the walls of the quarters, classrooms, or outhouses. He was forced to pay for all the glassware, chinaware, and furniture which he broke, either accidentally or deliberately. A violation of these rules usually meant expulsion for the guilty student.[23]

The curriculum consisted of five courses—a preparatory course open to boys who were at least thirteen years old, and freshman, sophomore, junior, and senior courses. The preparatory course consisted of spelling, reading, penmanship, geography, grammar, composition, arithmetic, elements of algebra, history, Latin grammar, Caesar, Greek grammar, and the Greek Testament. The courses in English (reading, grammar, etc.) were continued as long as the student was deficient in these subjects. The collegiate subjects were arranged in four groups, mathematics, languages, ethics and belles lettres, science and military tactics. The freshman schedule included algebra, geometry, trigonometry, mensuration, Latin and Greek, physiology, history, composition and elocution, and infantry and artillery drills.[24]

The sophomore course was simply a continuation of the freshman studies with the addition of surveying, navigation, and theology. However, the junior schedule included chemistry with "its application to agriculture," mineralogy, geology, and paleontology, and the seniors studied acoustics, optics, astronomy, and electromagnetism. The senior program included also political economy, ancient and modern history, international and constitutional law, and philosophy.[25]

When the school opened it was necessary for the cadet to take the entire course in order to receive the A.B. degree. Modern languages were not included in the regular curriculum and did not carry any credit towards the degree. However, in 1856 a complete scientific course was added and the institution began to grant the degree of bachelor of science. French and German

---

[23] *Annual Announcement of the University of Nashville,* 1855-1856, pp. 22-25.
[24] *Ibid.,* 15.   [25] *Ibid.,* 16.

now became a part of the scientific course and Spanish was considered an elective. Science students had the privilege of studying architecture and civil engineering. Fencing, bookkeeping, drawing, and painting (oils and water color) were offered as "extras" to both scientific and classical students.[26]

The entire four-year course was bound to give a diligent student a liberal education. The administration explained the purpose of the curriculum in the annual catalogue:

> The course here indicated is thoroughly taught. It has been selected with the view of training all the intellectual faculties and of avoiding that partial system which develops the capacities and energies of one portion of them to the neglect and even detriment of the other. It is believed that it combines the excellencies of the course pursued in our best literary institutions with the essential parts of that of our national military academy at West Point; and that while it adorns the mind of the student with literary graces, it will also inure him to habits of industry, and qualify him for the most accurate and difficult investigations. Under the uniform and economical distribution of time, and the habits of punctuality attained by military discipline, applied so as to protect the students from the allurements, the vices, and the dissipations usually incident to college life, the faculty can safely pledge themselves to secure more than ordinary results.[27]

In 1855 the tuition at the institute was $105 for a term of twenty weeks or $210 per academic year. This included board, laundry, fuel, linen, medical service, and the use of arms. Each student had to furnish his own room and supply himself with candles and one pair of good blankets. The matriculation fee was $5 and the graduation fee was $10. By 1860 the tuition had been raised $5 per term.

Although this military school was quite successful during the five years of its existence (1855-1860) it could not have been entirely satisfactory to John Berrien Lindsley, who was now Chancellor of the University of Nashville, and other supporters of higher education. However, after the university had been rebuilt (1853-1854) funds were so scarce that the trustees were "at their

---

[26] *Ibid.*, 1856-1857, pp. 13-16; *ibid.*, 1860-1861, p. 13.
[27] *Ibid.*, 1855-1856, pp. 16-17.

wits' end to know what to do with their grounds and buildings."[28] The combination military and literary college seemed to be the only solution to the problem.

The tradition that female academies originated in the South and remained peculiar to the South cannot be corroborated by the facts. In 1779, long before the Nashville Female Academy opened its doors in 1817, there was a school for young ladies in New Haven and a similar school in Newburyport, Massachusetts. Perhaps the first successful female schools were conducted by the Moravians in Bethlehem, Pennsylvania, and later in Philadelphia. At any rate, by 1780 the Moravian system had made such a good impression that Benjamin Rush and other educators established a female academy in Philadelphia. Before 1808 female academies had opened in Greenfield, Connecticut, and in Medford, Bradford, Concord, and Pittsfield, Massachusetts. In Lexington, Kentucky, one of Nashville's important rivals in the field of education, the first academy for young ladies was opened in 1805.[29]

In 1850 the Nashville Female Academy completed its thirty-third year of activity and for sustained success the school had an enviable reputation. It was more than self-sustaining; it was "self-enriching." "Its prosperity," claimed the *Nashville Daily News*, "has been unparalleled in the history of female schools."[30] According to the same newspaper, the academy buildings were the "most extensive in the United States devoted to female education."[31] They had a front on Church Street of one hundred and eighty feet and extended back two hundred and eighty feet. Most of the buildings were two stories high.[32]

The prosperity of the institution permitted frequent remodel-

[28] Edwin H. Ewing, *An Address by the Honorable Edwin H. Ewing at the Celebration of the Centennial Anniversary of the University of Nashville, December 10, 1885* (Nashville, 1885), 14-15; Lillian Foster, *Wayside Glimpses, North and South* (New York, 1860), 185.

[29] Wooldridge, *History of Nashville*, 400 n.; William Woodbridge, "Female Education in the United States Prior to 1800," in Barnard's *American Journal of Education* (Hartford, 1856-1881), XXVII (1877), 273; George B. Emerson, "Schools as they Should Be," in *ibid.*, XXVIII (1878), 257-274 and especially 269.

[30] *Nashville Daily News*, August 29, 1858.

[31] *Idem*. The academy was owned by fifty stockholders.

[32] Wooldridge (ed.), *History of Nashville*, 404.

ing and expansion. For example, in 1857 a new chapel was constructed and the number of dormitory rooms was increased. In the same year the buildings were entirely refurnished, and much of the equipment, including the chemical apparatus, was brought up to date.[33] In the following year $60,000 was spent on improvements, and by 1860 the entire plant was heated by steam and equipped with gas lamps. There were numerous bath rooms with hot and cold water, and the kitchen and laundry equipment was the best that money could buy. The buildings were connected by porticoes and covered walks to permit communication without exposure to the weather.[34]

The courses of study at the Nashville Female Academy were divided into three departments, called, respectively, preparatory, academic, and collegiate. The preparatory department was designed for girls under ten years of age. Here for one year the pupils studied the rudiments of spelling, reading, writing, and arithmetic. McGuffey's *Speller* and *First Reader* and Mitchel's *Primary Geography* were the only textbooks used.[35] The preparatory department had a large room, apart from all others, which was well supplied with maps and charts. There were special teachers for the small children whose activities, both academic and recreational, were distinct from those of the older girls.[36]

The classes in the academic department were called second junior, first junior, second senior, and first senior. Each class had one teacher for all the prescribed subjects, which were about the same for each year of the four-year course. These subjects included spelling, penmanship, vocal music, arithmetic, geography, grammar, composition, botany, history of the United States, and mythology.[37]

Instruction in the collegiate department was by "a college of teachers." The work in this upper division was on a four-year

---

[33] *Nashville Union and American*, April 15, 1857.
[34] *Nashville Daily News*, August 29, 1858; *Nashville City and Business Directory*, V (1860-1861), 31.
[35] *Idem; Nashville Female Academy*, July, 1852. (Pamphlet in Tennessee State Library).
[36] *Idem.*   [37] *Idem.*

basis and the curriculum included penmanship, grammar, physiology, zoology, physical geography, ancient and modern history, algebra, geometry, natural philosophy, elements of physics, chemistry, geology, astronomy, rhetoric, political science, Bible, and ethics. The course of study did not require languages. The administration declared that as much attention was given to the study of the English language as was usually given in colleges to "the Dead Languages."[38] The elimination of Greek and Latin was a bold step in an age when the classics were still regarded as a collegiate tradition that formed the foundation of any curriculum. However, Greek and Latin were taught when desired. The same was true with respect to French, Spanish, and German.

The "Ornamental Department" of the Nashville Female Academy was very popular with the young ladies.[39] The ornamental subjects were vocal music, instrumental music (piano, harp, and guitar), drawing, painting, and fancy needle work.[40] Many of the young ladies who lived in Nashville studied only music at the academy. Such students were called "parlor boarders" and no doubt there were times when their presence was regretted by the regular students. At any rate, after 1853 a special building was provided for the music students "thus rendering the boarding house more quiet and affording greater advantages to our music pupils."[41] Every June at commencement the seniors who had acquired some skill in drawing, painting, needlework, and music gave an exhibition and concert to the public.[42]

While the academy was non-sectarian it was operated on a Christian basis and the students were expected to attend the church to which their parents belonged. It will be recalled, too, that the Bible represented one unit in the regular course of studies.

[38] *Idem;* see also *Nashville Patriot,* August 6, 1859; *Southern Lady's Companion* (Nashville, 1847-1854), V (1851), 150.
[39] *Nashville Patriot,* August 6, 1859; J. C. Cooke, "Memories of Days of Long Ago Recalled," in *Nashville Banner,* September 6, 1931.
[40] *Republican Banner and Nashville Whig,* June 15, 1852; *Nashville Union and American,* April 15, 1857.
[41] *Nashville City and Business Directory,* I (1853), 98.
[42] John Berrien Lindsley, Diary, June 8, 1857.

The principal of the academy, Rev. C. D. Elliott (in office 1844-1866), was a man of sound religious principles. In 1857 he declared that the academy, at least in atmosphere, had become eminently religious. "So eminently so," he asserted, "that there have been in the last five years more conversions in the academy than in . . . any church in the city, if not in all put together."[43]

It is interesting to notice that considerable attention was given to physical training at the academy. The classes in calisthenics were held in a recreation hall one hundred and twenty feet long by forty feet wide.[44] Elliott considered dancing good exercise and introduced it for the sake of health, cheerfulness, and recreation, but at the same time "in a manner consistent with the spirit of piety and devotion."[45] John B. McFerrin, editor of the Methodist paper, the *Nashville Christian Advocate,* opposed dancing in any form or for any purpose, and consequently he objected to dancing in the gymnasium of the Nashville Female Academy. On the basis that his position as editor of a Christian paper gave him the right to call ministers to account before the world he started to attack Elliott through the *Advocate.* Elliott, although he believed the matter should have been settled quietly in a church conference, defended himself on the basis that the Bible, the laws of the churches interested in the academy, and the writings of Wesley all confirmed his opinion that dancing was not sinful if taught as a recreation.[46]

The climax to this controversy came in 1858 after a Saturday night party at the academy. It was customary for the students and teachers to give charades, tableaux, and concerts on Saturday evenings. The entertainment in question, however, was arranged by the Negro servants of the institution, and a Virginia break-

[43] *Nashville Female Academy—Dancing,* October 16, 1857 (a circular in Tennessee State Library).
[44] Mrs. Bennett D. Bell, "Female Schools in Tennessee Prior to 1861," in *Confederate Veteran* (Nashville, 1893-1932), XXXII (1924), 171; *Nashville City and Business Directory,* V (1860-1861), 31.
[45] *Nashville Female Academy—Dancing,* October 16, 1857.
[46] *Idem;* see also *The Parlor Visitor* (Nashville and Murfreesboro, 1854-1857), II (1854), 18; III (1855), 187-188.

down was included on the program. Elliott enjoyed the entertainment himself and there were thirty or forty teachers and Nashville citizens in the audience, people "with extreme modesty in taste, piety, refinement and social position," who seemed to be amused at the darkies. McFerrin, however, as soon as he heard of the entertainment denounced it as sinful and contrary to Christian principles. In reply to this attack, Elliott declared, "if it is a sin to see a darky dance the Virginia Breakdown and all who ever laughed at it are to be expelled from the church, I shall certainly find myself in good company."[47] But in spite of the fact that Elliott received the support of many friends, he was divested of his orders. McFerrin was too powerful to be denied.

The success of the Nashville Female Academy was due to its capable presidents, its liberal curriculum, and its well-trained teachers. During Elliott's administration the academy reached the peak of its development. In 1844, when he became principal of the school, there was an enrollment of 194 students. By 1860 the number had increased to 513. In 1844 Elliott had a staff of only ten teachers, but by 1860 this had increased to thirty-eight.[48] Judged by the standards of the day the teachers were above the average. The ornamental department was especially strong. "In painting, drawing and music," declared Elliott, "we have endeavored to secure for our patrons the very best talent in the country."[49]

Some of the teachers were importations from Europe. Thus in 1860 Elliott engaged two piano instructors who had studied at the Conservatoire Impérial and under Henri Herz, a well-known European musician.[50] The academy's method of teaching French is worthy of notice. As early as 1833 the French students were placed in a particular section of the dormitory where they were constantly under the supervision of the French instructor,

[47] *Nashville Female Academy*, April 2, 1858 (Circular in Tennessee State Library).
[48] Wooldridge (ed.), *History of Nashville*, 404.
[49] *Nashville Patriot*, August 6, 1859.
[50] *Ibid.*, January 13, 1860. The two piano teachers were Camille Brunet and Athalie Casche.

or perhaps a French matron. In the dining room a table was set apart for these students who conversed in French during meals. A similar plan is followed today in the better institutions devoted primarily to the study of languages.

The administration of the Nashville Female Academy felt a grave responsibility towards its students. Consequently, discipline was strict and there were many rules that must have proved irksome to the older girls. As already noticed, all students, accompanied by a teacher, were forced to attend church on Sunday. No company was allowed in the dormitories and no student could visit a friend in town without special permission. No student was allowed outside the academy yard without a chaperon. Novels were prohibited. It was against the rules for a student to have an account at any of the city stores or to spend money without permission from the principal.[51] The school was proud of what it called "the maternal care" given the girls and it was claimed that this special service cost the institution $3,000 annually.[52]

But the rules did not prevent the girls from enjoying healthful and innocent amusements. The Saturday night parties have been mentioned. Walking with a chaperon was approved and picnic suppers were popular in warm weather. The following extract from a student diary is suggestive: "The first of May our class marched in a long procession to Watkins Grove where we had speeches, one by Dr. Elliott, and our class presented an old flag to a military company. We then returned and had dinner spread on the grass on the academy yard, a band playing and plenty of boys at the gates."[53]

Many of the students enjoyed their years at the academy and looked back to them as one of the happiest periods in their lives. As one graduate declared, "I love these halls, desks, globes, maps, and school books, and that old Bible from which I have heard

[51] *Republican Banner and Nashville Whig*, June 15, 1852.
[52] *Southern Business Directory and General Commercial Advertiser*, I (Charleston, 1854), 70.
[53] The Lucy Southgate Diary quoted by J. C. Cooke, "Memories of Days of Long Ago Recalled," in *Nashville Banner*, September 13, 1931.

our beloved superintendents read so oft the morning and evening lessons; and I love that familiar old bell that has called us so faithfully to our studies; its tones are as the voice of an old acquaintance."[54]

There were two other educational institutions in Nashville during the decade under discussion that deserve more than passing mention. These schools were the Nashville Ladies College and the Shelby Medical College.

The Ladies College was incorporated on February 18, 1852,[55] and obviously took the Nashville Female Academy for its model. Rev. R. A. Lapsley was chosen president, and in the first annual catalogue of the institution he explained its policy and purpose. The legitimate object of education, he wrote, "is to render the mind a fit instrument for observing, applying and obeying the laws under which God has placed the universe. The result is secured by developing the moral, intellectual and physical faculties in proportion to their relative importance."[56] He believed that education for women could not be overemphasized. Their sex and their position in society gave them in a Christian community "next to absolute control of the destiny of the race." It was true, Lapsley continued, that parents could assist in the development of their daughter's mind, but it was education that gave the young woman the "power to guide the unfolding intellect in the path of honor and true greatness."[57]

The faculty of the college included John Berrien Lindsley, professor of experimental philosophy, chemistry, mineralogy, geology, natural history, and botany. Perhaps no other man in the state was equal to such a teaching assignment. Perhaps it was more remarkable that young women actually studied sciences but it was becoming the fashion for women to use scientific terms and many saw the practical relationship between chemistry and home economics. The editor of the *South-Western Monthly* gave

[54] *Southern Lady's Companion*, IV (1850), 137.
[55] Tennessee *Acts*, 1851-1852, p. 558.
[56] *Nashville Ladies College, First Annual Catalogue* (1853), 9.
[57] *Idem.*

expression to the new trend when he took up his pen "not to write a dissertation on female education, but to insist that young ladies be taught chemistry. They will thereby be better qualified to superintend domestic affairs, guard against many accidents to which households are subject, and perhaps be instrumental in saving life."[58]

The Shelby Medical College was chartered in 1857 and the first session began on November 1, 1858. That there was a need for another medical school in Nashville seems evident. "The Medical Department of the University of Nashville has succeeded beyond expectation," said the *Nashville Daily News*,[59] "and still a number of our most eminent physicians are satisfied of the demand for another institution of equal capacity; not for the purpose of rivalry, but that there may be abundant facilities for the swarms of pupils who prefer Nashville over other and less healthful localities in the South and who have no inclination to go North for their medical instruction."

With one exception, the faculty of the Shelby Medical College was chosen from Tennessee physicians. John Frederick May had been associated with Baltimore and Washington and when he accepted the professorship of surgery at the new medical school in Nashville he had a national reputation. ". . . one of the most distinguished surgeons in the country," said the *Republican Banner and Nashville Whig*,[60] "an eloquent lecturer, skillful operator, and profound scholar."

The plant of the Shelby Medical College included a museum, a laboratory, two lecture halls, and a private hospital. The laboratory was well equipped for the period, and the museum contained "a great variety of specimens, both natural and artificial."[61] The hospital received pauper patients from the city at the rate of $1.50 per week per patient. It also accommodated patients from the United States Marine service.

[58] *The South-Western Monthly, A Journal Devoted to Literature and Science, Education, the Mechanic Arts and Agriculture*, I (1852), 42-43.
[59] *Nashville Daily News*, July 17, 1858.
[60] *Republican Banner and Nashville Whig*, July 17, 1858.
[61] *Nashville Patriot*, October 17, 1859.

The agreement between the city administration and the college to care for paupers at $1.50 a week was not placidly accepted by the press. The editor of the *Daily News* did not believe that nurses could be employed and the patients fed properly at such a low rate. Furthermore, the *Daily News* was opposed to the principle of giving out a sick man's life to be cared for by the lowest bidder.[62] A correspondent of the same paper believed that the faculty wanted the paupers solely for the benefit of the medical students. "They want them to try experiments upon and lecture over," he declared, "while the patient is perhaps suffering from want of kind attention."[63]

The Shelby Medical College was opened at an unfortunate time. Scarcely had it perfected its organization when the Civil War interrupted its activities and soon put an end to its career.

In the decade under discussion there were three commercial colleges chartered in Nashville. The first of the three to come into existence was Carney's Nashville Commercial College, which was incorporated by the legislature on February 22, 1852. According to its charter this college was "an institution for the instruction of young gentlemen in mercantile knowledge, embracing all the branches requisite for thoroughly qualifying them for bookkeepers and business pursuits."[64] This school was short-lived, as it was abandoned in 1853.

The most successful of the commercial schools was the Southern Commercial College which was chartered on March 1, 1854. The curriculum consisted of bookkeeping, commercial law, commercial penmanship, and commercial arithmetic. By 1860 the Southern Commercial College, "free from contaminating influence of Northern fanatics,"[65] was widely known and hundreds of its graduates were either in business for themselves, or filling responsible positions as accountants and bookkeepers in Nashville and throughout the South.

[62] *Nashville Daily News*, July 24, 1858.
[63] *Ibid.*, July 24, 1856.
[64] Tennessee *Acts*, 1851-1852, p. 619.
[65] *Nashville City and Business Directory*, V (1860-1861), 280.

The third college of this type was the Nashville Commercial College which was chartered on March 20, 1858.[66] In addition to the regular business courses, this school offered surveying, civil engineering, and architectural drawing.

There would be no point in enumerating all the private schools of lesser importance in Nashville, so only a few of the more interesting ones will be mentioned. The Nashville Male Academy was operated by Nathaniel Cross and N. Davison Cross. Here for the sum of $210.00 per year, boys and young men were given a thorough mathematical and classical education. The tuition included room and board. The Nashville Female Institute was chartered in 1852. This school, which was under the direction of Rev. C. C. Bitting, held its sessions in the basement of a church. Miss Coleman's school for young ladies was described as "one of long and high standing" while Miss Nichols operated a superior private school for the children of the wealthy. At the beginning of the decade Alfred Hume's school was one of the best, while Bishop Miles' school for boys and the Academy of St. Cecelia (founded in 1860) should not be overlooked.[67]

One other school needs to be mentioned, not because the school itself was important, but because its proprietor, William Ferrel (1817-1891), was on the verge of a career in science and mathematics that was to bring him world recognition. Ferrel was born into poverty, but before his allotted time had run its course he was known as a distinguished American meteorologist. His early home in Fulton County, Pennsylvania, was a simple log cabin with a mud chimney. His second home in Berkeley County, Virginia, was little better, although here he had the advantage of a nearby log schoolhouse. From boyhood he showed an unusual interest in mathematics and the little money he earned by working in his neighbors' fields he spent for arithmetic and surveying books. He used a barn door for a blackboard and a

[66] Tennessee *Acts of a Private Nature*, 1857-1858, p. 381.

[67] Newspaper advertisements and notices throughout the period; see also, Tennessee *Acts*, 1851-1852, p. 272; *Nashville City and Business Directory*, I (1853), vi, vii; VIII (1872), 13; Mrs. O. Z. Bond, "Life of Brigadier General Felix Kirk Zollicoffer, C. S. A." (MS in Tennessee State Library), 5.

pitchfork tine for chalk but in spite of the handicaps he soon became an expert mathematician. In 1844 he graduated from Bethany College and began a teaching career. He taught in Liberty, Missouri, Todd County, Kentucky, and Clarksville, Tennessee, before he opened his school in Nashville in 1854.[68]

By this time he had developed a special interest in geography and meteorology although his first published paper indicates that he was interested also in geology. This paper appeared in 1854 in the *Nashville Journal of Medicine and Surgery*[69] and was entitled "On the Hypothesis of the Internal Fluidity of the Earth." Ferrel discredited this hypothesis and declared that the center of the earth was solid. During the next two years he was developing a theory pertaining to the effect of the rotation of the earth on the course of the winds and ocean currents. His ideas on this subject were announced in an essay entitled "The Winds and the Currents of the Ocean" which was published in the *Nashville Journal of Medicine and Surgery*[70] in 1856. In this essay he first propounded one of the fundamental principles on which the science of meteorology was to be based and which since has been known as Ferrel's Law.

The law may be defined as a meteorological generalization to the effect that the deflecting force exerted on the winds of the globe by the earth's rotation is inversely proportionate to the velocity of motion, increasing from zero at the equator to a maximum value at either pole. This force deflects the winds in the northern hemisphere to the right hand, and in the southern hemisphere to the left hand.[71]

The originality of Ferrel's meteorological attainments soon attracted attention at home and abroad, and in the spring of 1857 he was appointed assistant editor of the *American Ephemeris and Nautical Almanac* which was published in Cambridge, Massachusetts. His new duties took him to Cambridge during the

---

[68] W. J. Humphreys, "William Ferrel," in *Dictionary of American Biography*, 20 vols. (New York, 1928-1936), VI, 338-339.
[69] *Nashville Journal of Medicine and Surgery*, VII (1854), 199-203.
[70] *Ibid.*, XI (1856), 287-301, 375-389.
[71] *Nelson's Perpetual Loose-Leaf Encyclopaedia* (New York, 1921), V, 2.

summer of 1857, but in the fall he was back in Nashville operating his private school. The next year, however, he gave up teaching as a profession, turned his school over to a colleague, and returned to Cambridge. In 1867 he accepted a special appointment to the United States Coast Survey for Tidal Observations. While engaged in this work he invented a tide-predicting machine which was adopted by the government. He rounded out his long and varied career by holding a high position in the United States Signal Service.[72]

Professor Herman L. Fairchild of the University of Rochester in an article published in *Science,* November 11, 1932, gave a modern estimate of Ferrel's work. "Until the middle of the past century," wrote Fairchild, "the winds were supposed to be lawless. And it remained for a schoolteacher in Nashville, Tennessee, with a flair for mathematics, Mr. William Ferrel, to make the interesting and important discovery that the prevailing currents of the air are an effect of the earth's rotation. His analysis of the forces and his description of the winds, published during the years 1856-1889, yet remain authoritative."[73]

By 1850 Nashville was beginning to realize that the old system of private schools was inadequate, and before the close of the decade the city had laid the foundations for a public school system. In June, 1852, Alfred Hume (1808-1853), a prominent schoolteacher, was selected by the city council to examine the best public school systems then in operation in the United States. After a tour which took him to Cleveland, Boston, Providence, Philadelphia, and Baltimore, Hume returned to Nashville and on August 26, 1852, presented the report that became the basis of Nashville's public school system.[74]

In this report, Hume pointed out the advantages of public schools over private schools. "Buildings perfectly adapted to schools can be erected by the public," he asserted. "These build-

[72] *Idem.*
[73] Herman L. Fairchild, "Earth Rotation and River Erosion" in *Science* (New York, 1883-), LXXVI (1932), 423-424.
[74] Alfred Hume, *Report on the Subject of Public Schools in the City of Nashville* (Nashville, 1852).

ings can be furnished in better style, with all the necessary furniture and apparatus. Teachers of the highest qualifications can be procured always. Better work can be demanded of them, because they will be independent of the influence of parents, and because they will be compelled to teach a fewer number of subjects. And lastly: public schools can be subjected to a much more rigid examination than any private schools can possibly be."[75] It is apparent that Hume believed that the instruction in private schools was frequently superficial.

The Boston school system influenced Hume more than any other and it was taken as the model for the Nashville schools. The plan called for a board of education, and a primary, grammar, and high school. The board was given authority to elect and dismiss teachers, to fix salaries, to adopt the course of study pursued in each division of the schools, to recommend textbooks, to examine the pupils, to supervise the buildings, and to appoint a superintendent of schools.[76]

The primary school was intended for children from four to eight years old. These children might be safely divided into classes containing as many as sixty pupils. "Experience has proved that one teacher can properly instruct that number," said Hume, "all being nearly of the same age, and very little difference in their attainments."[77] On this point, of course, Hume was mistaken, but so were his pedagogical contemporaries. The pupils in the primary department were taught to read, spell, and do mental arithmetic. Vocal music and elements of drawing were also a part of the curriculum, while discipline and moral instruction were constantly emphasized.

The curriculum in the grammar and high school was typical of the times. In the grammar school the program consisted of English grammar and composition, geography, history, arithmetic, algebra, natural philosophy, elementary chemistry, vocal music, and (for the girls) instrumental music. In the high school more advanced mathematics and chemistry were offered. But a

[75] *Ibid.*, 13-14. [76] *Ibid.*, 15-16. [77] *Ibid.*, 17.

forerunner of a modern trend is seen in the fact that French and Spanish were added to the inevitable Latin and Greek.[78]

The public schools were maintained by a property tax and a poll tax. In 1852 the city council levied a tax of one fifth of one per cent on all property assessed in the city for the purpose of "building up and putting into operation a system of public schools."[79] For the same purpose, all free white males between the ages of twenty-one and fifty were obliged to pay an annual poll tax of two dollars.

By 1860 considerable progress had been made. According to the *Nashville Patriot* for January 27, 1860, the city had five schools in operation with a total enrollment of 1,892 pupils. In 1856 Lillian Foster found the high school "in a prosperous condition and provided with the very best teachers."[80] However, in 1860 there were only thirty-one teachers for the entire system, or an average of sixty-one pupils per teacher.[81]

Alfred Hume has been called "the father of the Nashville public schools." It is evident that he deserves the title, because not only did he draw up the plans for the original system but he gave unsparingly of his time and energy in order that it might operate as smoothly as possible. "The eyes of the people are turned to him," said the *Nashville Daily Gazette*,[82] "and they expect his judgment and experience to mould and perfect that system of schools to which thousands are looking with anxious eyes."

Hume was imbued with the same zeal, the same spirit, that had fired Philip Lindsley's ambitions in his youth. No doubt Hume had been influenced by Lindsley's pleas for common schools as the President of the University of Nashville had been interested in education at every level and campaigned for public schools as well as for the university. It was unfortunate that Hume died in 1853 before his work was complete. But imperfect

[78] *Ibid.*, 18.
[79] *Revised Laws of the City of Nashville*, 1806-1855 (Nashville, 1854 [*sic*]), II, 172.
[80] Lillian Foster, *Wayside Glimpses, North and South*, 187.
[81] *Nashville Patriot*, January 27, 1860.
[82] *Nashville Daily Gazette*, March 17, 1853.

as the school system was, at least the foundation was constructed by 1860. An efficient public school system cannot be created in seven years. Alfred Hume realized this when he said, "Many will perhaps look for a perfect revolution in the whole educational system of our country here at once; these will be sadly mistaken."[83] And they were.

[83] Hume, *Report on the Subject of Public Schools in the City of Nashville*, 23.

CHAPTER III

NASHVILLE PHYSICIANS AND THE
MEDICAL SCIENCE

WHILE a physical plant is a necessity, it is the faculty which determines in the final analysis the true value of any institution of learning. The medical department of the University of Nashville was peculiarly fortunate in its personnel. Judged on the basis of scientific knowledge and medical technique as it was known and practiced in the middle of the nineteenth century, the men who lectured in the halls of this school and who applied the scalpel in its clinics should be ranked collectively above the average.

Shortly after the new medical school opened, the *Boston Medical and Surgical Journal* announced, "it would not be surprising were Nashville to become a great medical center."[1] With respect to the faculty, the Boston journal asserted, "There are eight professors of acknowledged worth and strength to the Nashville college, which will record its name on the pages of medical history in a manner honorable to their memories in after times."[2]

The eight professors of acknowledged worth were: W. T. Briggs, J. M. Watson, A. H. Buchanan, C. K. Winston, Robert M. Porter, W. K. Bowling, Paul F. Eve, and John Berrien Lindsley. Porter died in 1856 after contracting blood poisoning while at work in the dissecting room. He was succeeded by T. R. Jennings, who was well known as a teacher of anatomy in Nashville, having opened dissecting rooms there in 1838.

While all these men were capable, three in particular deserve special attention: John Berrien Lindsley, William King Bowling, and Paul Fitzsimmons Eve. Lindsley's importance has been ex-

---

[1] *Boston Medical and Surgical Journal* (Boston, 1828-), XLVI (1852), 485.
[2] *Ibid.*, 365.

plained in another connection (Chapter II) and need not be repeated here. Bowling, who was to gain national prominence as editor of the *Nashville Journal of Medicine and Surgery* was born in Westmoreland County, Virginia, in 1807. When he was three years old he went with his parents to northern Kentucky. His education consisted of private instruction and courses in the Medical College of Ohio and the medical department of Cincinnati College. He graduated from the Cincinnati institution in 1836 and for the next fourteen years successfully practiced medicine in Logan County, Kentucky. In 1850, Bowling came to Nashville and coöperated with Lindsley and other Nashville educators in establishing the medical school of the University of Nashville.[3]

Paul Fitzsimmons Eve was born at Forest Hall on the Savannah River, near Augusta, Georgia, in 1806. At the age of twenty he was graduated with the A.B. degree from Franklin College (now the University of Georgia) at Athens. His medical and surgical training was secured in the office of Dr. Charles D. Meigs of Philadelphia, in the medical school of the University of Pennsylvania, and in the clinics of the most famous surgeons of London and Paris. In addition to clinical training, he had some unusual and valuable experiences as a surgeon in the July Revolution in Paris (1830), in the Polish Revolution (1831), and in the Mexican War.[4]

In 1832 Eve participated in the organization of the Medical College of Georgia and held the chair of surgery at that institution until 1850 when he resigned to accept a position at the University of Louisville. In the following year, 1851, he was appointed professor of surgery at the Medical School of the University of Nashville. This position he held for ten years when the advent

---

[3] W. W. Clayton, *History of Davidson County, Tennessee, with Illustrations and Biographical Sketches of Its Prominent Men and Pioneers* (Philadelphia, 1880), 410-412.

[4] Paul F. Eve, "Address, November 3, 1851," in *Addresses Delivered before the Medical Classes of the University of Nashville*, 32; Eve, "On Asiatic Cholera Morbus," in *American Journal of the Medical Sciences*, O. S. (Philadelphia, 1827-1832), X (1832), 524-526; Chalmers T. Dow, "Paul Fitzsimmons Eve, M.D.," in *Transactions of the American Medical Association* (Philadelphia, 1848-1882), XXIX (1878), 641-646.

of the Civil War called him to serve as surgeon in General Joseph E. Johnston's army.[5]

Without doubt, Eve became one of the leading surgeons of the South in the period from 1850 to 1877. However, his reputation was not sectional. He was well known throughout the United States and was personally acquainted with many of the distinguished surgeons of Europe.[6] The fact that he published during his life over six hundred articles on medicine and surgery enhanced his reputation.[7] In 1857 he was elected president of the American Medical Association and this office brought him additional prestige.

Warm hearted and impulsive by nature and possessing ability as a public speaker, Eve made friends easily wherever he went and he was able to hold large audiences by his eloquence and sincerity. He was well liked in Nashville where he was an ardent supporter of the medical school and where he enjoyed "an overwhelming practice." He was somewhat of a philosopher and his common-sense attitude towards life and towards his profession was one reason for his popularity. The following plea for professional coöperation is typical of the man.

Those who are continually dealing with disease and death, who daily see poor frail humanity in its worst estate; who know full well the uncertainty and difficulties of their act, and their own liability to mistakes, should be kind and forbearing to each other. Few can estimate the injury done to the profession of medicine, by its members judging harshly of the acts of each other, by exaggerating reports, by a want of strict conformity to the truth, by personal disputes or professional controversy, by hasty and inconsiderate publications. The character of our noble calling ought to induce a forgiving spirit, to subdue envy, jealousy, and every evil passion, and prevent the exposure of the imperfections of an erring brother.[8]

[5] *Ibid.*, 643.
[6] *Nashville Journal of Medicine and Surgery,* II (1852), 186; III (1852), 93 ff., 138 ff., 208 ff.
[7] Dow, "Paul Fitzsimmons Eve, M.D.," 645.
[8] Paul F. Eve, "An Introductory Lecture, Delivered in the Medical College of Georgia, November 5, 1849," partially quoted in *American Journal of the Medical Sciences,* N. S. (Philadelphia, 1832-1853), XIX (1850), 471-474.

In spite of his accomplishments and his gifts to medical and surgical science, Eve maintained an attitude of humility. "A truly wise man is always humble," he told his students at the medical school. He warned them against the misconception that the completion of their college work was the end of their medical education. "You have but commenced a science," he declared, "for the full acquisition of which, a life time is too short."[9]

Both Eve and Bowling were bitter opponents of the quacks and neither lost an opportunity to denounce them from the public platform or in the editorial columns of the *Nashville Journal of Medicine and Surgery*. In the fifties the public had not entirely accepted the medical profession and many people preferred the quack to the trained "sawbones." The competition of the quack must have been a discouraging obstacle in the path of the young physician. The temptation to discard science and to traffic in secret prescriptions was always before him. The honor of the profession, however, was usually maintained. The University of Nashville retained the privilege of revoking a medical degree if and when one of its graduates engaged in irregular practice.[10]

Eve possessed a particular grievance against certain members of the clergy because, he maintained, they encouraged quacks to advertise in church periodicals. In no uncertain words he condemned this practice, although his crusading enthusiasm caused him to exaggerate the situation. He looked upon ministers as divinely inspired men commissioned to spread the gospel and not to spread the fraud and secret medicines of the nostrum-venders who had immorality and dishonesty stamped upon them "in frozen impudence."[11] Should Christians and Christian organizations encourage such charlatans? Eve believed that such support was not only unethical but unchristian.

[9] Paul F. Eve, "An Address to the Graduating Class of the Medical Department of the University of Nashville, 1855," in *Addresses Delivered before the Medical Classes of the University of Nashville*, 16.
[10] *Ibid.*, 10, 11, 19, 21; Albert G. Handley, "The Medical Man," in Inaugural Dissertations Submitted to the University of Nashville for the Degree of Doctor of Medicine (MSS in Peabody College Library), No. 46 (1853), 6.
[11] Eve, "An Address to the Graduating Class . . . 1855," p. 14.

It should be noted that Eve was not anti-clerical. He held in veneration the minister humbly devoted to God and he believed there should be a closer coöperation between the clergy and physicians. But Eve denounced the hypocrite who used religion as a cloak to disguise his true designs.[12]

The editorial policy of the *Nashville Journal of Medicine and Surgery* was vehemently anti-quack. This journal expressed the sentiments not only of the medical department of the university, but of the Medical Society of the State of Tennessee.[13] With withering editorials, Bowling carried on the warfare against the venders of illicit medicine. That the quacks were numerous there can be no doubt. Every medical journal of any consequence in the country frequently denounced the irregular practitioners. As the editor of the *Buffalo Medical Journal* stated, scarcely a medical lecture or address was published which did not abound in "fulminations against quackery."[14]

Perhaps there was not an organ in the country that so persistently and boldly campaigned against medical charlatanism as the *Nashville Journal of Medicine and Surgery*. As this publication circulated throughout the United States and England,[15] the battle cries of its supporters were heard half way around the globe. Letters of praise poured in from North and South. A Nashville subscriber believed that the editorial policy of the journal was beginning to have a good effect on medical affairs in Tennessee. He expressed his mind in a letter to the editor, and declared that the bold, professional stand taken by the journal against quacks and irregular members of the profession was being felt throughout the state and all that was needed to put them to rout was "a little more grape."[16]

The use of medical journals to spread anti-quack propaganda was one method of attacking the charlatans. However, such a method was not entirely satisfactory. Of what use were medical

---

[12] *Ibid.*, 18.
[13] *Nashville Journal of Medicine and Surgery*, IV (1853), 62.
[14] Quoted in *ibid.*, II (1852), 282.
[15] *Ibid.*, VIII (1855), 335-336.   [16] *Ibid.*, VI (1854), 187.

journals in the hands of the illiterate or in the hands of those who were prejudiced against the medical profession? Obviously, something more fundamental was needed. First, a general diffusion of knowledge, and, second, medical schools with a sound and thorough curriculum.

Judged by the standards of the day, the course in medical science and surgery offered by the medical department of the University of Nashville was thorough and complete. In order to graduate with the degree of M.D., the student was required to spend three years in the office of a regular physician, attend two full courses of lectures at the medical school, write an acceptable thesis on some medical topic, and pass a satisfactory examination.[17]

With Eve in mind, it would seem to the twentieth-century student that the faculty of the medical school was farther advanced in the field of anatomy and surgery than it was in therapeutics. The remedies employed in the treatment of diseases such as pneumonia and typhoid fever seem very strongly akin to quackery, as will be pointed out later.

In Eve the students at Nashville found a skillful, brave, and experienced surgeon. He was well known in medical circles before he moved to Nashville. Already he had attracted attention by the skillful operations he had performed while connected with the medical school at Atlanta. Among these was the removal of the entire uterus from a Negro woman. In all probability, Eve was the first surgeon in America to accomplish this feat.[18] He was particularly successful in removing stones from the bladder. Out of twenty-five operations of this nature, only four resulted in fatalities and only one of these was due directly to the operation.[19]

In the surgical clinic of the medical school at Nashville, Eve performed many difficult and interesting operations with the

[17] *Ibid.*, II (1852), 186; *Annual Announcement of the University of Nashville, 1851*, p. 6.

[18] Nineteen similar operations had been performed in Europe prior to Eve's performance. Paul F. Eve, *A Collection of Remarkable Cases of Surgery* (Philadelphia, 1857), 481-483; *Western Journal of Medicine and Surgery* (Louisville, 1840-1855), VI (1846), 401-407.

[19] Paul F. Eve, "Report of Twenty-Five Cases of Urinary Calculus," in *The American Journal of Medical Sciences*, N. S., XXIV (1852), 41-53.

students as spectators. Fortunately for the historian, the surgeon wrote detailed reports of these operations. One of peculiar interest is reproduced here:

Report of the Surgical Clinic for the First Week of the Preliminary Lectures in the Nashville University. Case I. Cysto-Sarcoma, resembling somewhat Fungus Haematodes—Operation—Death on the sixth day after it.

Mr. A. of Montgomery county, aged 60, received an injury on the top of his left shoulder, by a fall from a horse some twenty-five years ago. There resulted a small tumor at the point stricken, which gave but little or no inconvenience until he made a trip on horseback to Virginia, three years since. It then began slowly to enlarge; for the past twelve months, and particularly during the last six, it has rapidly increased in volume. It is about the size of a child's head at birth; is situated over the external extremity of the clavicle and the acromion process of the scapula; is quite irregular on its surface, presenting besides varicosed veins, smooth, rounded nodules under the distended and attenuated skin, with the mass itself projecting forwards and upward; and although apparently springing from the bone, can be moved pretty freely over the shoulder in an antero-posterior direction, but not laterally. The scapulo-humeral articulation is not involved in the disease. The patient's general health is not good; he has lost much flesh and strength during the past four months, but which he attributes to the excessive heat of the past summer. He suffers, too, he thinks, occasionally from dyspepsia; has lost his teeth years ago . . . but still uses tobacco. He has also a very peculiar deformity in the skin, said by him to be congenital. The entire surface of the body, save the palms of the hands and the soles of the feet, is covered with numerous round projecting tumors, about the size of large warts. He presents the appearance of a small-pox patient at a little distance, only these bodies exist instead of the pits of the variola. Besides this affection of the dermoid structure, there are several hard tumors, occasionally found, nearly as large as pigeon or pullet eggs, under the skin, in the areolar tissue.

The patient is exceedingly anxious about his condition, and very urgent for an operation. He believes there is no connection between the large tumor on the shoulder and the extensive congenital deformity of the skin. He came to Nashville a week before being operated upon, and at the consultation, Drs. Jennings, Porter, Buchanan, Rawlings, Waters, Briggs and Watson were present. The majority were inclined to the opinion . . . that his disease was malignant, probably fungus haematodes; one or two present thought more favorably of it; and it was agreed to place him under preparatory treatment for an operation, but to be governed in its extent by the revelation of an exploratory incision to be made into the tumor.

On Monday, the 2nd of October (1854), Dr. Bowling being added to the counsel, a puncture was passed obliquely under the skin, and entered about the middle of the diseased mass. The narrow blade of the knife met with no resistance, though moved in several directions; blood alone escaped and was supposed to be derived chiefly from the integuments. At the earnest request of some present, a second puncture was made into the center of one of the protruding nodules, when *serum* flowed freely. This at once induced us to believe that the affection was benign, and arrangements were immediately commenced to remove, if possible, the entire tumor. Bringing the patient under the influence of a mixture of chloroform and ether, long elliptical incisions were made to include the redundancy of skin which otherwise would remain in removing so large a diseased mass; the outer flaps were dissected up, and then a cut made into the tumor to empty its cysts and thus diminish its volume. This latter proceeding revealed the nature of the affection, for blood and serum freely escaped. In addition to these fluids, there was a substance resembling lard in consistence, probably coagulated albumen, occupying some of the large cysts, which latter were thick and fibrous in structure. By a rapid use of the knife a large mass was exsected with the integuments included between the incisions, and twisted sutures around pins passed through the integuments over the chasm were applied to arrest the hemorrhage, which threatened to be profuse. The length of the wound when closed was about nine inches, and it was covered with adhesive plasters, compresses and a roller bandage.

This operation was very badly borne by the patient. The anaesthetic mixture did not act well, the system being at no time fully impressed by it. I don't recollect ever to have heard one complain more, during the dressing of a wound. I learnt subsequent to this period that he had at times freely indulged in drink; and his mind had no doubt suffered from his recent physical ailment; but it is due to his medical advisers to say, his case was fairly and candidly placed before him, as well as his son and daughter who accompanied him to this city. Indeed, the character of the professional gentlemen named is sufficient guarantee that the very best was done for him that could have been under the circumstances, independent of the chief actor in the operation. The difficulty in the diagnosis of the nature of the tumor was very great, and the decision to attempt its removal was a natural consequence, even from our cautious proceedings. I believe all present will bear evidence with how great reluctance I operated in the case, having yielded my judgment to the more favorable opinion expressed by others concerning it, though I shrink from no part of the responsibility in performing it. I believed I was in the path of duty when endeavoring to prolong life and ease pain, and this is quite enough for me.

The following two days after the operation, our patient promised that he might so far recover as to be able to return home, a distance of forty miles; but during the following one his mind began to wander; the wound discharged a very copious sanious and albuminous matter; the fly, notwithstanding every care, got access to it, and maggots were developed throughout it, causing a most offensive and irritating ulcer, which exhausted life on the sixth day. There was no secondary hemorrhage; the pins ulcerated through the skin about the fourth day; and the large tumor having greatly subsided, the shoulder had become nearly flat again, so as to resemble the opposite one.[20]

It will be noticed that Eve used a mixture of chloroform and ether as an anaesthesia. The first anaesthesia to be used extensively was sulphuric ether discovered by Crawford W. Long (1815-1878) in 1843 and William T. G. Morton (1819-1868), a Boston dentist, in 1846. However, in the fifties chloroform was gaining favor as the best anaesthesia to use during surgical operations, but the profession was still skeptical because of its occasional fatal effects.[21] Chloroform was discovered by Samuel Guthrie (1782-1848), a frontier chemist of Sacketts Harbor, New York, in 1830, but it remained for Sir James Y. Simpson of Edinburgh to discover its anaesthetic power in 1847. His adoption of it for all surgical operations and as a means of alleviating the suffering of women in childbirth stirred up a professional storm that had its reverberations in the United States. Certain members of the faculty of the Medical School of the University of Nashville, especially John M. Watson, did not approve of its use.[22]

[20] Reported in the *Nashville Journal of Medicine and Surgery*, VII (1854), 449-452.
[21] Emanuel J. Josey, "Anaesthetics," in Inaugural Dissertations submitted to the University of Nashville, No. 394 (1858), 5.
[22] L. W. Peacock, "Hygiene," in Inaugural Dissertations, . . . No. 448 (1859), 5.

It seems that some of the objections to the use of anaesthesia in midwifery had a religious and biblical foundation. Felix Grundy M'Gavock, in his dissertation entitled "Anaesthesia" stressed this point. He declared that the enemies of anaesthesia did not attack the use of chloroform in surgery "with the same vehemence as in midwifery for the simple reason that against the latter, as they think, they find a command in the Bible which says *in sorrow shall she bring forth*. This they take as their text and will preach until silenced by reason." Using the same text, M'Gavock attempted to refute this argument by proclaiming that the translators of the Bible had made a mistake when they chose the word *sorrow*. The word they should have used was labor. He carried his argument one step farther and in so doing proved himself to be a good fundamentalist. Anaesthesia was a gift from God, he declared. It was intended that man should use it to allay pain and suffering. Furthermore, not only did God give this remedy to man but he set man the example "by anaesthetising Adam when from his side he took Mother Eve."[23] Without doubt this proved his point to his own satisfaction.

The place of God in the study of medicine was frequently mentioned by the medical students in their dissertations. M'Gavock, for example, declared: "I know that our Maker has kindly given us nerves of sensation that we may feel the approach of disease and harm and guard against it."[24] John Charles Mathews, another medical student, frequently wandered in the field of metaphysical and theological speculation, in spite of the fact that the subject of his dissertation was nutrition. There was only one answer to all the questions which he could not otherwise explain—God. "Why are not all men as small as Tom Thumb? Why have crystals a peculiar shape, or shapes? Why do trees grow erect? Why do children resemble parents in color, features, etc.? Why is man who is changing the particles of his composition every hour, still one year is really the same man . . .

---

[23] Felix Grundy M'Gavock, "Anaesthesia," in *Inaugural Dissertations*, . . . No. 53 (1853), 16-17.   [24] *Ibid.*, 3.

that he was the year previous? We can answer them only by saying that they are the laws of God."[25]

At times Mathews allowed his pen to dip too deeply into the ink of sentimentalism. "Here at his given station man stands permanently till by the blasting of disease or approach of age ... sooner or later he sinks into the cold vault of the grave! Ah! Tis God, who is the beach against which the billows of nutrition break and recede through the pained declivities of time into the Matrix of Eternity." It should be admitted that Mathews wrote parenthetically after his name "Minister of Gospel."[26] The rhetoric of the pulpit and the terminology of the clinic did not mix so well.

It seems that no attempt was made by the teaching staff of the medical school to interfere with the personal religious views of the students. On the contrary, anxious parents were assured that their sons would not be disillusioned with respect to their personal conceptions of deity and immortality.[27]

The same broad-mindedness characterized the teaching of medicine. A careful study of the dissertations discloses the fact that the faculty was not dogmatic on the subject of therapeutics. While it is true that each member of the staff had his own ideas and his favorite remedies, no attempt was made to force these views on the students. A study was made of the best European and American authorities and the textual information was enriched by the individual conceptions and theories held by the various members of the teaching staff. These theories were put into practice in hospital and clinic so that the students were able to observe the actual effects of the remedies on disease.

The medical records of the day show that the physician of 1850 knew very little about either the cause or cure of disease. The Nashville physicians were quite frank in admitting their ignorance. John W. Richardson, speaking to the medical students

---

[25] John Charles Mathews, "Physiology of Nutrition," in *Inaugural Dissertations* ... No. 81 (1853), 44-45.   [26] *Ibid.*, 44, and title page.
[27] Thomas R. Jennings, "An Introductory Lecture, October 30, 1854," in *Addresses Delivered before the Medical Classes of the University of Nashville*, 39.

on the difficulties and responsibilities of physicians, stated that there were only a few specific causes then known to the profession.[28] Bowling declared that the physicians of the day knew nothing about consumption and that very few believed it was contagious.[29] The devastating effect of cholera shows that little if anything was known about this disease. Perhaps Eve knew more about cholera than the average American physician as he had studied European methods of treatment and knew from personal observations that they were quite effective.[30]

The most universal remedy for nearly all ailments was bloodletting. There were various methods of bleeding a patient. For localized bleeding a method known as "cupping" was employed. This method required the use of a cupping glass by means of which blood was extracted from the surface veins. When bleeding children, the physician used a leech, an apparatus for drawing blood by suction. Fresh-water leeches or blood-sucking worms, especially the European variety known as *Hirudo medicinalis*, were used for the same purpose. Physicians also used the scarificator. This instrument contained several lancets moved by a spring and was used to scratch or slightly cut the skin in order to draw small amounts of blood.[31]

There were times when it was considered expedient to draw large quantities of blood from the body and to do this a vein or an artery was opened. Venesection was the more common remedy and doctors usually opened the vein at the bend of the elbow because it was most convenient. Resort was made to arteriotomy only in emergency cases such as apoplexy.[32] In ordinary cases the phlebotomized patient might be expected to show several reactions to the treatment. After a certain amount of blood had been extracted the patient might be expected to show a slight

[28] John W. Richardson, "The Difficulties and Responsibilities of the Profession," in *ibid.*, 4.
[29] W. K. Bowling, "Character and Writings of Sydenham," in *ibid.*, 12.
[30] Paul F. Eve, "On Asiatic Cholera Morbus," in *American Journal of the Medical Sciences*, O. S., X (1832), 524-526.
[31] Benjamin Alfred, "Blood Letting and Its Therapeutic Effects," in Inaugural Dissertations . . ., No. 217 (1856), 3.   [32] *Ibid.*, 1-3.

degree of dizziness, singing in the ears, hurried respiration, enfeebled pulse, pale face, moist brow, nauseated stomach, and sometimes unconsciousness.[33]

Occasionally, a voice was raised in opposition to the practice of bleeding, but such voices were stilled by the great chorus of ridicule issuing from the ranks of the conservative physicians. Early in the fifties, William Turner of New York declared that the practice of bleeding patients was contrary to common sense and he petitioned the legislature of the state of New York to make blood-letting a penal offense. In Nashville Bowling jeered at the idea. He believed that Turner petitioned the legislature in order to win publicity for himself and the new quack remedies which he had, no doubt, up his sleeve. With appropriate sarcasm, Bowling concluded his notice. "We agree with him. It is a decided improvement upon the almanac plan."[34]

To the twentieth-century physician many of the remedies used by the doctors of medicine in the fifties seem to be little better than quack methods. It will be interesting to single out several common diseases, such as pneumonia and typhoid fever, and describe the causes and methods of treatment as taught to the students of medicine in Nashville.

Pneumonia was described in the census report of 1860 as "rather a southern than a northern malady." The fact that more Negroes than white people died of the disease did not alter the situation from the professional point of view. The following table[35] shows the order of states with respect to the fatality of pneumonia:

States	Ratio	States	Ratio
Arkansas	19.6	Georgia	11.6
Mississippi	14.3	Louisiana	10.8
South Carolina	12.4	Kansas	10.0
Alabama	12.3	Nebraska	9.7
Texas	11.8	Missouri	8.9

[33] *Ibid.*, 7.
[34] *Nashville Journal of Medicine and Surgery,* I (1851), 244.
[35] *Eighth Census of the United States,* 1860 (Statistics), 244. During the year ending June 1, 1860, there were 1,165 deaths from pneumonia in Tennessee. *Ibid.*, 29.

Tennessee	8.8	Connecticut	5.1
Virginia	8.6	New Hampshire	5.1
Iowa	8.6	Vermont	5.0
North Carolina	8.6	Massachusetts	4.8
Kentucky	8.3	Maryland	4.5
Indiana	8.2	Maine	4.0
Michigan	8.1	New Jersey	3.9
Oregon	7.0	Pennsylvania	3.9
Minnesota	6.7	Delaware	3.6
District of Col.	6.7	California	3.3
Wisconsin	6.5	Washington	2.0
Rhode Island	5.7	Utah	1.8
Ohio	5.3	New Mexico	1.2

Because of the prevalence of pneumonia in Tennessee there is little wonder that so much attention was given to this disease by the physicians and students at Nashville. It was generally believed that the most frequent causes of pneumonia could be traced to changeable weather conditions. Sudden exposure to cold, wearing damp clothes, sleeping in damp beds, wearing clothes too thin for the season, running in a sharp cold atmosphere, heavy blows on the chest, poisonous inhalations, sudden constipation, over indulgence in liquor, and major surgical operations were listed among the causes of this disease.[36] The excessive use of the voice was considered by some to be a contributing factor.[37] James L. Griffin, a graduate of the medical school, was of the opinion that malaria was the most important cause of pneumonia in the South.[38]

In the treatment of pneumonia there were three remedies, blood-letting, a good cathartic, and the use of mercury. Blood-letting was considered the most important treatment. As all the blood in the system was necessarily forced through the congested lungs which were incapable of functioning properly and hence

[36] Samuel B. Brown, "Acute Pneumonia," in Inaugural Dissertations . . ., No. 8 (1851), 29.
[37] Harris Diggs, "Pneumonia," in Inaugural Dissertations . . ., No. 413 (1859), 8.
[38] James L. Griffin, "Pneumonia," in Inaugural Dissertations . . ., No. 45 (1853), 15.

caused the patient much distress, it was believed that by reducing the amount of blood in the body the pressure on the lungs would be lessened.[39]

The amount of blood drawn depended on the stage of the disease, the condition of the pulse, and the constitution of the patient. In general, blood was allowed to flow from a large vein until the pulse improved, the pressure about the chest was relieved, or the patient showed signs of fainting. This process was repeated in twelve or twenty-four hours, provided there was no improvement and provided the patient's pulse and general condition indicated that he could stand it.[40]

It was considered a good practice to give the patient a dose of castor oil after the first bleeding. After the oil had taken effect, small doses of tartar emetic were administered every hour or two during the day. After several days had passed, a pill consisting of ipecac (one grain), opium (one grain), and calomel (two or three grains), was prescribed for the patient. This pill was taken at night and, in combination with the doses of tartar emetic which were continued during the day, was supposed to produce relaxation and sleep, to lessen the cough, and to prepare the patient for a possible subsequent mecurial treatment.[41]

Mustard plasters, called "blisters," were used by some physicians at any stage of the disease. After the crisis had been passed the patient was given an expectorant. This might consist of "syrup of squills and seneca in combination with wine of ipecac."[42]

According to the United States census for 1860, typhoid fever ranked third as a destroyer of human life in Tennessee. In the year ending June 1, 1860, 918 Tennesseans succumbed to this disease, while consumption, in first place, claimed 1,440, and pneumonia, in second place, claimed 1,165.[43]

Typhoid was a mystery to the medical profession. As yet, no

---

[39] Brown, "Acute Pneumonia," 32 ff. [40] *Ibid.*, 13.
[41] Brown, "Acute Pneumonia," 32 ff.; Diggs, "Pneumonia," 9 ff.
[42] *Ibid.*, 12.
[43] *Eighth Census of the United States*, 1860 (Statistics), 29.

one had come to any clear conclusions with respect to the causes or the treatment of the disease. The variations of the disease made it doubly difficult for any single plan of treatment to be developed. As one medical student asserted, "There is no disease, perhaps, common to this or any other country about which there are more conflicting opinions among medical men relative to its nature and treatment than typhoid fever; affording sufficient evidence to my mind that it is not clearly understood by the profession."[44]

J. Boyde Talbot, a student with more than ordinary interest in original observation and research, claimed that the obscurity which enveloped typhoid was due to the lack of original investigations on the part of the younger physicians and too great a dependence on the so-called authorities. But even this young scientist, after spending five years in observation and study, including autopsies on those who had died of typhoid, presented a treatment for the disease that differed little from that of the authorities he so easily criticized.[45]

At that time, of course, the typhoid bacillus was unknown and some of the attempts to explain the cause of the disease seem humorous to the twentieth-century scientist. One Nashville student claimed that the primary cause of typhoid was some latent poisonous principle afloat in the air, which being inhaled into the lungs, and absorbed, contaminated the blood and brought about "that peculiar condition of the system termed . . . typhoid."[46]

Treatment for this peculiar condition of the system was complicated, but began simply enough with a cathartic such as calomel and rhubarb. Bleeding was not overlooked, especially if there was much "inflammatory action, headaches or delirium," although the amount of blood drawn from the patient was small compared to the amount taken from a pneumonia victim. If the

[44] S. P. Crawford, "Typhoid Fever," in Inaugural Dissertations . . ., No. 68 (1853), 1.
[45] J. Boyde Talbot, "Typhoid Fever," in ibid., No. 87 (1853), 1, 2, 21-28.
[46] J. G. W. Taylor, "Typhoid Fever," in ibid., No. 461 (1859), 1.

typhoid patient became very feverish, leeches were applied to the temples and cold water or an ice pack was placed on the head after the hair had been shaved off. To induce perspiration and to calm the nerves a mixture composed of citrate of potassa, ipecac, and sweet spirit of niter was used.

If the patient was unable to sleep, small quantities of sulphate of morphia and sulphuric acid were administered. In case of mental derangement, aqua ammonia was prescribed. For the scaly or flaky tongue that accompanied the disease, most physicians prescribed oil of turpentine disguised with sugar and arabic gum to make it more palatable. This disguise prevented the vomiting that usually occurred when the oil of turpentine was taken straight. Diarrhea, another characteristic of typhoid, was held in check by iodide of potassium combined with opium and iodide ointment rubbed on the abdomen.[47]

Having to undergo such a treatment it is little wonder that typhoid patients had sinking spells. At such a time a stimulant was necessary. For this purpose wine and brandy were mixed into a drink. Sponge baths of warm water and brandy were also popular. For nourishment the patient was given vegetable gruels and meat broths.[48]

Some "authorities" on typhoid believed that the best way to treat the disease was to let it run its course. One of the students at Nashville declared that the best treatment was to let the patient and the disease alone as long as they "agreed together."[49] However, if the disease began to take unfair advantage of the patient, such as making an attack on the brain or lungs, then the physician was justified in using all the orthodox remedies. Those who believed in this method considered typhoid a disease that required no active treatment but one that should be watched closely for complications. The fact that the dangerous nature of

---

[47] The above discussion of typhoid treatment is based on the following dissertations: T. B. LaRue, "Typhoid Fever," in Inaugural Dissertations . . ., No. 13 (1851), 18 ff.; Austin A. Shipp, "Typhoid Fever," in *ibid.*, No. 10 (1851), 17; Joseph Field, "Typhoid Fever," in *ibid.*, No. 52 (1853), 15, 17.

[48] LaRue, "Typhoid Fever," 18 ff.   [49] Taylor, "Typhoid Fever," 13.

the complications likely to develop was realized by the profession was a hopeful sign.

While the power of medicine and the effectiveness of internal treatment was generally acknowledged by the medical profession, there were non-medical remedies with widespread popularity. One of these was the use of cold water and ice. It was claimed by the supporters of the cold water cure that one of the best methods to obtain relief from bilious fever was to sponge the body from head to foot with cold water. Ice held in the mouth was recommended for nauseated stomachs and quinine taken with plenty of cold water was considered an excellent remedy for fevers.

When a person collapsed from malignant intermittent fever and called a doctor who believed in the cold water formula, he would be stripped of his clothes and doused with fifteen or twenty buckets of cold water in rapid succession. Then the patient was rubbed dry with a coarse towel or hair brush and put in bed between blankets. If this treatment failed the doctor was in despair and the patient had little chance to recover.[50] Thus cold water, considered both a stimulant and a sedative, was used "to keep a man from burning up . . . and to keep him from freezing."[51]

Because of its "styptic influence over the blood," cold water was considered by some doctors as a great aid in the treatment of wounds, uteral hemorrhage, and surgery. The *Nashville Journal of Medicine and Surgery* recorded the case of a young man who "was stabbed in five places with a large pocket knife. One stab severed part of the deltoid muscle [which covers the shoulder joint], one between the spine and inferior angle of left scapula [shoulder blade], another immediately below this, a fourth but slight wound immediately under the armpit, and the fifth and worst of them all about midway between the spine and sternum [breastbone], entering between the sixth and seventh ribs, wound-

[50] J. W. Baird, "The Use of Cold Water in the Treatment of Disease," in Inaugural Dissertations . . ., No. 105 (1854).   [51] *Ibid.*, 8-9.

ing a lung. This last was bleeding copiously, air was bubbling out at every respiration." Cold water compresses, adhesive tape, and a dose of salts brought about "a rapid recovery."[52]

The use of cold water as described above must not be confused with the so-called "water cures" that were given so much publicity in the forties and fifties. There were several versions of the water cure but they were all quack methods. The most common method consisted in wrapping the naked body in cold wet sheets in order to relieve various types of ailments. The popularity of the water cure is amazing. Even Harriett Martineau tried it and apparently was more than satisfied with the results. The *Nashville Journal of Medicine and Surgery* gives the following account of her experience:

Miss Martineau, the celebrated English traveler, has also tested the efficacy of cold sheets upon her virgin corporosity—and she was enraptured.... All her various and complicated aches and groans were magically drawn out by the wet sheet, and in an elysian state of half consciousness she could see the legion of demons which inhabited her chaste and virgin organism leaping madly from the pores of her skin and submitting to quiet suffocation in the folds of the reeking linen![53]

To return to medicine, a progressive trend is seen in the increased emphasis placed on hygiene during the fifties. "The chief end now of medicine," Eve declared, "is the prevention of disease, hence the importance given to hygiene and sanitary regulations."[54] In his dissertation on hygiene, L. H. Peacock stated that hygiene "offers more to remove disease and to disarm pestilence of its strength than all that has been done for the healing art, and strange to say until within a few years this subject has been almost entirely neglected."[55] From a study of this dissertation and several others on the same subject, it is evident that the faculty

---

[52] B. S. Hopkins, "Cold Water in Surgery," in the *Nashville Journal of Medicine and Surgery*, VIII (1855), 270-272.
[53] *Ibid.*, VI (1854), 60.
[54] Paul F. Eve, "Claims of Medicine to be regarded as a Science," in *Address Delivered before the Medical Classes of the University of Nashville*, 28.
[55] L. H. Peacock, "Hygiene," in Inaugural Dissertations ..., No. 448 (1859), 10.

of the medical school stressed the importance of regularity in bathing, eating, and exercising. Both warm and cold baths were recommended, the warm bath never to be heated over 90°. It was believed that a cold bath every morning would improve the appetite, equalize the circulation, compose the nerves, and increase the activity of the mind.[56] With respect to nourishment, one was urged to use common sense and to eat in proportion to the amount of exercise taken in any given day. As one student wrote, "Food is the steam of life and he that eats and drinks too much and does not keep up his machinery, his paddles and his wheels at work must finally burst his boiler."[57]

The medical students and the professors were not immune to public sentiment and there is no doubt that the scientific angles of the pro-slavery doctrine made an impression on all those connected with the medical school.

In 1854 Josiah Clark Nott (1804-1873), a physician of Mobile, Alabama, collaborating with George B. Gliddon, published a book on ethnology entitled *The Types of Mankind*. The success of this book was amazing, no less than ten editions being necessary to satisfy the public demand, and this in an era when only one book out of every two hundred ran into a second edition.[58] *The Types of Mankind* was undoubtedly the most important work of its kind prior to Darwin's *Origin of Species*. But for the slave-holding states, this ethnological study had a peculiar and special value because the authors attempted to prove that each of the different races of man sprang from a fixed type. The Negro race, for example, had an origin quite different from the white race and was probably much younger. Furthermore, Nott and Gliddon believed that the Negro common to the United States had the same ethnological features as the type of Negro known and enslaved by the Egyptians in the fourteenth century before Christ. All the intervening centuries, even a new environ-

---

[56] Baird, "The Use of Cold Water in the Treatment of Disease," 19.
[57] L. A. Upshaw, "Hygiene," in Inaugural Dissertations . . ., No. 465 (1858), 19.
[58] *Nashville Union and American*, September 6, 1856.

ment in America, had failed to alter these outstanding Negro characteristics.[59]

In reply to those who believed that the Negro would develop eventually an intellect equal to the whites, Nott declared that such a contention had no scientific basis and was disproved by cranial measurements. Of course, Nott admitted that the Negroes in the United States were more intelligent and better developed physically than their African ancestors. This was a natural but limited reaction to increased comforts, better food and constant contact with the superior Caucasians. "Wild horses, cattle, asses, and other brutes," wrote Nott, "are greatly improved in like manner by domestication; but neither climate nor food can transmute an ass into a horse, or a buffalo into an ox."[60] Nor could climate and food change a Negro into a white man.

Such a scientific thesis was admirably suited to the needs of the pro-slavery philosophers, propagandists, and politicians. Did not these scientists show that the Negro was an entirely separate and inferior race of man? How could the two races ever meet as equals on the same social and cultural level? Here at last was a definite scientific answer to the doctrine of equality preached by the abolitionists. The beauty of the southern defense lay in the fact that it was based to a large extent on the studies of a northern scientist as Nott and Gliddon indicated in the preface to their book.[61]

As *The Types of Mankind* ran through ten editions, it is safe to assume that every wide-awake scientist and physician in the South either read the book or heard of Nott's doctrine indirectly. Certainly the staff of the Medical School of the University of Nashville was acquainted with the work and it would be safe to assume that a majority of the students had heard of it. Indeed, two medical students presented dissertations in which they attempted to prove that the Negro belonged to a distinct and in-

---

[59] Josiah Clark Nott and George R. Gliddon, *The Types of Mankind* (Philadelphia, 1857), 249-250, 255, 259-260.   [60] *Ibid.*, 260.
[61] *Ibid.*, ix-xiii. For some interesting comments on Nott see William Howard Russell, *My Diary North and South* (Boston, 1863), 226.

ferior race. The first dissertation was presented in 1855 and the second in 1858 and these dates correspond with the period when *The Types of Mankind* was becoming so popular. The arguments presented by the two students reflect the medical angle but in general they harmonize with the popular interpretation.

"We take the ground that the Negro is a separate being," wrote Theodore Westmoreland in his dissertation, and a few years later another medical student, Newton C. Miller, expressed the same opinion.[62] Both students declared that to prove the diversity of the two races was a simple matter of science and both leaned heavily on the obvious anatomical differences. Upon examination, it was discovered that the cranium of the Negro was much thicker and the brain cavity smaller than that of a white man. With respect to the shape of the head, a very marked dissimilarity was noted, the head of the white man being described as round and symmetrical with an elevated and expanded forehead, while that of the Negro was flat with a retreating forehead. There was a difference observable in the facial angle of the two races. That of the white man was estimated at 80 degrees on the average while that of the Negro was declared to be about 70 degrees. The difference was attributed to the protrusion of the upper jaw in the case of the Negro. Other anatomical differences were noticed in the shape of the nose, the size of the nasal apertures and the construction of the ear. Furthermore, the pelvis of the Negro was found to be longer and narrower and the iliac bones more vertical than in the white man. Differences in legs and feet were also noted. The distinctive differences in the hair of the white man and the hair of the Negro were given much attention. Under the microscope the white man's hair proved to be straight, flowing, or curled; that of the Negro crisped, frizzled, or spirally twisted. The magnifying lens showed structural differences in the hair. That of the white man was

[62] Theodore Westmoreland, "The Anatomical and Physiological Differences in the Ethiopian and the White Man," in Inaugural Dissertations, No. 148 (1855); Newton C. Miller, "The Diversity of the Human Species," in *ibid.*, No. 319 (1858).

found to be oval or cylindrical in shape; while the Negro's hair was described as "excentrically elliptical or flat." Furthermore, microscopy showed that the central duct carrying the coloring matter in the hair of the white man was absent in the hair of the Negro, in which the coloring matter was diffused in the cortex or superficial outward section of the hair. Finally, it was demonstrated by experiment that the hair of the white man could not be rolled or pressed into felt, whereas the Negro's hair could be felted without much difficulty. "From the foregoing facts," wrote Miller, "it would appear that the hair of the Negro's head bears a very close resemblance to wool and in the opinion of many, the resemblance is so close as to make it impossible to distinguish any anatomical or physical differences between them."[68]

There were two other characteristics of the Negro that were placed under the spotlight of scientific analysis, the dark color of the skin and the peculiar Negro odor. There were two theories (perhaps more) that attempted to explain the cause of the dusky hue of the Negro skin. The first may be called the climatic theory. Certain physiologists believed that the pigment cells which determine the color of the skin were greatly influenced by light. Comparisons were made to plants which depended on the light of the sun for their color and which faded when placed in a dark room. Thus the tropical sun operating on the skin of the African Negro for generations had gradually turned his skin black. This theory was not accepted by all scientists and a southern scientist was almost in duty bound to reject it.

Miller, whose dissertation is one of the most interesting turned out by the medical students, believed the analogy between the Negro and the plant to be fallacious. "In the case of the plant," he declared, "the change of color effected is nothing more than a chemical change produced by the absence of light. . . . Now if the analogy be a good one, the skin of the Negro ought to return to its original fair hue when removed from . . . the strong

[68] *Ibid.*, 19.

light of the tropics and he would propagate a white offspring according to his former type." This, of course, had never happened, hence the climatic theory was denounced as unsound and the differences in color could only be explained scientifically by resorting to the theory of the diversity of the origin of the human species.[64]

The characteristic odor of the Negro was evidently a point at issue between the slaveholders and the abolitionists. The latter, running true to form, maintained that the odor was due to filthy, unsanitary conditions of the slave quarters. In the essay by Westmoreland mentioned above, this argument was refuted by a simple statement to the effect that white men when exposed to filthy surroundings did not smell like Negroes. This young doctor hoped that the day was not far distant when physiologists would be able to clearly demonstrate that the odor of the black man was inherent in him and not due to any environmental factors associated with slavery. Such scientific proof would, no doubt, "give a quietus to some of our modern self-styled philanthropists who contend for an equality of mankind."[65]

Another peculiar habit of the Negro, according to Miller, was "the almost universal custom . . . when he sleeps to shut out the pure oxygen from the air passages by covering his head and face with a portion of his covering."[66] This was a habit practiced the year around regardless of the temperature of the atmosphere. White men did not do this, as a matter of fact, could not without suffering great discomfort. Was there any connection between this bedtime habit and the low mentality of the Negro race? Miller had no proof, but he assumed that there was and he based his assumption on the theory that high intellectual activity necessitated a constant flow of oxygenated blood to the brain. As the Negro breathed the same air over and over again all through the night, the amount of oxygen he inhaled decreased and the amount of carbon dioxide increased in proportion. Consequently,

[64] *Ibid.,* 26. See also, Westmoreland, "The Anatomical and Physiological Differences in the Ethiopian and the White Man," 3-4.   [65] *Ibid.,* 7.
[66] Miller, "The Diversity of the Human Species," 28.

as this was a nightly, lifetime habit, there was little wonder that the brain of the Negro functioned rather weakly and inefficiently.[67]

The entire nervous system of the Negro was considered coarse. Consequently, he lacked refined feeling and was incapable of elevated sentiment. "Who is it that has lived in the southern states of this Confederacy," asked Westmoreland, "that has not noticed the total indifference of father, mother, son, and daughter towards each other while in distress? They are but little affected by the loss of a relative whether it be wife, husband, son or daughter."[68] Here was one answer to Harriet Beecher Stowe and all other philanthropists who sought in the slave market sentimental grist for their mill.

Westmoreland, waving the banner of the slave owners, strongly suspected that there was a difference in the structure of the Negro stomach. This alone, he thought, could account for the strange desire of the Negro to eat certain things that a white man could hardly digest. He neglected to list these unusual articles of food as he was anxious to make his next point, namely, that the Negro was relatively free of stomach ache and other disturbances of the digestive organs. This was not due to the fact that the Negroes were slaves and were denied the opportunity to eat the rich food to be found on the table of the white master, because the poor whites in the North lived on a diet similar to that of the slaves and were suffering constantly from dyspepsia. Therefore, the explanation of the Negro's immunity from indigestion under ordinary circumstances was not to be found in the quality or quantity of the food, but in the "peculiar organization of the digestive apparatus."[69]

The difference between whites and blacks did not end here. The Negro was considered racially peculiar in other respects. He did not react to medical treatment in the same way that a white man did. For example, he could not stand the loss of

---

[67] *Ibid.*, 28-30.
[68] Westmoreland, "The Anatomical and Physiological Differences in the Ethiopian and the White Man," 16.   [69] *Idem.*

blood, so the common practice of bleeding was seldom effective on the dusky patient. On the other hand, experience showed that a Negro could bear physical pain better than a white man and so surgical operations were not such hardships for the black man provided he did not lose much blood. It was related that a Negro would "lie upon a table and have a limb amputated without scarcely a murmur and then die from the loss of a little blood."[70]

Why all these differences in physiology and anatomy? Why these strange immunities and strange reactions? To Westmoreland the answer was simple. The Negroes possessed an inferior physical organization due to the fact that as a race they had developed much later than the Caucasian, probably after Noah and the flood. They were low in the scale of human beings, "approaching in their conformation and sensualities the monkey tribe."[71]

Miller had no sympathy for the "miserable and degraded class of abolition fanatics" who assumed the role of philanthropist and argued the absolute equality of the races. The fact that the Negro had never attempted to break the chains that bound him to Africa's soil was considered proof that he did not possess the intellect or the initiative of the white man. But Miller did not stop here. With pertinent questions he presented his case.

What has the negro done to entitle him to be called the equal of the white man? . . . Who is the wooly head that has commanded the admiration of the world by the masterly policy with which he has conducted a nation on to power and prosperity? Where are the kinky headed Demosthenes or Ciceros who have electrified large audiences of their fellow citizens with their eloquence? Where are the flat nosed Websters, Clays and Calhouns whose effusions in the Senate of the United States afford the most perfect models of oratory and logic extant? Where will you look for the flat footed Story or Taney whose opinions have received the sanction of law and become supreme authority of the land? Finally, who is the colored gentleman that has won imperishable renown to himself and conferred benefits incalculable upon his race by his skill in . . . the profession of medicine? . . . They have never yet appeared upon the earth, nor shall they until

[70] Ibid., 25.   [71] Ibid., 18.

the Creator shall by his omnipotent fiat endow the negro with a new physical constitution. Abolitionists and negro sympathisers may assert the equality of the negro and the white man but stubborn facts will ever prove the falsity of the assertions.[72]

And so Nashville medical students, relying upon osteology and ethnology, or more specifically, relying on the scientific theories of Nott and Gliddon, gave their support to the pro-slavery argument. They were able to prove, at least to their own satisfaction, that the Negro was not, never had been, and probably never could be the equal of the dominating Causasians. The inferiority of the Negro, his peculiar anatomical characteristics, could be explained only on the basis that he belonged to a race whose origin and development was in no way connected with the progeny of Adam and Eve. The idea that the Garden of Eden had been the incunabula of the black man was almost inconceivable.

It is not surprising that Darwin's *Origin of Species* was given a cool reception by many southern scientists. Darwin discountenanced Nott's theory that the white man and the Negro had distinct origins and claimed instead that both had risen from a common origin. The typical attitude of Nashville physicians towards Darwin's theory may be summed up in the words of Dr. John Watson. "There may be anthropoid apes morally," he declared, "but none zoologically."[73]

It would be unjust to be too critical of the medical men of the fifties. They must be judged on the basis of their contemporary civilization. They were pioneering and although some were still in the deep woods, others were approaching the clearings where the light was brighter and the path of progress less encumbered with ancient and foolish doctrines.

Certainly Paul Eve made valuable contributions, especially in the field of surgery. His place in the medical history of the na-

---

[72] Miller, "The Diversity of the Human Species," 36-38.
[73] John Watson, "An Introductory Address, October 30, 1855," in *Addresses Delivered before the Medical Classes of the University of Nashville*, 16.

tion is assured. Bowling and John Berrien Lindsley deserve high praise for the roles they played in establishing the Medical School of the University of Nashville. This school was the foundation for one of the nation's medical centers at the present time.

CHAPTER IV
RELIGIOUS LEADERS IN PULPIT AND PRESS

RELIGION has always played an important role in American life and religious leaders, especially brilliant and energetic ministers, have made many contributions to the intellectual life as well as the spiritual life of the nation. It has been pointed out in the introductory chapter of this study that frontier conditions produced some strange cults and some eccentric figures even in the orthodox denominations. By 1850, however, the frontier influences had been greatly modified, and in the city of Nashville had almost disappeared. But there remained a certain amount of intolerance and bigotry and what may be termed theological conservatism which was constantly on guard against the newer forces of the nineteenth century such as Universalism and spiritualism.

In Nashville, most of the prominent denominations were well entrenched by 1850. If numbers mean power then the Methodists and Baptists had the advantage, but the Disciples of Christ (Christians) and the Presbyterians exerted considerable influence. The Episcopal and Catholic churches were also represented and by 1859 the Jews and Lutherans had organized congregations. In the period under review, each of these denominations, with the exception of the last two, produced an outstanding leader who made more than a local impression either as a preacher or as the editor of a religious journal. First to be considered is the Methodist minister and editor, John B. McFerrin.

As early as the first decade of the nineteenth century Nashville was included in a Tennessee Methodist circuit. By 1812 the little city on the rocks had become the head of the Nashville district which had a staff of ten preachers and one presiding elder. In 1818 Nashville became a "station" with a resident preacher in charge of Methodist activities. It seems that the first church was built about 1812. Before that time, the Methodists had met in a private room in the county jail, quarters which were not entirely satisfactory. When at last they had a church one of the more prominent members of the pioneer congregation declared that he felt "thankful to God that Methodism has got out of jail."[1]

Once out of jail, the Methodist church in Nashville grew rapidly and became increasingly important in the affairs of Tennessee Methodism. During this period of growth a number of young preachers, eager to make an impression and anxious to make as many converts as possible, came to Nashville for a few months, or a year, and then moved on, perhaps never to return again in any official capacity. But there was one in particular who did return and by 1850 he had become an integral part of the city's maturing religious and intellectual life. This man was the Rev. John B. McFerrin.

According to tradition, McFerrin was "born in a cane brake and cradled in a sugar trough." The tradition may exaggerate the facts, but it is known that he was born in Rutherford County, Tennessee, in 1807 and the environment was typical of the frontier. His grandfather had been a patriot during the American Revolution, and his father, James McFerrin, followed Jackson during the War of 1812. When he was thirteen John McFerrin was converted at a Methodist camp meeting and soon joined the Methodist Church, much to the surprise of the neighbors who knew that the McFerrins, on both sides of the family, had been Scotch Presbyterians.[2]

Young McFerrin's first service as a member of the church was to offer a prayer at a small gathering of frontiersmen. This was an humble beginning for a man who one day was to represent

[1] John B. McFerrin, *History of Methodism in Tennessee*, 3 vols. (Nashville, 1875), III, 73; Nashville *Daily American*, March 20, 1887. The jailer himself was a Methodist. *Idem.*

[2] "Bishop McTyeire's Sermon at the Funeral of Dr. McFerrin," in *Nashville Christian Advocate*, May 21, 1887; O. P. Fitzgerald, *John B. McFerrin, A Biography* (Nashville, 1888), 11.

the Methodists of the United States at a world conference. From 1825 to 1840, McFerrin rode the circuits of Tennessee and Alabama, carried the Gospel to the Cherokee Indians, and occasionally occupied a pulpit in a village or city. In 1831 he was sent to Nashville for a year, an appointment that complimented his ability. Busy years followed, years crowded with traveling, with preaching, with church building, with establishing a family of his own. In 1835 he was back in Nashville, but not to stay. Only when he was appointed editor of the *South-Western Christian Advocate* in 1840 did he establish a permanent residence in the growing city on the Cumberland.[3]

The editorship came as a surprise and McFerrin was not pleased. "I could not positively rebel," he wrote in later years, "and yet I begged to be excused. The paper was still in debt, the subscription list was small, and I was without much experience."[4] McFerrin hated debts and he worked diligently to relieve the *Advocate* of its financial embarrassment. His great physical energy enabled him to do the work of an entire staff. He wrote editorials, obituaries, and articles. He read all the volunteered poetry and this called for courage and stamina. He clipped selections, acted as mail clerk, promoted subscription campaigns, and hired and directed the printers. In addition, he preached at camp meetings and revivals, attended conferences, and sharpened thunderbolts for theological controversies.

In 1846 the name of the paper was changed to the *Nashville Christian Advocate* and by 1849 the editor was able to announce that the enterprise paid a handsome dividend to the several conferences sustaining it. In 1851 the *Louisville Christian Advocate* ran into financial difficulties that could be solved only by a merger with the Nashville paper. This transaction increased the circulation of the paper and McFerrin believed the time had come to enlarge the organization and to improve its equipment. Consequently, a better grade of paper was used, new type was

[3] John B. McFerrin, "Valedictory," in *Nashville Christian Advocate*, July 1, 1858.
[4] Quoted in Fitzgerald, *John B. McFerrin, A Biography*, 119. In 1845, M. M. Henkle became co-editor with McFerrin.

introduced, and a new Hoe power press was purchased. The new press was so complicated compared to the antiquated one formerly used that the operators ruined an entire issue of the paper before they learned how to handle it.[5]

McFerrin was more than a good editor, he was an excellent business manager as well. When he gave up the editorship in 1858 the mailing list of the *Advocate* contained the names of over twelve thousand subscribers who paid in advance. This was an increase of about eight thousand over the circulation figures for 1840. Furthermore, all debts had been paid and the paper was a source of revenue to the church.[6]

In 1858 McFerrin was appointed book agent, or general manager, of the Publishing House of the Methodist Episcopal Church, South, which had been established in Nashville by the General Conference of 1854. McFerrin himself had been influential in establishing the need for a book concern and he had promoted Nashville as the most logical place for it.[7] He had not, however, promoted himself for the position of book agent and he accepted his new responsibilities with mixed emotions. In 1840 he had been loath to accept the editorship of the *Advocate* but after managing it for eighteen years he discovered that he could not give it up without some regrets. He admitted that the excitement of an editorial life suited his temper but he expected to find excitement and also a challenge to his ability in the new position.

As general book agent, McFerrin had charge of the funds, stock, fixtures, real estate and other properties of the publishing house as well as the depositories and periodicals belonging to the general conference.[8] By 1858 the book concern was already well

[5] *Nashville and Louisville Christian Advocate*, February 13, 1851.
[6] McFerrin, "Valedictory," in *Nashville Christian Advocate*, July 1, 1858.
[7] A number of civic leaders not connected with the Methodist Church were interested in the publishing house and aided in the campaign to raise the necessary capital. John B. Lindsley was active in this connection. By 1860 the publishing house was operating twelve presses. *Nashville City and Business Directory*, V (1860-1861), 88.
[8] "Report of the General Conference of 1858," in *Nashville Christian Advocate*, June 10, 1858.

established and a large staff was necessary to operate the composition rooms, the pressrooms, and the bindery. All this, of course, involved considerable expense but under McFerrin's leadership the publishing house began to do a flourishing business. "After reviewing the whole history of our publishing enterprises," he wrote a number of years later, "I am surprised at the success that attended them."[9]

If popular acclaim is to be taken as a criterion, McFerrin was among the best preachers of the day. But he was not a great orator, being handicapped by a high-pitched, almost unpleasant voice. He made an impression because of his quaint remarks, his genuine spiritual qualities, his personal magnetism, and his "distinctly individualized personality."[10] He acted like a father to all young preachers and he was a sympathetic listener to all those who came to him with their troubles.[11]

As a controversialist, McFerrin fought for what he believed was the truth, just as his Scotch ancestors had fought for their ideals. He joined the Methodist Church at a time when it was a church militant. Enemies, real and imaginary, seemed to be on all sides. The youthful preacher was told that he would either have to fight or flee and being a McFerrin he fought. But the mellowing philosophy of his lengthening years tended to soften his attack and to make him wary of controversies involving personalities. In 1858 he looked back across the years and attempted to justify the methods he had employed against his adversaries, many of whom he secretly respected. He admitted that at times he had given "too keen an edge" to his weapons.[12] He opposed what he considered to be wrong and he "honestly and faithfully ... applied the knife where amputation was necessary to the life of the patient."[13]

McFerrin was a conservative and a God-fearing Methodist,

---

[9] Quoted in Fitzgerald, *John B. McFerrin, A Biography*, 237.

[10] "Dr. Cottrell's Letter," in *Nashville Christian Advocate*, May 21, 1887.

[11] O. P. Fitzgerald, "Dr. McFerrin as a Man," in Nashville *Daily American*, May 17, 1887.

[12] McFerrin, "Valedictory," in *Nashville Christian Advocate*, July 1, 1858.

[13] *Idem.*

but his conservatism was elastic. There were times when he showed a remarkable appreciation of tolerance. He opposed dancing,[14] various popular amusements, and "new fangled ideas," and yet he published some Baptist literature that the *Tennessee Baptist* refused to publish, and he supported education for women. "A virtuous and well educated woman," he wrote, "is more to be prized than rubies."[15]

As a writer, McFerrin's most ambitious contribution was his *History of Methodism in Tennessee* which was published in three volumes in 1875. This work covers only the first part of the nineteenth century but it presents a clear account of aggressive Methodism on the march in those early years. The book is not philosophical and cannot be called interpretative. It simply tells what was done by Tennessee Methodists and who did it. With respect to this history, perhaps the most remarkable fact is that the author found time to write it in the midst of his many activities.

There is an old tradition in Tennessee to the effect that in the early days there was a gentleman's agreement between the Presbyterians and the Baptists that limited the activities of the former to the towns and of the latter to the rural districts. The chief evidence in support of this tradition is the fact that Presbyterian churches were usually founded in the towns before the Baptists arrived in sufficient numbers to organize a congregation. This was the situation in Nashville where the Presbyterians organized their first church about 1813.[16] This was about seven years before the first organization of Nashville Baptists was dignified by the term "church."

The first congregation of Nashville Presbyterians was gathered together by Rev. William Hume, a Scotchman, who came to the little frontier town in 1801. In 1813, under the guidance

---

[14] As indicated in Chapter II.
[15] *Nashville Christian Advocate*, February 27, 1851.
[16] Some sources give 1814, but the Records of the First Presbyterian Church indicate that 1813 may be a more accurate date. (Microfilm copies of these records are in Vanderbilt University Library).

of Rev. Gideon Blackburn, the congregation became the First Presbyterian Church of Nashville. During the years from 1810 to 1813, and probably later, the Sunday services were held in the woods just off the public square as the first church building was not ready for occupancy until 1816. Although always comparatively small, the Presbyterian Church in Nashville, because of the high ideals and intelligence of its leaders, exerted an influence beyond its numerical strength. For several generations after its creation, the church was fortunate to be led by zealous and self-sacrificing pastors who slowly but surely built the foundations deep into Nashville soil. The last of these "foundation builders" was the Rev. John Todd Edgar (1792-1860).[17]

Edgar, who was a Princeton graduate, was serving in the Presbyterian Church in Frankfort, Kentucky, when he was offered the pastorate of the First Church in Nashville. This was in 1833 and until his death in 1860 he was one of Nashville's leading citizens. He was interested in all civic affairs and he was always ready to promote any project that would add distinction to the life of the city. His church, of course, was his greatest interest and under his leadership it grew in numbers and in influence.

Edgar's success in Nashville was the result of his ability to overcome unexpected obstacles and to rise above unpleasant and even tragic situations. Such a situation was created by the burning of the First Presbyterian Church on September 14, 1848.[18] The records of the church reveal Edgar as a practical leader and businessman who immediately faced the problem of building a new church. From insurance $8000 was realized, about $400 was received for the old materials in the ruins, and thousands more were raised by subscription. A building committee was appointed and Edgar took an active part in the business of this committee throughout its existence.[19]

[17] Rev. William S. Jacobs (ed.), *Presbyterianism in Nashville* (Nashville, 1904), 20.
[18] Records of the First Presbyterian Church, September 15, 1848.
[19] *Ibid.*, September 16, October 23, December 15, 1848; Report of the Building Committee (in the church records), October 26, 1848.

Several sets of plans were examined by the committee and finally it voted to accept those submitted by William Strickland, the Philadelphia architect who had been brought to Nashville to design the new capitol building.[20] The cornerstone of the new church was laid with elaborate ceremonies on April 28, 1849. Obeying a request from Edgar and the building committee, Strickland provided a zinc box into which was placed a copy of the Bible, a confession of faith, an almanac for 1849, a silver plate which contained the names of the pastor and other church officials, the building committee, the architect, the masons and carpenters, the mayor, the governor, and the president of the United States. Several other items were engraved on the plate, including the population of Nashville and the number of members in the First Presbyterian Church. After copies of the city papers had been added to the collection, the box was closed and carefully placed in the cornerstone.[21]

Although services were held in the basement as early as January 5, 1850, the new church, which cost over fifty thousand dollars, was not completed until the spring of 1851. With patience and common sense and with the aid of his brilliant and forceful personality, Edgar held his congregation together during the difficult years immediately following the fire and finally he was able to lead his flock once more into green pastures. There seems to be no doubt about his ability as a preacher. While still at Frankfort he had attracted the attention of Henry Clay who regarded him as an accomplished orator. In Nashville, year by year, he added new laurels to his fame until the time came when even the new church could not hold the large audiences that came to hear him.[22]

Edgar was a thorough Calvinist and believed in the biblical statement that man must rule in the church as well as in the

---

[20] Records of the First Presbyterian Church, December 15, 1848.
[21] Records of the First Presbyterian Church, April 19, 1849.
[22] *The First Presbyterian Church, Nashville; the Addresses Delivered in Connection with the Observances of the One Hundredth Anniversary* (Nashville, 1915), 80; Jacobs (ed.), *Presbyterianism in Nashville*, 20.

home. However, he was not a theological tyrant but a gracious and accomplished gentleman, although he reflected some of the rough characteristics of the age. He called a spade a spade but he was able to do so without inflicting a personal injury. He lived in Nashville for twenty-seven years and apparently was a force for good during the entire period. He won the love and commanded the respect of all classes of people which was, perhaps, his greatest accomplishment.[23]

The Baptist Church of Nashville was organized in 1820 and the first regular preacher took charge of the congregation in 1822. This was Richard Dabbs, of Virginia, who died in 1825. Dabbs was followed by Philip S. Fall who soon came under the spell of Alexander Campbell's oratory and joined the "Reformers" who later became the Disciples of Christ or Christians. Fall carried most of the congregation with him, and this schism almost destroyed the original Baptist Church of Nashville before it was a decade old. Only five members of the congregation remained true to the old Baptist faith but this did not prevent them from organizing the First Baptist Church of Nashville. For several years this little group met in school houses, public halls, and the courthouse and in 1834 numbered only thirty members. In that year the Rev. Robert B. C. Howell became pastor and thereafter the congregation grew rapidly. But this church, born of controversy, continued to experience doctrinal difficulties and the most striking episode of its history during the fifties was a serious personal controversy that involved Howell and Rev. J. R. Graves, editor of the *Tennessee Baptist*.

James Robinson Graves (1820-1893) was born in Chester, Vermont, the son of Zuinglius Calvin and Lois Schnell Graves. While he was still an infant his father died and because of poor financial circumstances his mother was unable to give him more than a rudimentary education. His mother was a Congregationalist but young Graves became a Baptist in 1835 and from 1839 to 1845 he taught school in Ohio and Kentucky while he pre-

---

[23] Records of the First Presbyterian Church, July 29, 1859.

pared himself for the ministry. In July, 1845, he opened an academy in Nashville. Towards the close of the same year he was appointed pastor of Central Baptist Church but he was to make his greatest impression as an editor and not as a minister. In 1846 he began to edit the *Tennessee Baptist* and nine years later, with Rev. J. M. Pendleton as co-editor, he launched the *Southern Baptist Review and Eclectic*.[24]

Through his own publications, Graves proved his often expressed contention that the press was a powerful instrument. Since "all the abettors of evil used the press" he thought the best way to fight the enemy was to attack them with their own weapons. The *Southern Baptist Review and Eclectic* was founded expressly for such a purpose. It had other aims, however, among which was the desire to preserve what Graves considered to be the best Baptist thought. Newspapers, he believed, were too fragile for such a purpose.[25]

According to Graves, who was a conservative, the best Baptist thought was impregnated with the following beliefs: (1) The Baptists were not sectarians because they alone had the proper understanding of the Bible. (2) Infant baptism was unorthodox. (3) Immersion was the only correct way to baptize. There was no Gospel justification for sprinkling or pouring. (4) Justification by faith should precede baptism in all cases. It was claimed that baptism alone was not enough to make the conscience good, and all those who taught that baptism was essential to justification were automatically classified as dogmatic modern reformers.[26]

To many of his contemporaries, Graves himself seemed extremely dogmatic, but apparently he was sincere in his beliefs, and being a dynamo of energy, it was quite natural for him to prosecute a press war against all denominations not within the

---

[24] J. J. Burnett, *Sketches of Tennessee's Pioneer Baptist Preachers* (Nashville, 1919), 184-200; J. H. Spencer, *A History of Kentucky Baptists* from 1769 to 1885, 2 vols. (Cincinnati, 1885), 353-354.
[25] *Southern Baptist Review and Eclectic* (Nashville, 1855-1861?), I (1855), 2.
[26] *Ibid.*, 4-5.

sacred realm of conservative Baptists. He believed that the Catholic Church and all non-Baptist protestant sects were agencies operating for the overthrow of republican institutions.[27] Reflecting the spirit of the times, he was especially opposed to "Romanism" and he could see the Catholic Church only as a den of thieves and blood-thirsty persecutors, an institution stained with the blood of martyrs. The strength of the Roman Church, he claimed, was to be found in its mastery of the minds of its members from infancy. "The papacy," he wrote, "depends for its existence and power upon kidnapping and enslaving the infancy of humanity in its cradle."[28] Inspired by the memory of Baptists burned at the stake or frozen to death in Apline passes, Graves lifted his hands and proclaimed a crusade against "this infant slave trade."

But could the Baptists depend upon the other Protestant organizations for coöperation in this attempt to convert the Catholics and lead them back into the ways of Christ? Graves was convinced that the answer to this question was in the negative since the Protestants were disunited and could not act as a unit against the Roman Church. Even if they could bury the denominational war hatchets, the Protestants, because of their historical background, could not judge the Catholics without condemning themselves. Did not the Protestant sects grow out of the Roman Church and were they not, therefore, tainted with the corruption of the mother church? "If the fountain is corrupt," asserted Graves, "all the waters that flow from it are also corrupt."[29]

At this point in his argument Graves emphasized his main contention: only the Baptists had a pure and apostolic origin. The Presbyterian, Lutheran, and Episcopal churches were the daughters of the Catholic Church, while the Methodist Church was a granddaughter and, although too noisy, possessed a marked resemblance to her grandmother.[30] And so, thought Graves, the

[27] J. R. Graves, *The Watchman's Reply* (Nashville, 1853), 20.
[28] *Ibid.*, 28 ff.
[29] *Ibid.*, 42.
[30] *Ibid.*, 43-44.

Baptists were encircled with enemies, and if they were to maintain their position, convert their opponents, and eventually lead the world back to the true religion, they would have to gain more power. This could be done through the press, the pulpit, and by means of education. "We must have an educated ministry," Graves declared, "to maintain our standing before the world with the denominations that oppose us."[31]

His interest in an educated ministry is significant. Apparently he was aware of the changing social and cultural life around him. He saw that society, year by year, was becoming better educated and better equipped to meet the increasing complexities of life. This was one of the few progressive ideas that he exhibited, but it was an important one. He realized that illiterate preachers might be orthodox but at the same time they did not have the background or the command of words necessary to defend the "pure Apostolic Church" against the criticisms of a society that was slowly but surely raising its cultural level and developing new intellectual patterns.

Graves himself did not need any further training in order to carry on his warfare with the opposing denominations. He knew how to give virulent expression to his thoughts on Romanism and Methodism, as the columns of the *Tennessee Baptist* proved. But his masterful criticism of the Methodist Church was to be found in his book *The Great Iron Wheel*. One of the best passages in the book is an imaginative description of a Methodist revival which is so amusing that it is quoted here in full:

Listen to the character of the preaching; the doctrines advanced; observe all the multiform and questionable appliances and ingenious expedients brought into requisition. The pulpit or stand is a Mount Sinai hung with the blackness of darkness, crested with fire, and shaken with thunderings, and wreathed with fierce lightnings; wrath and fury, "hell-fire and damnation" are the themes of sermon and exhortation. The membership must be roused to action. The preacher says he wants to hear "a shout raised in the camp of Israel"—that the walls of Jericho never fell down until Israel raised the shout; and he

[31] *Ibid.*, 78.

never knew anything done until some sister "got happy." "Lord, make these sisters here *shouting* happy, right now." What appeals follow upon this to the passions—to the affections and fears! What scenes are depicted of dying fathers, dying mothers, dying children and infants (violent sobbing), death-scenes, hell-scenes (a lady faints here, and another screams), and judgment-scenes—friends in heaven meeting fathers and mothers there, meeting children, and the dear little babes lost. Hear that Shout—(had the *Lord* answered the prayer?)—and another—and another; and now it becomes general—the preacher's voice rises like trumpet-tone over all—"Fire! Fire! Send down fi-re." "Baptize all this congregation in the Holy Ghost and fi-re." "Pow-er! Pow-er!—Come in thy mighty pow-er!" Now, the excitement being at the right stage, the straw being prepared, the door of the altar is thrown open and sinners are called upon to come forward before they drop into hell. In the midst of the uproar, parents drag their excited and terrified children into the altar, and others from alarm, others from pure nervous excitement, and others from sympathy, rush forward; the altar is crowded. Now follows what some preachers call a "sanctified row." The mourners are exhorted to pray mightily—and a season of prayer commences. A brother who has a strong voice is called upon to pray and all the mourners are exhorted to pray at once, and all Christians to pray—call mightily upon God. And who can describe the scene that follows for the next half hour—men and women, girls and boys, of all ages, are mingled and commingled in one conglomerated mass in the straw, rolling and tumbling, and throwing their arms and limbs about in every conceivable direction; forty or fifty "mourners" crying, screaming, some shouting, some swooning, some with the powers; the shrill voice of the leader ever and anon rising above the din, calling for "fire," "power!" and the ministers shouting the loud and deep "A-men! a-men! do, Lord! Hallelujah!" This lasts until ten or eleven, with the simple variation of a song instead of a prayer, when the noise, uproar and confusion is, if possible, far greater! . . . and there, how those ministers are beating them upon their backs as though religion was a wedge to be driven in between the shoulder-blades![32]

Graves' theory of baptism coupled with his truculent attitude and his scathing editorials, eventually produced a temporary disaffection among Nashville Baptists. He was particularly impatient with the Pedobaptists and declared that they had no real

[32] J. R. Graves, *The Great Iron Wheel* (Nashville, 1856), 531-533.

baptism, that they did not follow the Bible, and that they were not Christians. Consequently, from his point of view, their ministers had no real authority to preach or even to pray in Baptist churches. Because of these beliefs, Graves denounced what had become more or less common in the Southwest, the practice of inviting Pedobaptists to preach in Baptist pulpits and to take part in Baptist conventions.[33]

Naturally such bigoted doctrines produced a critical reaction in various quarters. One of the most important critics was John L. Waller (1809-1854), the vigorous leader of Kentucky Baptists, who used the columns of the *Western Baptist Review* as a medium through which he expressed his disapproval. This was in 1853. Graves, of course, did not appreciate Waller's censorship but rather than make a reply himself he induced his friend, J. M. Pendleton, to write a series of articles for the *Tennessee Baptist* which demonstrated the impropriety of pulpit communion with Pedobaptists. Graves was well pleased with the articles and in 1854 collected them into a tract with the intention of having it published by the Tennessee Baptist Publishing Society. It seems that there were several Kentucky Baptists in Nashville who were associated with the publishing concern. These men supported Waller and refused to publish Graves' tract. Graves, however, defied them and published the treatise at the Southwestern Publishing House, a firm which he himself had established.[34]

The publication of the tract[35] tended to widen the breach between the truculent editor and the more liberal faction of Nashville Baptists. From 1854 to 1857 fertile brains were seeking ways to knock Graves from his high perch and to destroy his paper which was becoming more abusive. In 1857 correspondence was opened with the Rev. R. B. C. Howell, then in Richmond, Virginia, and finally he was invited to Nashville to direct

[33] J. M. Pendleton, *An Old Landmark Reset* (Nashville, 1854), 8-13; *Both Sides: A Full Investigation of the Charges Preferred Against Elder J. R. Graves by R. B. C. Howell and Others* (Nashville, 1859), 14-15.   [34] *Ibid.*, 15.
[35] The tract was J. M. Pendleton's *An Old Landmark Reset*.

the First Baptist Church and also to lead a crusade against Graves and his henchmen.[36]

R. B. C. Howell was born in Wayne County, Virginia, in 1801, the son of Ralph and Jane Crawford Howell. He received a better education than Graves and when he first accepted the call to Nashville in 1834 he had already held two pastorates of some importance. He was well received in Nashville and he remained until 1850 when he was transferred to Richmond, Virginia. When he returned to Nashville in 1857 to take part in the campaign against Graves, he had written nothing to mark him as a more liberal man than his intended opponent. On the contrary he had asserted that he believed the scriptures to be the word of God and that they revealed all men should know about the way to salvation. Apparently he accepted the narrative of the fall of man in the shade of the Edenic apple tree as genuine history. On several occasions he had expressed his belief in complete immersion as the only orthodox method to use in the ceremony of baptism.[37] Howell, however, was more tolerant and less truculent than Graves. But it was obvious that Howell could not attack Graves because of the latter's anti-sprinkling theories without laying himself open to criticism on the grounds of inconsistency. So it was decided that Graves' editorial policy was to be censored and the integrity of his personal character was to be publicly questioned. The fact that Graves had been born in New England was helpful because if all else failed it would be possible to fall back on the damn Yankee theme. As a matter of fact Graves' birthplace was held against him throughout the controversy.[38]

The affair reached a climax on the evening of October 2, 1858, when Howell summoned Graves to trial at the First Baptist Church. A large crowd gathered in the church and spilled

[36] *Both Sides: A Full Investigation of the Charges Preferred Against Elder J. R. Graves by R. B. C. Howell and Others*, 15-19.
[37] Burnett, *Sketches of Tennessee Pioneer Baptist Preachers*, 246-252; Nashville, *Republican Banner*, April 7, 8, 1858.
[38] *Both Sides: A Full Investigation of the Charges Preferred Against Elder J. R. Graves by R. B. C. Howell and Others*, 34, 37.

down the front steps. This audience was composed of members of both factions and many others were present out of curiosity. This peculiar trial continued far into the night and gradually became a battle of words between the two chief contestants. Howell, tall, commanding, with a round, red face, presented a dramatic figure. Graves, small in stature but loud of voice, tried to freeze his adversary into submission with the cold logic of his arguments. The audience, too, became more expressive as the hours went by and as the two star performers warmed to the occasion their speeches and tirades were acclaimed by loud applause, the stamping of feet, and general disorder.[39]

At midnight the general assembly adjourned to reconvene at a later date, but all those who supported Graves and who considered the trial an unorthodox and unchristian procedure remained until two o'clock in the morning. In these early hours a resolution favoring the organization of a new church was adopted and Graves requested that a committee be appointed to confer with the different Baptist associations and to arrange for a general meeting to investigate the charges brought against him. The request was granted and preparations were made to call a general Baptist council. Thereafter, Graves refused to recognize Howell's "court" and the trial proceeded without his presence.[40]

The special committee appointed in the early morning hours of October 3, 1858, soon went to work to build up support for the "misjudged" Graves. As a result of the committee's exertions, a council representative of the Baptist association of Middle Tennessee and Northern Alabama met in Lebanon, Tennessee, October 23, 1858. Graves was elected moderator, a rather strange move when it is considered that he was actually on trial.

The findings of this October council were not conclusive and another council was called which met in Nashville in March, 1859. This body appointed a committee of seven to consider all the evidence in the case and to bring in a decision. The com-

[39] *Nashville Daily Gazette*, October 4, 1858.
[40] *Ibid.*, October 26, 1858.

mittee was actually a packed jury which was supposed to clear Graves of all the charges brought against him by the Howell faction. The charges were based for the most part upon his reckless editorial policy which had been unethical, to say the least. But with the defense guiding the prosecution there could be only one outcome. The committee of seven, after considering the mass of testimonials presented to it, decided that the Howell group was simply a faction without scriptural authority, and had no right to bring Graves to trial.[41]

Graves' exoneration was more than a personal triumph. It was a victory for the conservative, "Old Landmark" doctrines which he represented and which had become so widespread that it was virtually a movement. Graves continued to live in Nashville until the Civil War ruined his publishing business. About 1870 he moved to Memphis. On the other hand, Howell's reputation was not impaired by his participation in the movement to dethrone Graves. He continued to hold his pastorate in Nashville until ill health forced his resignation in 1867.

The origin of the Disciple or Christian Church in Nashville has been explained in connection with the early history of the Baptist Church. By 1850 the chief congregation of this denomination in Nashville was known as the Church of Christ and this organization was regarded as a model by many Christians in Middle Tennessee. The influence exerted by this church was the result of the management of its very active and well-known pastor, Jesse B. Ferguson, who had been in charge of the congregation since 1847.

Jesse B. Ferguson (1819-1870), the son of Robert and Hannah Ferguson, was born in Philadelphia, but while he was still an infant he was taken by his parents to a rural community near Winchester, Virginia. Very little is known about his life until 1838 when, at the age of nineteen, he began to write for the *Heretic Detector,* a Christian periodical published in Middleburg,

[41] *Both Sides: A full Investigation of the Charges Preferred Against Elder Graves . . .,* 231 ff.

Ohio, by Arthur Crichfield.[42] At this time (May, 1838) Ferguson, in all probability, had had some experiences as a minister.[43] In December, 1839, Crichfield was so busy with editorial duties that he began to turn over some of the *Detector's* correspondence to Ferguson. From conductor of the answer department, young Ferguson rose to be joint editor of the paper (1841) and so he added journalism to his daily life, already replete with the duties of a preacher and debater.[44]

After various experiences in Ohio and Kentucky, Ferguson visited Nashville in 1842. In that city he preached before the congregation of the Church of Christ and was so well received that in 1846 he was asked to return as assistant pastor. He accepted the call and after serving a brief apprenticeship he became pastor of the church in 1847.[45] In 1848 he began to publish one of the most successful religious journals of the day, the *Christian Magazine*.

At the age of twenty-nine, Ferguson had risen to a position of prominence. His popularity was almost phenomenal and can be accounted for by his polished manners, his fascinating personality, and his eloquence in the pulpit. Even those who disapproved of his doctrines declared that "never was a man so honored and caressed by the Disciples of Christ in the South West."[46] His followers were not confined to the members of his church. His appeal was universal and tramps, gamblers, streetwalkers, and the worldly minded sat spellbound by his oratory. With a combination of personality and well-chosen words he was able to weave a sermonic web that caught the dregs of society as well as the social butterflies.[47]

Under Ferguson's leadership, the congregation grew and pros-

[42] *Heretic Detector* (Middleburg, 1837-1841), II (1839), 188-192 and *passim*.
[43] H. Leo Boles, "J. B. Ferguson," in *Biographical Sketches of Gospel Preachers* (Nashville, 1932), 187.
[44] *Heretic Detector*, III (1839), 355; IV (1840), 224-226, 287.
[45] *History and True Position of the Church of Christ in Nashville, with an Examination of the Speculative Theology Recently Introduced from Neologists, Universalists, etc.* (Nashville, 1854), 12. [46] *Ibid.*, 12.
[47] *Ibid.*, 12-13; Robert Richardson (ed.), *Memoirs of Alexander Campbell*, 2 vols. (Philadelphia, 1870), 603; Randall W. MacGavock, Diary, December 13, 1857.

pered and in 1852, with considerable pomp and ceremony, a new church was opened to the public. The new edifice, Greek Corinthian in style with a lofty spire rising to a height of one hundred fifty feet, could seat about twelve hundred persons in its white walnut, crimson-cushioned pews.[48]

But Ferguson's success was not achieved without creating a feeling of envy among the older members of the congregation who previous to 1847 had played more important roles in the life and administration of the church. His opponents could not deny his eloquence but they doubted that it converted the heathen to the ways of Christ. They could not deny that he attracted the crowds, "but," they declared, "the stage and the opera please many of the same persons quite as well." They could not understand the fact that he attracted "the idle, frolicksome, theatrical, sensual, and profane part of the community."[49]

So the older members of the congregation, pious and unimaginative, began to doubt the sincerity of their pastor and to question his faithfulness to the creed of the Disciples. They waited for an opportunity to denounce him publicly and they were given their chance when he published some of his doctrinal views in the *Christian Magazine* (April, 1852) and subsequently became involved in a controversy with Alexander Campbell. The article in question was entitled "The Spirits in Prison" and seems to have been published at the request of his friends.[50] Using as his text I Peter, 3:18-20 and 4:1-6, Ferguson developed the thesis that God intended all men to be saved whether or not they knew the scriptures or had ever heard of Christ. He believed that there was a spiritual ministry and that the souls of heathens still had a chance in the future world to learn of Christ through the teachings of the spirit preachers.[51]

"From our souls," wrote Ferguson, "we pity the spiritual darkness of any man or sect of men whose earthly and selfish

---

[48] Nashville *Daily Union*, June 1, 1852; *Christian Magazine* (Nashville, 1848-1853), V (1852), 237-239.
[49] *History and True Position of the Church of Christ in Nashville*, 12-13.
[50] *Christian Magazine*, V (1852), 113-115. [51] *Ibid.*, 114-115.

views limit the benefits of the mission of Christ to the comparatively few who hear of Him and learn His ways while they remain in the flesh. Infants, idiots, pagans, and the countless thousands whose external circumstances remove them far from the light of the blessed gospels as it shines through earthen mirrors, are thus consigned to a perdition revolting to every just conception of God, of Christ, or the benevolent purpose of life."[52]

But to Alexander Campbell, Ferguson's views were not only revolting, they were unorthodox to the point of being revolutionary. Ferguson must be silenced, and with this end in view, Campbell published a criticism of Ferguson's ideas under the caption "A New Discovery" and with biting sarcasm denounced Ferguson's vision of a ghostly priesthood as a new type of Universalism. "Rapt in sublime vision," wrote Campbell, "he [Ferguson] sees not merely the present or future living nations of the earth converted to Christ, but in the far distance of coming cycles of ages without end, he rejoices to see obstinate Jews and idolatrous pagans, who heard in vain both Moses and the Prophets, bowing to the ghostly ministers of mercy sent from the schools of hades."[53]

Campbell believed that Ferguson's doctrine was unscriptural and incompatible with the principles of the Christian Church. It was dangerous because it tended to neutralize the work of the ministers preaching that sinners must repent or else be lost forever. It was difficult enough for the orthodox ministers to combat the wages of evil without having to compete with a pastoral ghost brigade. Had Ferguson recanted and returned to the fold all would have been forgiven, but he objected to the dictatorial attitude taken by Campbell and proceeded to compare him with the Pope. At the same time he said with refreshing simplicity, "I desire no controversy on this subject."[54]

It was in keeping with the spirit of the times, of course, for Protestants to protest against what they called papal tyranny;

[52] *Idem.*
[53] *Millennial Harbinger* (Bethany, 1830-1870), II (1852), 313-329.
[54] *Christian Magazine,* V (1852), 244-245.

but to mention the name of Alexander Campbell in the same breath with popery was a shameless transgression of the bounds of ministerial ethics. "But alas!" Campbell protested with great indignation, "has it come to this, that such comparison shall be instituted, whispered, named, talked of, printed, published at Nashville and applied to Alexander Campbell!"[55] The ire of the Old Man of Bethany was fully aroused and he decided to put on his Christian harness, to unsheath the sword of righteousness, and to enter the field in defense of true scriptural religion. With an editorial fanfare he announced a declaration of war and called for help from all the orthodox brethren. The Church Campbellite had become the church bellicose.

Campbell's appeal for support was not in vain. In Pennsylvania, Ohio, Kentucky, and Tennessee his faithful friends and followers came to his aid with editorials and letters. From many quarters, Ferguson was denounced as a Universalist, a heretic, and an unbeliever. Samuel Church of Pittsburgh thought Ferguson had gone "sissy" and condemned his new theory as a mere sentiment that attempted to cushion the road to hell.[56] Church preferred the "blunt, rough, honest method." He desired no honeyed words and no feather pillows for ungodly men. A spade should be called a spade, a sinner should be called a sinner, and every man should be made to face the question, "How can you escape the damnation of hell?" He believed that Ferguson was making religion so easy that people could "slip into the lake of fire and brimstone with the same ease that a vessel slides over its greased ways into the sea."[57]

In general, those who censured Ferguson's doctrine saw in it only an attempt to lighten the penalties attached to gospel law. From their point of view this was a grave offense. It did not produce benevolence but irreverence and impiety. It tended to belittle the tragedy of the cross and to diminish the bitterness of sin. It was maintained that one of the sweetest rewards waiting

---

[55] *Millennial Harbinger*, II (1852), 493.
[56] *Ibid.*, 505-508.   [57] *Ibid.*, 507.

for the true Christian who suffers and repents was the redeeming love of God. But if the punishment of sin was made less severe, and many believed this would be the result of Ferguson's preaching, then the redeeming love would be less beautiful.

At first, Ferguson refused to re-publish Campbell's criticisms in the *Christian Magazine* on the grounds that his journal represented the Church of Christ in the state of Tennessee and consequently had no space for essays created in the heat of personal controversy. But Campbell did not appreciate the editorial ethics involved and he declared that it was unfair to ignore his statements. Piqued by this neglect, he requested that his articles be reprinted in the *Christian Magazine* so that everyone in Tennessee might realize that Ferguson was an egotistical editor who cherished the unique hope of being an evangelist in hades.[58]

Finally, after the regular December (1852) number of the *Magazine* had appeared, Ferguson brought out a thirty-two page extra in which he published everything that Campbell had written in connection with the controversy. Ferguson, who was failing in health, was tired of the whole affair, and he hoped that the extra edition would quiet his opponent and bring the quarrel to an end. He believed that personal feuds colored with hard names exhibited bad taste and should be avoided if possible. He wished to place the matter in the hands of his own congregation either to reject or to sustain him. With complete faith in his Nashville friends he went South for the winter to regain his health.[59]

During his absence the charge of Universalism was brought against him once more. For some time, as noted above, the minority group in his church had doubted his faithfulness to the creed and now they became openly hostile. His personal influence, however, was still so strong that at the church election held early in 1853 he was sustained by a majority vote, and throughout 1853 his popularity seemed to increase rather than decrease

[58] *Ibid.*, 634.
[59] *Christian Magazine*, VI (1853), 20, 32.

as a result of his difficulties with Campbell. He received many invitations to speak in churches in Tennessee and neighboring states. Winchester, Memphis, Clarksville, Hopkinsville, New Orleans, and other towns made him offers. Throughout the year letters came in from all parts of the country praising him for his attitude and for his doctrinal theories.

Campbell, however, never gave up. With the support of some of his strongest allies, including Benjamin Franklin (1812-1878), editor of the *Christian Age,* he continued his campaign against Ferguson. The voices of these two men were chiefly responsible for the formal protest made by the conservative group in the Nashville church later in the year.[60] On November 27, 1853, twenty-five members of the church entered a protest against the re-election of their pastor on the grounds that his sermons contained "strange sounds, such as Moses and the Prophets, Christ and the Apostles never heard or authorized," in short, that he was a Universalist.[61]

In spite of the opposition, Ferguson continued to hold his pastorate. Late in 1854, Campbell arrived in Nashville to preach and probably with the hope of a debate with the younger minister who had strayed from the beaten path of orthodoxy. But by this time Ferguson had taken up spiritualism and in a seance he claimed that he received a message from William E. Channing[62] which urged him to stay away from Campbell and to dispense with his spiritual meetings while Campbell was in Nashville.[63]

Campbell, denied the privilege of an interview with Ferguson, or better still, a debate, was forced to stage a one-man show. This he was quite capable of doing. He gave his first sermons in a Methodist Church which was opened to him at the suggestion of John B. McFerrin who had no use for Ferguson

---

[60] Joseph Franklin and J. A. Headington, *The Life and Times of Benjamin Franklin* (St. Louis, 1879), 211-213; *The Christian Age* (Cincinnati, 1849-1856), VIII (1852), 198; IX (1853), 18.

[61] *History and True Position of the Church of Christ in Nashville,* 13, 17-19.

[62] Channing (1780-1842), the Unitarian divine and writer.

[63] Richardson (ed.), *Memoirs of Alexander Campbell,* 612.

after he joined the spirit knockers. However, after his opening addresses, Campbell moved into Ferguson's church and preached as often as three times a day before large audiences.[64] Apparently he was well received in this storm center of controversy and his personal influence plus Ferguson's fraternization with the spiritualists considerably weakened the latter's position in the Church of Christ.

It was Ferguson's interest in spiritualism, more than his doctrine of universalism, that finally split his church into two hostile camps. Since both parties claimed the church property, it became necessary to take the case into court. The decision was against Ferguson and his friends and soon afterwards, either by accident or by design, the church burned.[65] Ferguson was now a pastor without a church, but for several years he continued to ride his wave of popularity and preached sporadically at the theater, at Odd Fellows Hall, and before various civic organizations.[66] On these occasions he drew large and attentive audiences and the Nashville *Daily Gazette* referred to him as "a great independent preacher."[67] Finally, disillusioned and in poor health, he left Nashville to become the wandering preacher of the Southwest. He lived for a time in Mississippi, Alabama, and Missouri. He dabbled in politics and in real estate and in 1870 he returned to Nashville. He died on September 3, 1870, and his death was hardly noticed in the city where he had been so popular a few years before.[68] His downfall marked a victory for the conservative Disciples in Nashville and they have maintained their supremacy to the present time.

In a region where the Protestants had had an overwhelming majority from frontier days, it was inevitable that the Catholic Church in Nashville and in Tennessee in general should be

[64] *Idem.*
[65] John T. Brown, *Churches of Christ, an Historical, Biographical, and Pictorial History of the Churches of Christ in the United States, Australia, England, and Canada* (Louisville, 1904), 358.
[66] Randall W. MacGavock, Diary, January 7, 1858; *Nashville Daily Gazette*, October 22, 26, 31, 1858. [67] *Ibid.*, October 26, 1858.
[68] The *Gospel Advocate*, September 22, 1870.

forced to tolerate a barrage of indignities issuing from the Protestant press and pulpits. It should be emphasized, however, that this criticism of Catholicism was by no means limited to Tennessee. It was a local expression of a national conflict that had its political outlet in the Know Nothing party. In Nashville the representatives of this party embarrassed the Catholics at every opportunity and on one occasion attempted to incite a riot. This was the infamous mob scene staged by the Know Nothings in front of the Catholic Cathedral on Christmas night, 1855. Fortunately the plot was discovered in time to warn many Catholics not to attend the special mass and those who did come were urged to ignore the demonstrators. During the mass the Know Nothings, who were crowded into the street in front of the church, roared and cursed and cat-called but when they realized that their insults were being ignored they dispersed.[69]

Catholic schools were also subjected to severe criticism by some of the more intolerant Protestants. John B. McFerrin allowed some of this anti-Catholic propaganda to appear in the Nashville *Christian Advocate* and the commercial press carried its share. To some critics Catholic schools were dark, secretive dens, evils that could be destroyed by building public schools. In some cases the Protestant attack was based on the idea that the Roman Church was undermining American democratic institutions and hence there was a patriotic as well as a sectarian appeal. One book of Protestant propaganda published in Nashville in 1856 bore the interesting title *Americanism Versus Romanism or the Cis-Atlantic Battle Between Sam and the Pope*. The Author, James L. Chapman, was a Methodist and with little attention to historical truth he related what he thought the Catholic Church had done for the world. As he saw it, the Catholics had substituted a Pope for an Emperor, images of saints for heathen idols, crafty Jesuits for the Apostles and the inquisition

---

[69] Rev. V. F. O'Daniel, *The Father of the Church in Tennessee, or the Life, Times, and Character of the Right Reverend Richard Pius Miles, O.P., The First Bishop of Nashville* (Washington, 1926), 523-524.

for the temple of liberty.[70] Furthermore, according to Chapman, the Roman Church, drunk with power, never regretted the outrages committed against the glorious past. "Romanism cared not, heeded not, shed not a tear of regret over its bloodstained acts, damnable policies, and hellish inventions."[71]

Fortunately for the Catholics in Tennessee, their first bishop, Richard Pius Miles, was a man of wisdom, patience, and education. He was a man who could maintain his dignity in the midst of intolerant attacks and soon he won the confidence and the friendship of many broad-minded Protestant leaders. Richard Miles was born in Maryland in 1791, the son of Nicholas and Ann Miles. Nicholas Miles was a carpenter and planter and shortly after the birth of Richard he moved his family to Nelson County, Kentucky, believing that there were better opportunities for success in the new West. So the future Bishop of Nashville was brought up in a frontier environment where schools were scarce; but Nicholas Miles provided a tutor for his children. In 1806, when he was fifteen, Richard entered the newly established Dominican school near Springfield, Kentucky. Here he came under the influence of several well-educated churchmen including Rev. Samuel T. Wilson who has been described as one of the most learned divines in America.[72]

Richard Miles had a thirst for education and he enjoyed his thorough course in history, languages, and music. This collegiate course was the prelude to his theological training. Either in 1809 or 1810 he took the vows in the order of St. Dominic. In 1816 he was ordained a priest. From this date until 1837, when he became bishop of the new diocese of Nashville, the young priest had various experiences as teacher, church builder, and missionary. These experiences gave him the necessary courage to face the difficulties presented by his new office in Ten-

[70] James L. Chapman, *Americanism Versus Romanism or the Cis-Atlantic Battle Between Sam and the Pope* (Nashville, 1856), *passim*.
[71] *Ibid.*, 173.
[72] O'Daniel, *The Father of the Church in Tennessee*, 71 ff; *Nashville Gazette*, February 22, 1860.

nessee. In 1837 he became a Bishop of the Roman Catholic Church, he became the spiritual leader of a diocese, and yet "all that he or his diocese possessed in temporal good was a dilapidated brick church, fifty-five by fifty-five feet, which stood on the northern declivity of a barren knob, covered with dwarf cedars, in the outskirts of Nashville."[73]

Bishop Miles was as aggressive as he was pious. By 1850 he had organized his diocese, founded a seminary and a school for boys, gathered around him a number of capable priests and nuns, established an orphan asylum and a hospital, and built a cathedral. A trip to Europe had improved his wardrobe and his treasury.[74] He had been accepted as a friend by many of the Protestants of Nashville. Some of these tolerant men and women, partly as a protest against their intolerant fellow citizens, had helped the Bishop with his work and some of them had attended, and continued to attend, the special Catholic services. They thought, as did the editor of the *Nashville Union and American*, that persecution of Catholics was "a disgrace to the intelligence of the age."[75]

One of Miles' greatest contributions was the beautiful Cathedral of the Seven Dolors, now called St. Mary's. This church, a monument to the efforts and perseverance of Tennessee's first Catholic Bishop, was dedicated with the proper ceremonies on October 31, 1847. The dedicatory services were opened by a procession of robed priests and bishops which circled the new building. As they walked with solemn dignity, the clergy sang the fifty-first psalm and sprinkled the walls of the church with holy water. In this way the church was purified and dedicated to the services of Bishop Miles, who, as master of ceremonies, brought up the rear of the procession. The services were concluded within the church, a building which was described by a contemporary as "a neat and chaste specimen of Grecian archi-

---

[73] O'Daniel, *The Father of the Church in Tennessee*, 315.

[74] *Ibid.*, 342-343; *Catholic Advocate*, March 21, 1840, October 23, 1841; *Daily Union*, November 3, 1847.

[75] *Nashville Union and American*, August 30, 1856.

tecture, which reflects credit upon its architect."[76] The architect referred to was William Strickland.[77]

The work of a bishop was never finished and Miles' task did not become much easier as he approached the end of his life. The diocese was well organized, churches had been constructed, and many converts had been made, but there was always a certain amount of suspicion and hostility that impeded his progress and there were always creditors who could not be satisfied entirely. Because of the comparatively small number of Catholics in the Nashville Diocese, the Catholic authorities in America neglected its financial needs and Miles was often thrown upon his own resources. He needed money for the Sisters of Charity whom he brought from Kentucky. He needed money for his boys' school and for the hospital. There seemed to be only one way to solve this financial difficulty and that was to sell his home and estate. And so in 1855 he gave up his spacious house and moved into what he called a "rat-trap." With the proceeds from the sale of his property to the local gas company and the Nashville and Northwestern Railroad he was able to establish his charities on a firm basis.[78]

In spite of poor health and advancing years, Bishop Miles was to build another church in Nashville before he died. This was the German Catholic Church in North Nashville which became known as the Church of the Assumption. As early as 1850 he realized that the Germans needed a church of their own and when the little old church on Capitol Hill burned in that year he sold the lot but carefully saved the bricks for the church he hoped to build in North Nashville.[79] Nearly a decade went by before the Bishop's plans were realized. The lot for the church was given by a generous citizen of Nashville and the stained glass windows and interior furnishings were the gifts of various members of the German parish. After many delays, the Church

[76] *Daily Union*, November 3, 1847.   [77] On Strickland see Chapter IX.
[78] O'Daniel, *The Father of the Church in Tennessee*, 525.
[79] "Assumption, Pioneer Parish of North Nashville," in the *Columbian* (Nashville, 1918—), VIII (1926), No. 1, p. 1.

of the Assumption, a simple Gothic structure, was dedicated on August 14, 1859. By this time Bishop Miles, partly because of his illness, had become "old and gray and full of sleep," but he was not denied the privilege of officiating at the dedication of the church which he had planned for so many years.[80]

The Church of the Assumption was Bishop Miles' last important contribution. He died the following year (1860) following a sudden stroke of paralysis.[81] At the time of his death, Catholic notables expressed the opinion that he had accomplished more in the Nashville Diocese than had been hoped for and that the foundation which he built would receive in time "a noble superstructure."

There were Episcopalians in Nashville at an early date but they remained unorganized until 1826. In that year a few families created an informal congregation that became the genesis of Christ Church. In 1829 a lot suitable for a church building was purchased and about 1830 the First Church of Christ was ready to be used.[82] Under the watchful eyes of Bishop James Otey and other prominent Tennessee Episcopalians, the Nashville church steadily grew in size and when the capable James Tomes became pastor in 1848 the congregation was worthy of his intelligence and aggressiveness.

Tomes, a native of England, was a prosperous businessman in New York City when he came under the influence of Bishop Otey and decided to enter the ministry. He was ordained in 1844, married the Bishop's daughter in 1846, and under the guidance of his father-in-law he rose rapidly in his new profession. After performing services for the church in several states he was called to Christ Church in Nashville in 1848.[83]

---

[80] O'Daniel, *The Father of the Church in Tennessee*, 551-552.

[81] *Nashville Gazette*, February 22, 1860.

[82] *National Banner and Nashville Whig*, September 11, 1829; *Christ Church, Nashville* (Nashville, 1929), 74 ff.

[83] William Mercer Green, *Memoir of the Rt. Rev. James Hervey Otey, D. D, LL. D., The First Bishop of Tennessee* (New York, 1885), 88, 161; Rev. Arthur Howard Noll, *History of the Church in the Diocese of Tennessee* (New York, 1900), 108, 111, 131.

Tomes was a man of wisdom and experience, of cheerfulness and optimism. Old and young brought their problems to him to solve and the poor and the destitute were regarded as his special wards. Tomes was not a "Sabbath Day preacher." He was a tireless worker both in the church and out, and he carried the gospel and also the inspiration of his own personality into the homes of the poor every day of the week. He conducted two services in the church every day throughout the year regardless of the weather, regardless of plagues or other calamities.[84]

Tomes did not believe in some of the aristocratic traditions of the Episcopal Church and he was openly opposed to the practice of renting pews to the members of the congregation. His kindness and many services won for him a host of friends who wanted to come to his church but there were no accommodations for them since the pews were rented or owned by older members of the congregation. Tomes was not an isolated democratic figure in the Episcopal Church as ministers in other cities were agitating for free pews in order that the poor might not be excluded from church.

His appeal for free pews brought considerable opposition from certain members of Christ Church and so the matter was dropped, as he did not wish to cause a schism. However, a few close friends who were in sympathy with him and who had no hope of making the church free, withdrew and formed a new congregation called the Church of the Advent.[85] Tomes took no part in this movement directly.

The new congregation was established "for the purpose of securing to themselves and posterity, the preaching of the true word of God, and the duly administering of the sacraments according to Christ's ordinance; of providing freely for all alike the same sacred privileges, and of enlarging the borders of the Redeemer's Kingdom."[86] In case there was any doubt about their attitude on a free church, members of the vestry of the new

---

[84] Reverend Charles Tomes, *An Unfinished Sermon* (Nashville, 1857), 5-11.
[85] *Ibid.*, 7-8.   [86] *Ibid.*, 18.

congregation drew up a resolution which stated rather bluntly that the system of rented pews and reserved seats was an obstruction to the dissemination of religious thought.[87] The church and its missions were to be supported by the free offerings of the worshippers. In April, 1857, Tomes was invited to take over the ministerial duties of the new church. He accepted the call as he believed there would be a greater opportunity in the free church to spread his beliefs among the poor.

The German Lutherans and the Jews produced no outstanding leaders during the period but their churches deserve to be mentioned. German Lutherans had become so numerous in Tennessee by the second decade of the nineteenth century that a separate Tennessee Synod was formed in 1820.[88] However, there was no Lutheran Church in Nashville before 1859. In May of that year, Rev. W. Jenkins, the Lutheran pastor in Shelbyville, Tennessee, attended the General Lutheran Synod in Pittsburgh and convinced Rev. Herman Eggers that he was needed in Nashville to direct the Lutherans in that city. On the last Sunday in July, 1859, Eggers preached his first sermon in Nashville and on August 11 "a Lutheran Evangelical Congregation" was organized. The Civil War broke up this congregation temporarily and they did not complete their church building until 1867.[89]

The Jews in Nashville organized for the first time in October, 1851. A Jewish benevolent society was organized and a cemetery was purchased. At first a rented room served as a synagogue but after the arrival of Rabbi Alexander Iser, a Russian Pole, the society was reorganized as a church and was chartered under the name of "Kaal a Kodish Mogen David," which meant a Holy Congregation—the Shield of David.[90] The Jewish church was declared to be a body corporate and politic with the right to own real estate and personal property of any nature provided

---

[87] *Ibid.*, Appendix, 19-20.
[88] Albert Bernhardt Faust, *The German Element in the United States*, 2 vols. (Boston and New York, 1909), I, 388.
[89] *Directory of the First Lutheran Church* (Nashville, 1926), 5.
[90] Tennessee *Acts*, 1853-1854, pp. 555-557.

the value of the property did not exceed at any time $100,000. Only Israelites could be admitted. The church was represented by one Parnas (President), one Gabah Sedoakah (Vice-President or President of Charity), one Gabah Beth Chayion (President of the Burial Grounds), one treasurer, one secretary, and four trustees. The charter referred to the congregation as a company and declared that the funds of the company should not be employed in banking, but were to be used for burial grounds, temples, and schools.[91] The first act of the new organization was to rent a hall large enough to hold all the members. This original congregation was orthodox and followed the strict rituals of the Polish Jewish Church.

The Young Men's Christian Association, organized in Nashville in January, 1855, deserves to be mentioned here as it was an organization that supplemented the work of the ministers and the churches. The purpose of the organization as stated by the constitution was to improve the spiritual, mental, and social conditions of the young men of Nashville. Each member of the association was expected to aid newcomers to the city in any way possible. Strangers were to be guided to suitable lodgings and they were to be assisted if they sought employment. If the strangers desired Christian associates and healthful recreation, it was the duty of the members of the Y. M. C. A. to provide these needs. It was also their duty to induce newcomers to join a church or Sunday school, and, of course, to join the Y. M. C. A. if they were considered good material.[92]

Another aim of this organization was to establish and maintain mission Sunday schools and Bible classes in the slum districts. Each school, according to the constitution, was to be managed by a superintendent, an associate superintendent, and a secretary. Information relative to this phase of the program is scant but there is some evidence that indicates that Bible classes were actually organized.[93]

[91] *Ibid.*, 556.
[92] *Constitution of the Young Men's Christian Association* (Nashville, 1857), 5.
[93] *Nashville Daily Gazette*, October 21, 1858.

The officers of the association were elected annually by ballot at the first regular meeting in October. The president presided at all meetings, preserved order, and called special meetings at the written request of three members. There was one vice-president for each denomination represented in the association. The vice-presidents (there were five in 1857) constituted a committee on membership. In addition to the officers named above, there was a corresponding secretary, a recording secretary, and a treasurer. There was an executive committee composed of all the officers and in addition standing committees on publications, lectures, library, sick members, finance, statistics, and employment. If these committees were active it may be assumed that the first Young Men's Christian Association in Nashville made a worthwhile contribution to the community.

It is difficult to form a just estimate of some of the religious leaders in Nashville during the period under review. This is especially true of the men whom the historian sees only through the smoke screen of doctrinal battles. In general it may be said that the ministers whose careers have been sketched in this chapter were unusually aggressive in their attempts to diffuse what each thought to be the true religious philosophy. Some were tolerant, some were intolerant, and some grew more liberal as they progressed with the times; all of them stood forth as leaders who made an impression on the city and on the state. Perhaps the church historians are correct when they say that there were giants in those days.

CHAPTER V

THE NASHVILLE THEATER: DRAMA AND OPERA,
1850-1860

I

ONE INDEX to the cultural level of a city is the attitude of its citizens towards the theater—the theater taken as the symbol of musical expression and dramatic arts. It has already been noted that Nashville possessed a crude theater as early as 1817 and that its citizens were considered to be musically inclined. It is the purpose of this chapter and the one to follow to describe the musical and dramatic opportunities presented in Nashville from 1850 to 1860 and to note the reaction of these entertainments on the public mind.

The history of the American theater in the nineteenth century offers enough unexploited dramatic material to inspire playwrights and novelists, to say nothing of historians, for decades to come. American actors and actresses of the old school were not pampered hot-house flowers basking in the limelight of fashionable society.[1] On the contrary, they were red-blooded troupers who braved the hardships of travel by mule-drawn canal boats, by crude steamboats, by rattling trains and careening stagecoaches in order that semi-frontier towns scattered from the Appalachians to the gold fields of California might have a taste of the Thespian art. Indeed, there were times when the itinerant actor did not have the price of a stagecoach seat and was forced to walk the dusty or muddy roads in order to keep his appointments.[2]

Among these traveling comedians and tragedians was to be

[1] Arthur Hornblow, *A History of the Theatre in America from its Beginnings to the Present Time*, 2 vols. (Philadelphia and London, 1919), I, 329.
[2] Joseph Jefferson, *Autobiography*, 45-46; Brander Matthews and Lawrence Hutton, *The Life and Art of Edwin Booth and His Contemporaries* (Boston, 1886), 61.

found the best talent of the day. Such names as Charlotte Cushman, James Murdock, John Drew, and Edwin Booth appeared upon the boards in prairie towns and river towns as well as on Broadway and Philadelphia's Chestnut Street. In the fifties the theater was more of a national institution than it is today.

From 1825 to 1850 the theater in Nashville had a precarious existence and during the forties in particular it had a difficult time. With the advent of the fifties, the cause of the drama brightened. In 1849 the state legislature of Tennessee passed an act which created by charter the Adelphi Theatre Company with a capital of $10,000. Stock in the new company was divided into shares of $25.00 each. Each year one fourth of one per cent of the capital stock was turned over to the state for common school purposes.[3]

The company was operated by a board of nine directors chosen from among the stockholders.[4] The president of the board was chosen by the board members. The object of the theater company was "to erect in the city of Nashville an appropriate and handsome building for the legitimate drama, and by proper rules and regulations to elevate the character of the stage representations."[5]

It was not to be an easy task to elevate the character of the stage presentations and Nashvillians were to discover that a theater devoted to the best attractions was not always successful. The competition of the circus and the minstrels was a potent force working against the legitimate stage.[6] In Nashville, perhaps the people themselves were the worst enemy of the theater. Certainly Nashville audiences were not always intelligent or refined. Frequently they lacked sound critical judgment and were apt to applaud when the actors least merited the compliment. At times such behavior must have chagrined the actor himself or

[3] Tennessee *Acts,* 1849-1850, pp. 447-448.
[4] *Idem.*   [5] *Idem.*
[6] Even in New York City during the forties the drama suffered a decline due to "jugglers and Negro singers." William B. Wood, *Personal Recollections of the Stage* (Philadelphia, 1855), 465.

else caused him "to laugh in his sleeve at the sweet simplicity of his hearers."[7]

According to the *Nashville Daily News,* the majority of the citizens preferred a low type of entertainment. ". . . it pains the eyes," declared this paper, "to see the popular favor bestowed upon roving circuses, clap-trap mountebanks and thieving fortune tellers."[8] Some people went to the theater merely to satisfy their curiosity and they took the manners of the circus and the saloon into the galleries and even into the dress circle. Cries and owl calls from the pit were not uncommon and occasionally fist fights took place in the aisles.[9]

But even the educated and appreciative minority failed to support the theater at times. This was due to the fact that the theater failed them. There were times when poor management resulted in poor plays and mediocre actors. The more discriminating citizens refused to support such entertainment. If their amusement was to be cheap, it was better to go to a minstrel and perhaps be pleasantly surprised than to attend the theater and be disappointed.

The Adelphi Theater, which was built on the west side of Cherry Street (now Fourth Ave.), a few doors below Cedar, opened on July 1, 1850, under the management of John Green.[10] The building, exclusive of decorations, cost about $25,000. There were separate entrances to each part of the house, that is, the entrance to the parquette and the first tier of boxes was on the front, while the second tier of boxes was reached by a side entrance.[11] It was claimed that the new theater possessed the second largest stage in the United States.[12]

In spite of the fact that the dramatic company consisted chiefly of local talent, the initial season was long and quite suc-

[7] *Nashville Daily Gazette,* April 16, 1852.
[8] *Nashville Daily News,* December 3, 1858.
[9] *Nashville Daily Gazette,* December 19, 1855; January 15, 1857.
[10] J. C. Guild, *Old Times in Tennessee, with Historical, Personal, and Political Scraps and Sketches* (Nashville, 1878), 487.
[11] *Daily Union,* June 12, 1850.
[12] Mrs. O. Z. Bond, "Life of Brigadier General Felix Kirk Zollicoffer, C.S.A.," 7.

cessful. Success was due in part to the novelty of a new theater and to the fact that the programs were changed every day. Furthermore, each program included songs and at least one farce in addition to the feature attraction. The price of admission was fifty and seventy-five cents.

From 1830 to about 1880, farces were very much in vogue and were considered "side dishes on the theatrical bills of fare."[13] But they were more than side dishes. They had a definite place in the dramatic literature of the period. Farces treated life bluntly, and at times, coarsely, but the better ones were witty and shrewdly displayed common human faults.[14] The farce on the regular program was not, therefore, peculiar to the Nashville stage. It was a practice recognized as good showmanship throughout the nation.

During the Adelphi's initial season, the first outstanding success was the play *Lucille*, by William Boyle Bernard. This drama was praised by the press for its literary merits as well as for its dramatic action. The *Nashville Daily Gazette* declared, "Its eloquence is like the surges of the sea. It is full of passion; and its author has embellished it with all the beautiful garniture to be found in the kingdom of nature, poetry and art."[15]

The production schedule of this local company was truly ambitious. Such plays as the *Merchant of Venice, Othello, Richard the Third, Hamlet, William Tell, Richelieu, Henry the Fourth,* and *The Lady of the Lake*, were presented in rapid succession and apparently to the satisfaction of the Nashville theater-going public.[16] The presentation of so many serious dramas is indicative of the fact that stock companies in the nineteenth century followed a standardized repertoire consisting chiefly of the works of Shakespeare.[17] For this reason, stars of the stage such as James Murdock and Edwin Booth traveled without a company of their

---

[13] Henry Austin Clapp, "Reminiscences of a Dramatic Critic," in *The Atlantic Monthly* (Boston, 1857—), LXXXVIII (1901), 158.
[14] *Idem.*
[15] *Nashville Daily Gazette*, July 26, 1850.
[16] *Ibid.*, August 6, 28, 30; September 1, 5; October 2, 5, 16, 1850.
[17] John Drew, *My Years on the Stage* (New York, 1922), 33.

own and for support depended on the local stock companies in the towns on their itinerary.[18]

From time to time, actors and actresses with a national reputation were engaged to appear with the Nashville company. During the first season, patrons of the Adelphi were given the opportunity to see Julia Dean and Eliza Logan. Julia Dean (1830-1863) was not a great actress, but her beauty, her gentle personality, and the naturalness of her acting brought her fame.[19] In 1850, she appeared twice in Nashville and starred in *Lucrezia Borgia, Evadne or the Statue, Romeo and Juliet, Macbeth, Fazio or the Italian Wife,* and *The Merchant of Venice.*[20]

Of all the actresses to visit Nashville in the fifties Eliza Logan (1829-1872) became the most popular, and by 1858, her influence over Nashville audiences was almost phenomenal. Her closest rival was Charlotte Cushman and even this eminent actress had to be content with second place where Nashville theater patrons were concerned. After an appearance at the Adelphi Theater on April 10, 1858, Eliza Logan was given one of the greatest ovations of her career. According to an eyewitness "at the close of the play, it seemed as if the audience, in the wildness and phrensy of their delight, would pull down the very walls of the theatre."[21]

Such popularity must have been deserved. In attempting to account for it the *Republican Banner and Nashville Whig* declared, "The difference between Miss Cushman and Miss Logan is the difference between the bold, earnest and vehement speaker, who grapples a subject with a giant's strength and yet with a giant's rudeness, and the chaste, elegant and classic orator, whose periods are all beautifully rounded and polished with elaborate care and exquisite taste. Miss Cushman is a bold and powerful actress; Miss Logan is chaste, soft and elegant. . . . In a word,

[18] *Idem.*
[19] Joseph Jefferson, *Autobiography,* 147-148.
[20] *Nashville Daily Gazette,* August 14, 16, 17, 24, 25; November 6, 1850.
[21] *Republican Banner and Nashville Whig,* April 10, 1858. In 1859, Eliza Logan married George Wood, a theatrical manager, and soon retired from the stage to live in Cincinnati.

Miss Cushman is the greatest, Miss Logan the most popular actress. Miss Cushman would please most the scholar and the thinker—while Miss Logan would be the favorite of the masses, and especially the favorite of the light-hearted, the gay, the sensitive and the refined."[22]

Charlotte Cushman (1816-1876) has been described as the only American actress of the nineteenth century to whom the adjective "great" can be aptly applied.[23] She was born in Boston, made her first public appearance in Boston (as a singer), and died in Boston. One of her paternal ancestors, Robert Cushman, came over in the Mayflower but even this impressive lineage failed to bring her immediate recognition as an artist.[24] Having failed in opera she fought her way into prominence as an underpaid stock actress at the old Bowery and Park theaters in New York.[25] In 1843 she supported the English actor, William Macready, and made such a favorable impression that he invited her to play with him when he returned to New York in 1844.[26] It is believed that her fame was due, in no small degree, to Macready's recognition of her ability.[27]

Cushman made her first appearance in Nashville on April 28, 1851,[28] and Nashville dramatic critics were given the opportunity to witness for themselves "the figure, the gait, the look, the gesture, the tone, by which she puts beauty and passion into language the most indifferent."[29]

John L. Marling, at that time editor of the *Nashville Daily Gazette*, was favorably impressed with her interpretation of Lady Macbeth. "There is a freshness, an originality, in the part as

---

[22] *Republican Banner and Nashville Whig*, April 10, 1858. See also *ibid.*, April 20, 1859; *Nashville Patriot*, March 7, 1859.

[23] Clapp, "Reminiscences of a Dramatic Critic," in *The Atlantic Monthly*, LXXXVIII (1901), 352.

[24] William Winter, *The Wallet of Time*, 2 vols. (New York, 1913), I, 161; Thomas Low Nichols, *Forty Years of American Life, 1821-1861*, 219.

[25] Mrs. John Drew, *Autobiographical Sketch* (New York, 1899), 185.

[26] William Charles Macready, *Reminiscences* (New York, 1875), 534.

[27] William Winter, *Shadows of the Stage* (New York, 1900), 208-209.

[28] *Nashville Daily Gazette*, April 28, 1851.

[29] W. Clark Russell, *Representative Actors* (London, n.d.), 408.

played by Miss Cushman," he declared, "and a depth of feeling too, which together imprison the heart and cause the audience to feel all that the words of the part imply."[30] On another occasion he declared that she was "decidedly the greatest tragic actress of the stage."[31] This was high praise to come from Nashville's most brilliant journalist, but his judgment was to be sustained by time.

In 1858, the engagement of Charlotte Cushman at the Gaiety was *the* event of the theatrical season. The press was liberal with its praise. "Miss Cushman is a genius," declared the *Republican Banner and Nashville Whig,* "a genius of the highest order. In witnessing her performances we see the difference between *genius* and mere *talent.* There is genius in all her motions, in every gesture, every look and every word. . . . The Gaiety is now truly a temple of art, and while the peerless Cushman is the presiding deity, it is pleasing and profitable to worship at the shrine."[32] On the following day, the same journal asserted with bold assurance ". . . There never was such acting done in Nashville."[33] During this engagement, in addition to her famous Lady Macbeth, Cushman appeared as Romeo and as Rosalind.[34]

In addition to Charlotte Cushman, the spring season of 1851 was noteworthy for the appearance of Mr. and Mrs. J. M. Field, Charles Burke, Mr. and Mrs. G. C. Howard, and the tragedian, Richard Graham. Field (1810-1856) was a dramatist as well as an actor. Among his creations were *Oregon, Victoria, Family Ties,* and *Such As It Is. Oregon* was written in 1846 while its author was connected with the Mobile Theatre Company, and the play reflected the national interest in Manifest Destiny and the western boundaries. *Victoria* must have been a literary curiosity. In it the chief characters were the young queen of Eng-

[30] *Nashville Daily Gazette,* April 29, 1851.
[31] *Ibid.,* April 28. Cushman began her dramatic career as Lady Macbeth (New Orleans, 1835). See Winter, *Wallet of Time,* I, 162.
[32] *Republican Banner and Nashville Whig,* March 31, 1858.
[33] *Ibid.,* April 1, 1858.
[34] *Ibid.,* March 29, and subsequent issues. She played three male roles with success: Romeo, Wolsey, and Hamlet. Winter, *Wallet of Time,* I, 167.

land and James Gordon Bennett, editor of the New York *Herald*. Not one of Field's plays has survived.[35]

During their Nashville engagement in 1851, the Fields appeared in *Gabrielle, or the Wager*, the popular melodrama *The Lady of Lyons, Trevanion or the False Position*, and *The Barricade Room*.[36]

Charles Burke (1822-1854) was a popular comedian and was well received in Nashville. In all probability he was the first to introduce his version of the play *Rip Van Winkle* to Nashville audiences. It was this play, with some revision, that was to make his half-brother, Joseph Jefferson the third, so justly famous in the last half of the century.[37] In 1851, however, Rip was not as popular a stage character as the Yankee, Solon Shingle, in Joseph Stevens Jones' play, *The People's Lawyer*. It was in this play that Burke opened his Nashville engagement in 1851. *The People's Lawyer* was a conventional play of false incrimination in which the hero, Charles Otis, is defended and cleared by Robert Howard, the "people's lawyer." The villain was forced to confess that he committed perjury. Solon Shingle had little to do with the plot but offered comic relief, especially in the court scene, where he fell asleep and upon awakening believed that Charles Otis was being tried for robbing him of his apple sauce.

When *The People's Lawyer* first appeared (Boston, 1839) Solon Shingle was acted as a young man. It seems that Charles Burke was the first actor who saw the possibilities of making Solon an *old* Yankee and so represented him.[38] In Burke's hands "he became the simple-minded, phenomenally shrewd old man from New England, with a soul that soared no higher than the financial value of a 'bar'l of applesass.'"[39] Such was the character as presented in Nashville.

---

[35] A. H. Quinn, *A History of the American Drama from the Beginning to the Civil War* (New York, 1923), 284.

[36] *Nashville Daily Gazette*, April 12, 15, 20, 24, 1851.

[37] Quinn, *History of the American Drama from the Beginning to the Civil War*, 328-329; *Nashville Daily Gazette*, May 23, 1851.

[38] Lawrence Hutton, *Curiosities of the American Stage* (New York, 1891), 40.

[39] *Idem*.

Burke closed his Nashville engagement with *The Forrest Rose* by Samuel Woodworth. Like *The People's Lawyer*, this play depended on a rustic character for its appeal and in Jonathan Ploughboy, Woodworth created a masterpiece. Burke was ideally suited to play the part and his acting in this play, in *Rip Van Winkle*, and in *The People's Lawyer*, caused John L. Marling, Nashville's outstanding journalist, to describe him as "The greatest comedian on the boards."[40]

The fall season (1851) opened on October 1 with Eliza Logan appearing as Pauline in *The Lady of Lyons*. On October 17, this popular actress presented *London Assurance*, a play tediously long but interesting because of its historical significance. It was the first successful play written by Dion Boucicault, the Dublin playwright, who, after entering the United States in 1853, exercised a powerful influence on American drama. In all, Boucicault wrote over four hundred plays and adaptations.[41]

During the course of the same season, J. B. Roberts and Julia Dean performed at the Adelphi. Roberts possessed considerable experience which he had gained at home and abroad. In 1836, when he was only a youth of eighteen, good fortune had smiled on him and had given him the opportunity to play in Philadelphia's Chestnut Street Theatre with the old master J. B. Booth.[42] His most important offerings at this time in Nashville were *Sir Giles Overreach* and *Hamlet*. Julia Dean was pleasing in *Romeo and Juliet* and *The Duke's Wages*. The latter was Fanny Kemble's adaptation of Alexander Dumas' *Mademoiselle de Belle-Isle*.[43]

After December 18, 1851, Nashville was devoid of dramatic entertainment for several months. In April the manager of the Adelphi proposed "to produce in the course of the season

---

[40] *Nashville Daily Gazette*, May 14, 1851.

[41] *Ibid.*, October 18, 1851; Quinn, *History of the American Drama from the Beginning to the Civil War*, 368 ff.

[42] Appleton's *Cyclopedia of American Biography*, 8 vols. (New York, 1887-1889), V, 273.

[43] *Nashville Daily Gazette*, October 28, November 29, December 7, 13, 1851; Leota S. Driver, *Fanny Kemble* (Chapel Hill, 1933), 125.

spectacles and extravaganzas in a style hitherto unattempted in Nashville."[44] To carry out this plan, a company of experienced actors, a scenic artist, and a symphony orchestra were engaged. The opening program consisted of Sheridan Knowles' play, *The Love Chase*, and a farce, *Nipped in the Bud*.

It was not until May 12 that the first of the promised extravaganzas appeared. In the intervening period (April 14-May 6) *Romeo and Juliet*, *Macbeth*, *Hamlet* (twice), *Richard the Third*, *Othello*, *Julius Caesar*, *Richelieu*, and Byron's tragedy *Werner* were produced with the aid of such stars as Conrad Clarke and J. B. Roberts.[45]

The dramatic spectacle that was presented to the Nashville public on May 12 bore the title *Cherry and Fair Star*. The action took place against a background of grottos and hanging woods, moonlit vales, fairy glens, and serpent's dens. Finally the lovers, Cherry and Fair Star, were conducted through the mystic cloud-palace of the fairy queen to a palace of their own and they live happily forevermore.[46] This production ran for six nights and was so successful that the management staged another spectacle, *The Forty Thieves*, later in the month.[47] The season closed on June 9 with a benefit for the manager of the theater.

The Adelphi reopened under new management January 22, 1853, but aside from the appearance of Eliza Logan and J. B. Roberts, there was nothing distinctive about the short season which came to an end on February 16.[48] The fall season opened early (September 19) and in a three-act comedy, *The Honey Moon*, Nashville theater patrons had their first opportunity to criticize the new stock company headed by Mrs. Coleman Pope. Evidently the troupe was lacking in talent with the exception of Mrs. Pope who was not a permanent member but a visiting star. Indeed, the press, especially the *Nashville Daily Gazette*, was so disgusted with the low quality of the acting that it refused to

[44] *Republican Banner and Nashville Whig*, April 12, 1852.
[45] *Ibid.*, April 14, 1852, and subsequent issues.
[46] *Ibid.*, May 12, 1852.   [47] *Ibid.*, May 24, 1852.
[48] *Nashville Daily Gazette*, January 22, 1853, and subsequent issues.

make comments for several weeks. Only after Eliza Logan superseded Mrs. Pope did the *Gazette* disclose its real sentiments regarding the stock company. "Miss Logan . . . fully sustained the high histrionic reputation which is so deservedly hers, but her appearance among the rest of the corps was like throwing a brilliant gem 'mid nubian darkness—her brightness only rendered the contrast still more gloomy."[49]

But even little Eliza had her troubles with the thoroughly aroused critics. *The Hunchback,* a comedy by J. Sheridan Knowles, was one of her favorite plays but as presented on September 29, 1853, it became a dismal failure. The *Gazette* ridiculed the production and asserted, "*The Hunchback* was put upon the boards on Wednesday evening and its execution was admirable. When the curtain dropped at the end of the last scene, we left, not waiting to see the farce to follow, being perfectly contented with the one just concluded."[50]

After a number of mediocre billings, the Shakespearean actor, J. B. Roberts, began a nine-day engagement on November 1, 1853. By this time he was a "decided favorite" in Nashville and was praised especially for his *Richard the Third*. No such welcome awaited the actor J. A. Neafie who appeared for the first time in Nashville on December 13, 1853, in a prize-winning play by George H. Miles entitled *Mahommed, The Arabian Prophet*.[51] Neafie was heralded as a dramatic star, but he received little notice in the press on this occasion. When he returned to Nashville in 1856 he was described as a coxcomb, an imitator of Forrest, and an actor who might do well at the head of an ordinary stock company, but one who could not qualify as a star.[52] Probably the vehicle in which he made his Nashville debut was partly responsible for the bad impression he made on the critics, because *Mahommed,* like many prize-winning plays, had little popular appeal.

The stock company at the Adelphi in the fall of 1854 was

---

[49] *Ibid.*, September 30, 1853.
[51] *Ibid.*, December 13, 1853.
[50] *Idem.*
[52] *Ibid.*, December 9, 1856.

much superior to its predecessors. It was described by the press as the best troupe ever to appear in a Nashville theater.[53] G. K. Dickenson, an experienced London actor, headed the company and he was given the support of E. L. Litton, a favorite in New York, and the popular comedian, Joe Cowel. A six-piece orchestra was an added feature throughout the season. The desire for stars was fulfilled by the appearance of Eliza Logan, George Jameson, and Annett Ince.

Eliza Logan was as popular as ever, but it is interesting to note her apparent failure in the play *Adrienne the Actress* which had been made famous by the currently prominent French actress, Rachelle.[54] With remarkable acumen, the editor of the *Nashville Daily Gazette* composed a lengthy criticism of the production. His main point was that the play had suffered in translation:

> We do know that however effective it may be when presented to a French audience in the original language, it is almost next to an impossibility to give it the same force, spirit and effect in a translation. This remark holds true, not only to this one play, but also in regard to every literary production whatever, but more especially in reference to the drama. In a translation, the very soul, the animating spirit, which pervades and gives life and vigor to the whole, is frequently lost, owing to the fact that there are niceties of words and expression in one language which are not translatable into another, and without which the aim and meaning of the play become vague, disconnected, obscure in meaning, when, of course, it is without point or interest and is not unfrequently thus rendered ridiculous.[55]

In general, this is sound criticism and could be legitimately applied to innumerable translations. But Eliza Logan might have been unequal to the character she attempted to portray. At least, it is interesting and suggestive to note that during her engagement in Nashville in 1857, the English actress, Jean Davenport, presented *Adrienne the Actress* twice because of popular

[53] *Ibid.*, September 8, 1854.
[54] Eliza or Elizabeth Felix, 1821-1858. Rachelle was her stage name. She achieved her greatest success in plays of Corneille and Racine.
[55] *Nashville Daily Gazette*, September 28, 1854.

demand.[56] Furthermore, Eliza Logan was criticized in other cities for attempting the character of *Adrienne*.[57]

It would seem that this production, disappointing as it was, in no way detracted from Eliza Logan's popularity in Nashville. She was not considered at fault and her acting ability was not questioned. The trouble lay in the vehicle she had chosen. Apparently the play cramped and confined "into unworthy limits the pre-eminent powers of dramatic delineation which Miss Logan most unquestionably possesses."[58]

One of the most interesting plays presented in 1854 was *The Old Plantation, or The Real Uncle Tom*. In spite of the fact that this propaganda drama, a southern reply to *Uncle Tom's Cabin*, ran for several nights in succession it roused little comment in the press until a year later when it was presented once more. "We have always regarded theatrical representation of negro life as in bad taste," declared the *Nashville Daily Gazette*, "especially so when attempted by a theatrical company. . . . Negro shows and the drama are two very separate and distinct things, each doing very well when kept to itself, but producing a flat and insipid effect when mixed. . . . We strike against all unions that mar beauty and promote discord."[59]

This was a plea for art, beauty, and good taste with abolitionism but vaguely suggested, but in the following declaration, the increasing bitterness of sectionalism is obvious. "To the play of *Uncle Tom*," said the *Daily Gazette*, "and all others of a like ilk, however well they may be rendered, we believe the majority of people have a decided aversion. In witnessing a representation of Dame Stowe's misrepresentations dramatized at the North a year ago we . . . were chagrined that the stage had become so prostituted as to pander to the vulgar sympathies of a vitiated taste. There is no good to be accomplished by such representations—increased mischief and sectional prejudice rather."[60]

[56] *Ibid.*, January 15, 18, 1857.
[57] Clapp, "Reminiscences of a Dramatic Critic," in *The Atlantic Monthly*, LXXXVIII (1901), 346.
[58] *Nashville Daily Gazette*, September 28, 1854.
[59] *Ibid.*, October 10, 1855.
[60] *Ibid.*, October 19, 1855.

The most important event at the Adelphi during the fall season of 1855 was the engagement for several weeks of James E. Murdock (1811-1893). This actor made a good impression in Nashville, which was not surprising, as he was popular throughout the United States and possessed an international reputation as an elocutionist. In an age when the sins of the acting profession were mechanical staring, ranting, overacting, and poor diction, Murdock stood out as a model of intelligent interpretation and artistic restraint. He was one of the best actors on the American stage and even in his declining years he remained young "with the immortal youth of the true artist."[61]

With respect to his personal appearance Murdock was not good looking and was sometimes mistaken for a farmer.[62] But in spite of his personal appearance it seems that he was impressive as Hamlet. Greater Hamlets had preceded him and greater Hamlets were to follow him, but for the moment, and especially in Nashville, his conception of the morbid prince was considered masterful. He spoke his lines with ease and naturalness and he seemed to lose his personal identity in the character he assumed. It appeared to his Nashville critics that they looked upon Hamlet and not Murdock.[63] The fourth scene of the third act, in which the ghost reappears before the half-distracted son, was especially outstanding in the Murdock production.

In 1856 there was a change of management at the Adelphi and the house now became known as The Nashville Theatre. The new manager, Joel Davis, spent $2,000 to repaint and redecorate the building. The first season of the new regime (1856-1857) was comparatively successful in spite of the fact that the new manager became increasingly unpopular. The engagement

---

[61] Clara Morris, *Life on the Stage, My Personal Experiences and Recollections* (New York, 1901), 66. See also, Mrs. John Drew, *Autobiographical Sketch*, Appendix, 199; Clement Scott, *Drama of Yesterday and Today*, 2 vols. (London, 1899), II, 85-86. Murdock wrote several books on elocution. See, for example, his *A Plea for Spoken Language* (New York, 1883), and *Analytic Elocution* (New York, 1884).

[62] Morris, *Life on the Stage, My Personal Experiences and Recollections*, 129-130.

[63] Drew, *Autobiographical Sketch*, 134; *Nashville Daily Gazette*, November 6, 1855.

of Jean Davenport (1829-1903), "Queen of the English Stage" created unusual interest. The *Nashville Daily Gazette* carried an editorial a column and a half in length in which the entire career of the actress was traced.[64] The *Nashville Union and American* declared, "She has achieved a reputation in her profession second to none at present on the English stage and we predict she will create a furor among those of our citizens who can appreciate the higher and more intellectual qualities of the drama."[65] The prediction came true. Each night of her engagement found the theater crowded with a "brilliant audience" and her benefit performance was rated the most successful in the history of the Nashville theater.[66]

With respect to the play *Adrienne the Actress,* it seems that Jean Davenport was the translator and the original representative of the title role on the English stage. As already noted, she presented this play twice during her Nashville engagement and unlike the reception given to the Logan production in 1854, it was well received by press and public. Over the play and the audience, aided, no doubt, by her lovely temperament and perfect enunciation, she was able to throw "a grace beyond the reach of art."[67]

Among the plays presented by Jean Davenport was *Mona Lisa; or Da Vinci's Masterpiece* which was based on certain incidents taken from French and Italian history. The play was described as being "one of the most painfully interesting histories and graphic dramatic compositions in the whole range of the drama."[68] The press was generous with its laudatory comments on the histrionics of the star. Rarely had Nashville playgoers "witnessed acting distinguished by such classic skill, taste and elegance."[69] The queen of the English stage also interpreted Julia in *The Hunchback* for her Nashville supporters and this

[64] *Ibid.,* January 13, 1857.
[65] *Nashville Union and American,* January 8, 1857.
[66] *Ibid.,* January 14, 18, 1857; *Nashville Daily Gazette,* January 17, 1857.
[67] *Ibid.,* January 15, 1857; Winter, *Wallet of Time,* I, 232.
[68] *Nashville Daily Gazette,* January 14, 1857.
[69] *Nashville Union and American,* January 14, 1857.

characterization was well received. The character of Julia had been made famous by Fanny Kemble and after her retirement it was claimed that Jean Davenport had no equal in this role.[70]

Towards the close of the Davis regime the theater was fortunate in billing an unusual attraction. This was the engagement of Mr. and Mrs. John Drew from October 2 to October 14, 1857. John Drew (1827-1862) was born in Dublin, Ireland, and made his first American appearance at the Richmond Hill Theatre, New York, in 1842. He began his career as an interpreter of Irish roles in the old Bowery Theatre in 1845. A year later he became associated with the Chestnut Street Theatre, Philadelphia, and in 1853 with the Arch Street Theatre in the same city. His wife, Louisa Lane Drew (1820-1897) was a clever actress and a level-headed business woman. After the death of her husband in 1862, she managed the Arch Street Theatre for thirty-one years and made it one of the best-known stock houses in the country.[71]

In Nashville the Drews were received in a friendly fashion although by this time there was considerable hostility shown towards the manager of the playhouse, Joel Davis. The first night of their engagement brought out a good crowd and according to the press "the parquette, boxes and galleries were crowded, while the aisles were filled with those who stood and looked upon the stage. The acting however was of a character that prepared a man to stand and not grow weary."[72]

The acting of both Drew and his wife was given high praise. Drew was the best delineator of Irish character that Nashville had ever seen. He adopted in minute detail not only the brogue, but all the mannerisms so characteristic of the reckless Irishman. As O'Brian in *The Irish Emigrant* he was considered "unapproachable." Mrs. Drew was described as "an accomplished

---

[70] Driver, *Fanny Kemble*, 50, 148; *Nashville Daily Gazette,* January 17, 1857.

[71] Drew, *Autobiographical Sketch*, 6, 141-142, 192-193; John Drew, *My Years on the Stage,* 22; Hornblow, *History of the Theatre in America, from Its Beginning to the Present Time,* 83-86.

[72] *Nashville Daily Gazette*, October 3, 1857.

lady and a fascinating actress."[73] Upon her first appearance in Nashville "her sprightliness, vivacity, and grace immediately rendered her a favorite."[74] There was one fact that Nashvillians did not know—that she was the head of the Drew family and her husband's severest critic.

From time to time throughout the season of 1856-1857 the unfriendly feeling towards Joel Davis, manager of the theater, was reflected in the columns of the local newspapers. This feud between press, public, and management was often embarrassing to the visiting actors. Such was the case during the engagement of C. W. Couldock in April, 1857. Couldock (1815-1898) was an actor of ability and experience[75] and deserved a better reception than that given him in Nashville. The current opinion seemed to be that he was neglected because of the unpopularity of Joel Davis.[76]

This controversy reached a climax in the fall of 1857. The press and the public believed that a theater when properly operated exercised a strong cultural and educational force in the community but a theater badly conducted was considered to be injurious both to the literary and moral taste of a people.[77] Manager Davis was accused of underestimating the intelligence of Nashville's drama patrons when he persisted in forcing on them a stock company of inferior caliber. "Our theatre-goers are longing for amusements," declared the *Republican Banner and Nashville Whig*, "but no extent of fasting would ever force them to patronize Manager Davis' company. When will our theatre manager learn that the amusement seekers of Nashville can discriminate between good acting and such ungainly and offensive antics and murdering of the king's English as they have had the affrontery to offer this season."[78]

---

[73] *Ibid.*, October 2, 1858; Hornblow, *History of the Theatre in America, from Its Beginning to the Present Time*, 85.
[74] *Nashville Daily Gazette*, October 3, 1857.
[75] Couldock had been introduced to the American stage by Charlotte Cushman.
[76] *Nashville Union and American*, April 18, 1857.
[77] *Republican Banner and Nashville Whig*, December 9, 1857.
[78] *Republican Banner and Nashville Whig*, October 3, 1857.

This journal was frank and unrelenting in its campaign for better dramatics. Finally, the people were urged to boycott the theater entirely until an improvement was seen. Davis defended himself by declaring that Nashville could not afford a stock company as good as those in the New York or Philadelphia theaters where they did not depend on stars for patronage. "In this city," he asserted, "we must have stars as all other attractions fail."[79] But because of the opposition to Davis even some of his stars were coldly received.

Under the circumstances it seemed best for Davis to withdraw from Nashville and so he closed the theater on November 14, 1857. His successor was William Crisp (1820-1874) who was one of the most capable and experienced managers in the country.[80] Under his leadership the theater became popular once more. The name was changed to the Gaiety and a neatly furnished club room was opened for the gentlemen. Here the men gathered between acts to gossip, scan the latest newspapers, or perhaps sip a glass of planter's punch.[81] Indeed, Crisp did all in his power to make the patrons of the theater comfortable and he seems to have exerted himself to bring before them some of the best dramatic talent of the country. Even the critical editor of the *Republican Banner and Nashville Whig* declared that Crisp's stock company was "most excellent" and that the Gaiety was "deserving of liberal patronage."

During the first season of the Crisp regime (winter, 1857-1858) the Gaiety presented J. E. Murdock, Julia Dean, Charlotte Cushman, and Eliza Logan. Although Crisp succeeded in pleasing the public, his theater did not pay expenses. Undoubtedly the financial panic of 1857 was partly responsible, perhaps wholly responsible, for the unsatisfactory box office receipts. In 1858 Nashville business fell off ten per cent although there were no bank or business failures.[82]

---

[79] *Nashville Daily Gazette*, October 24, 1857.

[80] *Republican Banner and Nashville Whig*, December 9, 1857.

[81] *Nashville Daily Gazette*, December 20, 25, 1857.

[82] *Nashville City and Business Directory*, IV (1859), 15; *Republican Banner and Nashville Whig*, April 11, 20, 1858.

The following season introduced Edwin Booth (1833-1893) to Nashville's theater patrons. Perhaps there is not a profession or an art with a history containing more instances of the inheritance of great ability from father and grandfather than the history of the acting profession. Witness in America alone the family history of the Joseph Jeffersons, the Drews, the Keans, and the Barrymores. The same was true of the Booths and Edwin Booth eclipsed the fame of his father, Junius B. Booth.

Edwin Booth was not only born into the atmosphere of the stage, but he was well endowed by nature with the physical requirements for a great tragedian. Physique and bodily fitness is almost essential for a career on the stage. The advantages of poise, of grace, of personal attractiveness cannot be overrated. Booth, with broad shoulders, slender hips, and tapering limbs was the personification of grace. His face was long and oval and his forehead high. His pale complexion was a striking contrast to his dark hair and his black luminous eyes.[83]

Booth began his engagement in Nashville on March 8, 1859, and played to capacity houses for two weeks. At this time he was only twenty-six years old, "a slight, pale youth, with black flowing hair, soft brown eyes full of tenderness and gentle timidity, a manner mixed with shyness and quiet repose."[84] He opened his Nashville engagement with *Richard the Third* "to the largest audience ever assembled within the walls of the theatre—possibly with the exception of the occasion of Jenny Lind's first concert."[85] The young tragedian lived up to expectations. "His Richard was unlike that of any of his predecessors. He studies the great Bard for himself and imitates no one. His genius scorns the petty mannerisms of the stage and soars into the region of the actual."[86] Booth repeated *Richard the Third* the last night of his Nashville engagement.

---

[83] E. C. Stedman, "Edwin Booth," in *The Atlantic Monthly*, XVII (1866), 586-587.
[84] Brander Matthews and Lawrence Hutton, *The Life and Art of Edwin Booth and His Contemporaries*, 62.
[85] *Nashville Patriot*, March 9, 1859. On Jenny Lind, see Chapter VI.
[86] *Ibid.*, March 10, 1859.

Booth, of course, was to become one of the famous Hamlets of the nineteenth century. *Hamlet* demands a great deal of an actor. Slow in action and with many soliloquies, the play depends entirely on the Prince of Denmark, the central figure. Hamlet is not only a prince, he is a refined, accomplished gentleman. He loves goodness and truth, is impatient with fools and scorns affectation. Moreover, he is a scholar, a student of history and philosophy. Students of this famous dramatic character have emphasized the point that Hamlet is living at that period of life following years of study when a young man is apt to become poetical and speculative. Hamlet, then, is prince, gentleman, scholar, and poet.

Such a character moving in normal circumstances would tax the ability of any first-rate actor. But Hamlet, during the period of the play, does not live a normal life. Murder, ghostly visitations, and political intrigue cast over him an abnormal cloud of morbidness that drives him on to his tragic end.

Nature gave to Edwin Booth the melancholy, romantic face, the graceful carriage, the poetic temperament, and the genius necessary for a masterful interpretation of Shakespeare's most famous character. He was able with delicate, subtle effects of the voice, eyes, and gestures, to indicate the agonized unrest that Hamlet experienced.[87] In many respects Booth's Hamlet was original and it was complete to the smallest detail. It reflected the intelligent and diligent study that was the foundation of Booth's success. Booth and Hamlet became synonymous. It seems that to many people Booth was Hamlet and Hamlet was Booth and any attempt at a representation of Hamlet which was not an imitation of Booth's Hamlet was considered bad taste.

Booth, perhaps, did more than any other actor before the advent of Walter Hampden to make Hamlet a human and understandable person and to educate the people to a proper appre-

---

[87] Hamlin Garland, *Roadside Meetings*, (New York, 1930), 48; William Winter, *Life and Art of Edwin Booth* (New York, 1896), 256; *Nashville Daily News*, March 10, 1859.

ciation of the beauty to be found in Shakespearean tragedy. After 1860, Booth became the ideal Hamlet of the nation.

When Booth presented Hamlet in Nashville, March 9, 1859, less than two years had gone by since he had first assumed the part when he was only twenty-four, at the Metropolitan Theatre in New York. But in spite of his youth, there is no doubt that he gave his Nashville patrons the most polished Hamlet they had ever witnessed.[88] However, certain members of the audience were interested neither in Hamlet nor in Booth and talked so loud that both patrons and actors were annoyed. On several occasions, too, the star's supporting cast became weak-kneed and the play was held together only by Booth's poise and artistry.

It is interesting to note that the editor of the *Nashville Daily News* did not quite approve of some of Booth's original touches. He thought the actor had taken too many liberties with the original drama and was of the opinion that "Shakespeare knew the nature of his gifts, and refrained from high aspirations as an actor. Mr. Booth, and other great actors, should, on imitation of his sagacity, refrain from attempting dramatic composition. Every man within his own sphere!"[89]

However, in spite of the fact that conditions in the Gaiety were not perfect and although a few questioning statements came from the press, Booth came to Nashville, saw and was seen, and added many converts to his growing list of admirers. The first engagement of this young tragedian was one of the most important events in the history of the Nashville theater.

During the summer of 1859 Crisp completely remodeled the Gaiety. Better stairways were constructed, additional seats were installed and new cushions were placed on the old seats. The number of gas lamps was doubled. Several new scenes and a new drop curtain were added to the stage properties. On September 5, 1859, the *Republican Banner* gave an extensive description of the redecorated building:

[88] *Nashville Daily News*, March 10, 1859.
[89] *Idem*.

The decoration of the auditorium is extremely beautiful, the colors being pale blue, violet, pink and stone white, ornamented with gold. The dome of the ceiling, which spreads over the entire parquette is a pure blue sky. A light arcade on the fluted pillars enclose the dress circle, and the front of the first tier is ornamented with twenty-eight crystal chandeliers. The stage has twenty-eight foot lights which cast a brilliance upon one of the prettiest act drops we ever saw. The proscenium has also been elegantly adorned and the side mirrors have been removed to give place to a prettily designed open shell, with ornamental tracings extending to the stage boxes, in front of which is suspended on each side a magnificent chandelier.

Profiting by the criticism of his company during the Booth engagement, and remembering the fate of Joel Davis, Crisp had endeavored during the summer months to bring together a first-rate corps of actors for the new season. Judging by newspaper comment, he succeeded.[90] In addition to Mrs. Crisp, who was a capable actress, the new company consisted of twenty-three actors and actresses, a prompter, a musical director, a scenic artist, a machinist, a property maker, and a treasurer. The first star of the season (1859-1860) was J. E. Murdock who opened on October 11 with Bulwer's comedy *Money*. On this and every night during his ten-day engagement the Gaiety was crowded. Even his interpretation of the title role in *Othello* won the sympathy of the audience and this was difficult to do in the South on the eve of the Civil War.[91]

On October 31, 1859, "The queen of comedy and burlesque," Joey Gougenheim made her first appearance in Nashville. Her production of *The Hidden Hand,* a dramatization by Robert Jones of one of Mrs. Southworth's blood and thunder stories was received with delight, much to the surprise of the editor of the *Nashville Patriot* who did not have a very good opinion of Mrs. Southworth.[92] The play was described as "a great dramatic humbug," and literary trash, but the people found it spicy and

---

[90] *Nashville Patriot*, September 24, October 15, 1859; *Nashville Daily Gazette*, November 11, 1859.
[91] *Nashville Patriot*, October 21, 1859.
[92] Emma D. E. N. Southworth, 1819-1899.

entertaining.⁹³ Joey Gougenheim appeared again in February, 1860, and repeated *The Hidden Hand*. Other comedies in her repertoire included *Masks and Maces, The Jealous Wife,* and *The Maniac Lover*.

The same season (1859-1860) was noteworthy for the return engagement of Jean Davenport in November. The English Actress put Nashville theatrical circles "in a buzz of admiration" for her production of a new play *Faith and Falsehood, or Mesalliance*.⁹⁴ She won additional praise from the Nashville press and public for her performance in *Camille,* a play which she had introduced in the United States.

II

OPERA, in spite of its artificiality, is more closely related to drama than any other type of theatrical performance. It is in reality drama set to music and involves in addition to the musical score, plot, suspense, and climax. As the citizens of Nashville had shown interest in music from an early date and as they had developed a taste for the drama, it would be logical to suppose that they would welcome the appearance of opera. Operatic selections had been presented in concert in the city before 1850, but the first full production of an opera occurred on May 26, 1854, when Signor Luigi Arditi's Italian Opera Company opened with Donizetti's *Lucia di Lammermoor*.

Luigi Arditi (1822-1903) was educated at the Conservatory of Music in Milan. Although he showed talent as a composer, his reputation in Europe and America rested upon his ability as a conductor. He was only thirty-two years old when he appeared in Nashville in 1854, but already he had won considerable recognition in the musical world.⁹⁵

The first American performance of *Lucia di Lammermoor* took place in New Orleans on December 28, 1841.⁹⁶ The plot

---

⁹³ *Nashville Daily Gazette,* November 4, 5, 1859.
⁹⁴ *Nashville Daily Gazette,* November 24, 1859.
⁹⁵ Grove's *Dictionary of Music and Musicians,* 6 vols. (New York, 1927-1928), I, 108.
⁹⁶ Samuel H. Rous, *The Victrola Book of the Opera* (Camden, 1917), 250. Gaetano

of *Lucia* is founded on Scott's novel, *The Bride of Lammermoor,* and for that reason alone should have attracted considerable attention in Nashville, where Scott was popular. The story is simple but tragic. Lucia's brother, Lord Henry Ashton, arranges a marriage between Lucia and a wealthy nobleman, Lord Arthur, in order to retrieve his depleted fortune. Lucia, however, is in love with Lord Arthur's enemy, Edgar of Ravenwood. Arthur, learning of Lucia's love for Edgar, intercepts her love letters and presents to her a forged paper which convinces her that her lover, Edgar, is false to her. As a result, she consents to marry Arthur in order to aid her brother.

Lucia has just signed the contract at the wedding when Edgar appears and denounces Lucia for her fickleness. Edgar is driven from the castle and Lucia, realizing what she has done, becomes insane, kills her husband and dies. Edgar, overwhelmed by the tragedy, commits suicide.

Although a large audience filled the Adelphi to see and hear this most popular of Donizetti's compositions, it seems that many Nashvillians did not understand opera technique. For this reason, their introduction to the art was not entirely satisfactory, and the brilliant recitatives and arias for the soprano (Lucia) in the Mad Scene (Act III) were not readily appreciated or understood. This lack of understanding is easily understood. To the uninitiated, the Mad Scene seems overdrawn and unnatural and Lucia, although demented, sings without hesitation passages that would be difficult for a sane person. The explanation, of course, is simple. Donizetti ignored dramatic plausibility in order to create a musical sensation.

Realizing that its subscribers needed instruction in opera appreciation, the *Nashville Daily Gazette* believed it a civic duty to assume the role of teacher:

Those who attend the opera must not find fault because they cannot reduce the performance to any rule of reason. If a man in his

---

Donizetti (1797-1848) wrote sixty-three operas. See Frederich H. Martens, *A Thousand and One Nights of Opera* (New York, 1926), 351-352.

death agony is heard to sing, the hearer must not become disgusted at the outrage thereby inflicted upon his ideas of natural proceedings, but, losing sight of all unpoetic actuality, catch in the mystic flow of song, the spirit of the dying man. Indeed, perfectly to appreciate and to drink in the music of an opera, the mind must be detached from its natural state, and go gaily floating through the realms of a fairy land, even like some one of those viewless embodiments of melody that find birth in the brain of the composer.[97]

In addition to *Lucia di Lammermoor,* Arditi's company presented Donizetti's *Lucrezia Borgia,* Rossini's *Barber of Seville,* Bellini's *Norma* and *La Somnambula,* and Verdi's *Ernani.* The prima donna, Rosa DeVries, could not reach the high notes of Jenny Lind, but all admitted that she was a greater artist than the Swedish Nightingale. DeVries' performance in *Norma* was a triumph, and after several curtain calls she "retired under a perfect deluge of bouquets."[98]

Norma, Bellini's greatest work, was one of the most popular operas of the nineteenth century. The first American performance took place at the Park Theatre in New York City, February 25, 1841. The following year it was produced at the New Orleans Opera House.[99] The scene is laid in Gaul shortly after the Roman conquest and the romantic story is rich in symbolism, sentiment, mother love, and sacrifice. The charming musical score had more appeal to the Nashville audience than the brilliantly technical passages of *Lucia.* Particularly impressive was Norma's prayer to the moon, the queen of heaven.

> Norma:
> Queen of Heaven, while thou art reigning
> Love upon us is still remaining,
> Clad in pureness, alone disdaining
> Grosser earth's nocturnal veil.
> Queen of Heaven, hallow'd by thy presence,
> Let its holier, sweeter essence,
> Quelling every lawless license,

[97] *Nashville Daily Gazette,* May 30, 1854.
[98] *Ibid.,* June 2, 1854.
[99] Marten, *A Thousand and One Nights of Opera,* 78; Rous, *The Victrola Book of the Opera,* 339.

> As above, so here prevail!
> All is ended, be now the forest
> Disencumber'd of aught mortal.

In order to satisfy those music lovers whose religious scruples would not permit them to enter the Adelphi, Rosa DeVries arranged a musical festival at Odd Fellows Hall in December, 1854. The program consisted of selections from the favorite operas and was repeated, with certain variations, for several nights.[100] As part of the program for the second concert, Madame DeVries sang for the first time in the United States Mozart's Magic Flute Aria.[101]

The second opera company to appear in Nashville was the New Orleans English Opera Troupe. This company opened on April 29, 1858, with *Fra Diavolo,* and presented thereafter the *Barber of Seville, Daughter of the Regiment, Bohemian Girl,* and *Il Trovatore.*[102] Of this group, only *Il Trovatore* had a tragic vein.

During January, 1860, Nashville music lovers had a third opportunity to witness a series of operas. This time the organization was Teresa Parodi's Italian Opera Company and the opening performance was Verdi's *Ernani,* followed by *Il Trovatore, Norma, La Traviata, Lucrezia Borgia, Barber of Seville,* and *Don Juan.*[103] This company consisted of Carolina Alarmo, "the great lyric cantatrice," Hattie Brown, a product of the United States, Signors Spriglia, Gnone, and Barili, tenor, baritone, and basso respectively, and Angelo Torriani, the conductor. The stars were supported by a full orchestra and chorus. Parodi, of course, was the prima donna.[104]

Parodi's opera was well received although the ever popular minstrels were performing at the same time in Odd Fellows Hall. This was a hopeful sign and the *Nashville Patriot* rejoiced

---

[100] *Nashville Daily Gazette,* December 8-15, 1854.
[101] *Ibid.,* December 9, 10, 1854.
[102] *Republican Banner and Nashville Whig,* April 29, 1858.
[103] *Nashville Patriot,* January 17-27, 1860.
[104] *Ibid.,* January 17, 1860. See also, George P. Upton, *Musical Memories; My Recollections of Celebrities of the Half-Century 1850-1900* (Chicago, 1908), 20.

to think that the citizens of Nashville had proved their appreciation of the highest type of musical art by their liberal patronage of the opera.[105]

No doubt Nashville theater audiences in 1860 were more discriminating in dramatic taste than similar gatherings had been in 1850. But they remained picturesque and colorful and represented a cross section of the social life of Middle Tennessee. Fashionable ladies and gentlemen occupied the dress circle and some of the boxes. Perhaps their country cousins from outlying plantations were with them.[106] It is logical to suppose that many politicians and statesmen were patrons of the drama as the theater was usually open when the state legislature was in session. In the parquette and the balcony sat the ordinary folk, and, of course, there was a special section for Negroes.

The fashionable women of Nashville dressed elegantly when they attended the theater. Moleskin, cassimer, and French otter hats were considered the last word in headgear. Silk quilted lace boots protected their feet from the muddy street in front of the theater. Fashionable ladies dressed with as many hoops as they could manage. The "Belle of the South" was a dress that could be had with any number of hoops from eight to fifty.[107] The conservative gentleman seen at the theater usually wore a swallow-tail, black broadcloth suit, stiff shirt, and a black bow tie. His vest was of velvet or silk. High boots and a silk top hat were considered good form.[108] Frequently, members of the younger generation were seen in sack coat, soft hat, flowing tie, and low cut shoes.[109]

The behavior of the men at the theater was not always above reproach. Little respect was shown the ladies on those occasions when men and boys rushed from the building for no apparent reason except that they wanted to get out in a hurry. Even some

---

[105] *Nashville Patriot,* January 26, 27, 1860.
[106] Jane Thomas, *Old Days in Nashville* (Nashville, 1897), 89.
[107] *Nashville Patriot,* January 2, 1860.
[108] Bond, "Life of Brigadier General Felix Kirk Zollicoffer, C. S. A.," 9.
[109] *Idem.*

of the gentlemen in the dress circle chewed tobacco and used the floor for a spittoon.[110] Drunkenness, too, was quite common. Until 1859, the theater had a saloon upstairs and a refreshment room downstairs. Men ran upstairs to get a drink between the first and second acts and downstairs to get a drink between the second and third acts. Sometimes before the end of the play they "emptied their overcharged stomachs in the dress circle."[111]

When Crisp remodeled the theater in 1859, he abolished the saloon and prohibited the sale of liquor in the theater. A refreshment room remained, however. Here the theater patron could purchase oranges, figs, raisins, candy, and flowers.[112]

Seldom, if ever, were clergymen seen in the theater. And many who did not wear the cloth looked upon the stage as hell's vestibule and on the actors as Satan's emissaries. B. W. P. Jones, editor of the *Parlor Visitor*,[113] expressed the views of the anti-theater group when he wrote the following passage in his magazine:

It is nowhere said in all the Bible . . . thou shalt not attend the theatre. But the Bible taught man to glorify God through the body and the spirit, which God claimed as his own. Can any man, recognizing these as the declarations of Divine Truth, regard any one whose taste leads him habitually to the theatre as a Christian? What, a Temple of the Holy Ghost in a theatre! Do men glorify God by taking their bodies and their spirits, which are God's, to such places? The idea is preposterous![114]

Even the *Christian Magazine*, under the editorship of the comparatively liberal Jesse B. Ferguson, condemned those who used scripture quotations to defend amusements such as dancing and the theater. Ferguson believed that the circus and the theater were haunts of frivolity and vanity and exerted a pernicious influence.[115] This attitude was not peculiar to Nashville clergymen as churchmen in every city either expressed opposition to the theater or questioned its value as a cultural institution.

---

[110] *Nashville Daily News*, October 29, 1859.   [111] *Ibid.*, September 8, 1859.
[112] *Idem.*   [113] On the *Parlor Visitor*, see Chapter VIII.
[114] B. W. P. Jones, "The Theatre and the Dance," in the *Parlor Visitor*, VI (1856), 45.
[115] *Christian Magazine*, II (1849), 33, 39; III (1850), 249-250.

CHAPTER VI

THE NASHVILLE THEATER: CONCERTS AND MINSTRELS, 1850-1860

I

THE OUTSTANDING musical event of the decade in Nashville was the appearance of Jenny Lind (1820-1887) on March 29, 1851. Long before her Nashville engagement she had become an international sensation. In the United States what was termed "Jenny Lind" fever ran wild. Stores in the eastern cities displayed Jenny Lind bonnets, gloves, coats, hats, parasols, combs, shawls, and jewelry.[1] Butchers advertised Jenny Lind sausages and hardware stores made a specialty of Jenny Lind teakettles. Restaurant proprietors caught the fever and inserted "à la Jenny Lind" after the choice dishes on the menu cards. Jenny Lind pancakes became famous.[2] In Nashville Jenny Lind hats and Jenny Lind billiard tables were advertised in the newspapers and Willard's restaurant on Cedar street had a "Jenny Lind Room."[3] Perhaps the name of no other celebrity has ever been exploited to such an extent.

The arrival of the Swedish Nightingale in Nashville meant also the arrival of her manager, P. T. Barnum (1810-1891) who was already becoming more myth than man. Early in the morning of March 29, curious children and eager men and women began to line the river banks and to crowd the bridge over the Cumberland. The news had spread like wildfire that the famous singer would arrive by boat about nine o'clock. The people were not disappointed. The boat did arrive at nine and Jenny

---

[1] Upton, *Musical Memories, My Recollections of Celebrities of the Half Century 1850-1900*, 19.
[2] *Ibid.*, 19-21.
[3] *Nashville City and Business Directory*, I (1852), 109.

Lind, Barnum, and the entire company landed while the crowd cheered.[4]

By the time the auction of tickets began the excitement was intense.[5] The first ticket was started at $50 and was finally sold for $200.[6] Others sold from 25c to $10. The sale of tickets at the first auction alone netted $2380. Tickets at the box office of the Adelphi, whose seating capacity had been temporarily increased,[7] sold from $4 to $5. Standing room tickets were cheap at $3. The price of admission to the auction room was ten cents and the money secured in this way was donated to the orphans of Nashville.[8] This was a typical Barnum gesture. The gross receipts of Jenny Lind's first concert in Nashville, which was her sixty-eighth in the United States,[9] amounted to $7,786.30. The sale of tickets for her second concert brought in $4,248. This is indicative, not of a smaller audience, but of more sensible bidding in the auction room.

Some of the persons who purchased tickets at a high price became penitent after their enthusiasm cooled. According to Barnum a proprietor of a Nashville dry goods store declared to his friends, "I'll give five dollars to any man who will take me out and give me a good horse-whipping! I deserve it, and am willing to pay for having it done. To think that I should have been such a fool as to have paid forty-eight dollars for four tickets for my wife, two daughters and myself, to listen to music for

---

[4] *Nashville Daily Gazette*, March 30, 31, 1851. Le Grand Smith, Barnum's business manager, was already in Nashville awaiting the arrival of the company. C. G. Rosenberg, *Jenny Lind in America* (New York, 1851), 189. Rosenberg was Jenny Lind's husband.

[5] P. T. Barnum, *Struggles and Triumphs, or Forty Years' Recollections* (Buffalo, 1873), 344.

[6] *Idem; Nashville Daily Gazette*, March 30, April 3, 1851; Rosenberg, *Jenny Lind in America*, 191.

[7] Guild, *Old Times in Tennessee*, 488; Rosenberg, *Jenny Lind in America*, 191.

[8] *Nashville Daily Gazette*, March 30, April 3, 1851.

[9] Barnum called it the sixty-sixth, but he did not count the first two concerts in New York which were not included in the contract. The entire tour consisted of ninety-five concerts and brought in $712,161.34. Jenny Lind's share of this was $176,675.09. Barnum, *Struggles and Triumphs, or Forty Years Recollections*, 353-354.

only two hours, makes me mad with myself, and I want to pay somebody for giving me a thundering good horse-whipping!"[10]

Hotels took advantage of the situation and charged their distinguished guests and the members of the company double and, in some cases, treble the customary rates. Managers of livery stables also saw an opportunity to swell their income and acted accordingly. Several members of Barnum's party protested and became involved in a general row with landlords and livery managers. Pistols and canes were brandished belligerently and one hot-headed landlord brought his cowhide whip into play. Barnum and his business manager, Le Grand Smith, were asleep when this unannounced side show was enacted.[11]

The Adelphi management had made preparations to increase the seating capacity of the theater before the time of the first concert. The repairs, however, were not completed on schedule and the patrons found just cause for complaint. Many of the seats were cushionless and in certain sections of the house unfinished planks had been hastily substituted for seats. Doors were down and the night wind blew through holes in walls and ceiling. Fortunately the weather was warm, otherwise the building would have been untenable.[12]

But all this was forgotten when Jenny Lind made her entrance on the stage of the Adelphi and "brought down the house in immense applause." Personally she presented the appearance of a "simple, chaste, and unaffected lady, with a face not handsome, nor to a stranger prepossessing, yet withal, not without a certain degree of attraction."[13] She was dressed in a very simple pink silk gown which emphasized her slenderness.[14]

Jenny Lind's singing was a disappointment to some Nashvillians, including John L. Marling, the young and promising editor of the *Nashville Daily Gazette*. In a criticism of her first

[10] *Ibid.*, 344.
[11] Rosenberg, *Jenny Lind in America*, 196-197.
[12] *Ibid.*, 191-92, 193.
[13] *Nashville Daily Gazette*, April 2, 1851.
[14] Thomas, *Old Days in Nashville*, 62.

offering, an aria from the opera *Lucia di Lammermoor,* Marling deplored the lack of melody.

"This piece being in the Italian language," he wrote, "of course we did not expect to appreciate it. But we did expect to find something in this song, as indeed in all, to enchant, instruct, or amuse an American audience. Instead of finding this, however, we witnessed a gladiatorial display of the strength and volume of the great songstress' voice which was certainly remarkable as such but which contained little of that melody which alone can captivate and ravish an American ear."[15]

The fame of Jenny Lind's "Bird Song" had gone before her and perhaps Nashvillians expected too much. At any rate, according to Marling the entire audience was disappointed with the "Bird Song" and also with Jenny Lind's rendering of "Home Sweet Home." It was believed that the Swedish singer was incapable of infusing enough sentiment into her voice to please an American and especially a Southern audience.[16]

This disappointment was not fairly attributable to her, but to the extravagant advertising and inimitable management of Barnum. It was his policy to praise Jenny Lind to the skies.[17] It seems evident that she was magnified out of all proportion to her merits. But Marling had not been deceived. From the beginning he had considered the Lind mania as "a magnificent humbug—successful beyond anything on record. Yet successful only because it was in the hands of the master humbugger."[18]

Marling was not the only critic in the country who believed that Jenny Lind was overrated. For example, on August 14, 1851, Walt Whitman wrote in the New York *Evening Post,* "The Swedish Swan, with all her blandishments, never touched my heart in the least. I wondered at so much vocal dexterity; and indeed they were all very pretty, those leaps and double

[15] *Nashville Daily Gazette,* April 2, 1851.
[16] *Idem.*
[17] Barnum, *Struggles and Triumphs, or Forty Years Recollections,* 173; Upton, *Musical Memories, My Recollections of Celebrities of the Half Century 1850-1900,* 19; C. G. Rosenberg, *You Have Heard of Them* (New York, 1854), 214.
[18] *Nashville Daily Gazette,* April 2, 3, 1851.

somersets. But even in the grandest religious airs, genuine masterpieces as they are, of the German composers, executed by this strangely overpraised woman in perfect scientific style, let critics say what they like, it was a failure; for there was a vacuum in the head of the performance. Beauty pervaded it no doubt, and that of a high order. It was the beauty of Adam before God breathed into his nostrils."

The *Republican Banner and Nashville Whig* followed the conservative course and praised Jenny Lind's voice with a string of superlatives, ". . . its compass, cadence, melody and ventriloquous witchery appear mysterious and wonderful."[19]

No doubt there were many members of Jenny Lind's Nashville audience who were impressed favorably. To some the Echo Song was especially beautiful. It was noticed that when Jenny Lind sang this song her throat swelled out like a bird and that the listener could hear the notes die out in the distance "just like an exact imitation of an echo."[20]

While at Nashville Jenny Lind and Barnum, together with other members of the company, visited the Hermitage. Here for the first time in her life the Swedish Nightingale heard mocking birds singing in the trees. She was delighted, "as she had never before heard them sing except in their wire-bound cages."[21]

The next musical event of any importance took place in April, 1853, when the violinist, Ole Bull, and the child prodigy, Patti, gave a series of concerts under the direction of Maurice Strakosch. Ole Bull (1810-1880), a self-taught violin virtuoso, was described as the man from Norway who could draw from his violin the music of the spheres. He appealed to all—to the educated and the uneducated—to men and women.[22]

Ole Bull was not identified with any school, but his personality "was so magnetic that even musicians overlooked his

---

[19] April 2, 1851.
[20] Jane Thomas, *Old Days in Nashville*, 62.
[21] Barnum, *Struggles and Triumphs, or Forty Years Recollections*, 315.
[22] Guild, *Old Times in Tennessee*, 491; *Nashville Daily Gazette*, April 5, 7, 1853; Grove's *Dictionary of Music and Musicians*, I, 495-496.

eccentricities and occasional trickeries of technic."[23] He knew his limitations and usually played only his own compositions in public. His violin was especially constructed. The bridge of the instrument was almost flat, an arrangement which enabled him to produce unusual effects by playing chords and passages in four parts. His bow was so long that a smaller man would have had difficulty handling it.[24]

Adelina Patti (1843-1919) at this time was only ten years old and was considered the greatest phenomenon of the age. She sang Jenny Lind's "Echo Song" and "Home Sweet Home" for her Nashville audience much to the delight of every one present. The child's voice was described as "more than human: Words fail to give the impression on the heart and ear, made by the little prodigy. No one can conceive of the power, richness and perfection of her voice until they have listened to her."[25]

Patti appeared again in Nashville in December, 1855. Ole Bull returned in March, 1856. In the meantime, in March, 1853, the Nightingale Opera Troupe, under the direction of George Kimpel, gave Nashvillians a taste of comic opera. The most popular of the new songs that were introduced was "Katy Darling."[26]

On June 3, 4, 5, 1858, music lovers of Nashville were given the opportunity to hear the pianist, Sigismund Thalberg (1812-1871), and Henry Vieutemps, the prominent violinist. Madame Elena D'Augri, a singer well known at the time in metropolitan music circles, accompanied the two instrumentalists. Thalberg had his own grand piano for his concerts. It was a beautiful instrument, constructed especially for him by a Philadelphia firm, and was valued at $1200.[27]

The people of Nashville were not a little excited at the appearance of the three artists, and the patrons of music paid wil-

---

[23] Upton, *Musical Memories, My Recollections of Celebrities of the Half Century 1850-1900*, 57.
[24] Grove's *Dictionary of Music and Musicians*, I, 496.
[25] *Nashville Daily Gazette*, April 10, 1853.
[26] *Ibid.*, March 11, 13, 1853.
[27] *Republican Banner and Nashville Whig*, May 27, June 2, 3, 5, 1858.

lingly $2 a ticket that they might hear them perform. Evidently Thalberg made the greatest impression. It seems that he had a peculiar power over the piano that made it "under his magic touch, a new and before unheard instrument."[28]

On the evening of June 4, 1858, Thalberg and Vieuxtemps gave a free concert to 1250 school children, orphans, and the blind. Teachers from the city schools and the members of the board of education were present also.[29] The occasion was a happy one, especially for the children. "It was indeed a pretty sight to see such an array of children all, apparently, as happy and cheerful as could be imagined."[30]

On January 3, 1859, Strakosch's concert company appeared at Odd Fellows Hall. After performing to crowded houses for three nights[31] the troupe moved to the Gaiety for two additional concerts. The company boasted two stars, Mlle. Parodi and Madame De Wilhorst. Parodi was considered an excellent singer by her contemporaries, but in spite of this, the programs that were offered in Nashville, consisting chiefly of selections from opera, were not entirely satisfactory. The chief criticism was based on the sparseness of American, English, Scottish, and Irish songs on the programs. For the most part, members of the Nashville audience were ignorant of Italian, and in a lesser degree of French and German, and when they did not understand the words of a song they could not fully appreciate the singer's efforts. Frequently they applauded or condemned a rendition according to whim and not according to understanding.[32] In this connection the *Nashville Daily News* commented on the "innocent clappings of hands, clatter of canes, and hammer of heels, at the close of each piece."[33] Nashville audiences, at least on certain occasions, were capable of applause that was anything but refined.

[28] *Nashville Patriot*, June 5, 1858.
[29] *Ibid.*, June 5, 1858; *Republican Banner and Nashville Whig*, June 5, 1858; John Berrien Lindsley Diary, June 4, 1858.
[30] *Nashville Daily Gazette*, June 5, 1858.
[31] *Nashville Daily News*, January 4, 1859.
[32] *Nashville Daily News*, January 7, 1859.   [33] *Idem.*

The final program presented by Strakosch's company was typical:

Part One

The Stabat Mater; presented for the first time in Nashville. (Rossini's sacred composition)

Part Two

Selections from *The Barber of Seville* (Rossini)
" " *Don Giovanni* (Mozart)
" " *Il Trovatore* (Verdi)
" " *L' Elixir d' Amore* (Donizetti)
" " *Lucrezia Borgia* (Donizetti)
"Good Night and Pleasant Dreams," ballad by Wallace

Part Three

A selection from *Semiramide* (Rossini)
"Then You Will Remember Me" (Balfe)
The Comic Quartetto "Don't Tickle me I Pray" (Martini)[34]

The price of admission for the Strakosch concerts ranged up to $1.00.

Before leaving the subject of concerts mention should be made of the Swiss Bell Ringers who performed periodically in Nashville. There were several organizations of bell ringers which toured the country, the most prominent in the South being the Peake family and the Blaisdell brothers. A concert performed on bells was somewhat of a novelty and on this score alone the Peakes and the Blaisdells enjoyed considerable popularity. The Peake family, which possessed a degree of proficiency always satisfactory to the public, offered vocal selections and harp solos in addition to the bells. During their 1857 engagement in Nashville the concert hall "was crammed to suffocation with the elite of the city."[35] The price of admission to these concerts was twenty-five to fifty cents.

Variety shows, which were half concert and half vaudeville, offered another type of entertainment. Apparently the Bailey

---

[34] *Idem.*
[35] *Nashville Union and American*, January 21, 1857; *Nashville Patriot*, February 24, 1860.

Troupe was the favorite company of this type to appear in Nashville. One Nashville paper[36] spoke of this organization as "a favorite concert company" so it may be assumed that its appeal was primarily musical.

At times the patrons of the theater and the concert were fooled by false advertisements. Such was the case with respect to Hunt and Baird's Ballette and Pantomime Company whose press agent was bold if not unscrupulous. The performance of the "Ballette" was a total failure. "The whole affair was too paltry even to aspire to the dignity of humbug," said the *Nashville Daily Gazette*.[37]

II

The importance of Negro minstrelsy as an element of American culture never has been fully appreciated. From the historical point of view the minstrel is important because it represents a form of entertainment developed by Americans from materials found on American soil. "It is the only branch of the dramatic art," observed Laurence Hutton in 1889, "which has had its origin in this country, while the melody it has inspired is certainly our only approach to a national music."[38]

At a later date (1915) Brander Matthews made a similar claim in behalf of the minstrels. "Of all the varied and manifold kinds of theatrical entertainment," he declared, "negro-minstrelsy is the one which is absolutely native to these states and which could not have come into existence anywhere else in the civilized world."[39]

American minstrelsy drew its material and its inspiration from the American Negro slave and the traditionally romantic conception of life on the old plantation. In the early years sincere attempts were made to give a true representation of Negro

---

[36] *Nashville Union and American*, August 30, 1856.
[37] January 19, 1853.
[38] Laurence Hutton, "The Negro on the Stage," in *Harpers Magazine* (New York, 1850—), LXXIX (1889), 133.
[39] Brander Matthews, "The Rise and Fall of Negro-Minstrelsy," in *Scribners* (New York, 1887—), LVII (1915), 754.

life and character but as the years went by these attempts became sporadic and eventually gave way entirely to the exaggerated and distorted characterizations generally associated with the minstrel show.

But in spite of its inaccurate representations, the importance of the minstrel show as a type of entertainment cannot be overlooked. Its appeal was broader than that of the theater or the circus and during the fifties minstrels became the most popular form of entertainment in the country. The circus, the variety show, and the medicine show fell under the spell of the knights of minstrelsy. P. T. Barnum added a Negro dancer to his first traveling exhibition[40] and Barnum himself blacked his face on several occasions.[41] Even such famous actors as Joseph Jefferson[42] and Edwin Booth[43] at one time or another used the makeup of minstrelsy.

Throughout the fifties Nashville was visited several times a year by numerous minstrel companies. There was Lynch's Harmoneon Troupe, Balfe's Original Sable Opera Troupe, Old Joe Swensy's Virginia Minstrels, the Empire Minstrels, Aeolian Minstrels, Sanford's Pioneer Minstrels, and Mat Peel's Campbell Minstrels. As far as Nashville was concerned Mat Peel's Campbell Minstrels was considered the best although it does not appear that it possessed more real talent than any other troupe which performed in the city.[44]

The name of this organization calls for a word of explanation. The original Campbell Minstrels was organized by John Campbell, a former restaurant keeper. This company became so popular that before the close of the fifties, scores of other troupes borrowed the name. Peel's organization was no exception, hence Mat Peel's Minstrels became Mat Peel's Campbell

---

[40] Barnum, *Struggles and Triumphs, or Forty Years Recollections*, 88.
[41] *Ibid.*, 90; Hutton, *Curiosities of the American Stage*, 111.
[42] Joseph Jefferson, *Autobiography*, 7.
[43] Hutton, *Curiosities of the American Stage*, 106.
[44] *Nashville Union and American*, March 24, 1857.

Minstrels.⁴⁵ Probably taking their cue from P. T. Barnum, Minstrel proprietors were not averse to humbug for the sake of business. Peel's Minstrels reached the high water mark of their popularity in 1857. They began an engagement of several weeks in Nashville on March 23 and according to the press accounts the theater had never been so densely crowded, not even when Jenny Lind had been the chief attraction. Not for one night, or two nights, but night after night for over a week the house was "crammed from pit to dome without any abatement in appreciation or enthusiasm."⁴⁶

On April 3, 1857, the *Nashville Union and American* gave up half a column of its valuable space to an editorial on Peel's Campbells. This may be taken as an indication of their popularity and importance. Praise of the troupe was unstinted. "Either respectively or collectively, the Campbells stand unequalled for versatility and talent, whether as vocalists, negro delineators, or instrumentalists, or organized as a brass band, orchestra, or dramatic company. In all undertakings they are not only pleasing but actually super-excellent. Throughout the land the Campbells are ... successful; and wherever they go the compliments of the press and public strew their way, while hundreds nightly witness with delight and astonishment their inimitable doings, retiring with the lisp of satisfaction, rearing garlands of praise to their already high reputation."

Mat Peel himself was one reason for the popularity of the Campbells. Too frequently in the portrayal of Negro character the actor disregarded nature and was guilty of misrepresentations, both in actions and in words. It was maintained that Peel was never guilty of these sins against true minstrel art. His characterizations were natural, the result of long experience in the musical profession and close observation of Negro life as it was found in Southern cities and on the plantations. No false intonations or meaningless utterances weakened the roles he as-

---

⁴⁵ Carl Wittke, *Tambo and Bones: A History of the American Minstrel Stage* (Durham, 1930), 56, 72.

⁴⁶ *Nashville Union and American,* April 3, 1857.

sumed. In the use of dialect and in the use of the eyes, he was the model for many a hopeful minstrelite.[47]

Another talented member of the Campbell troupe was W. W. Newcomb. He was especially adept at representing "the placid, quiet negro, whose every act and saying is full of simplicity and unconscious wit, of slow understanding and apparent indifference to the ways of life."[48] As a tambourinist, comedian, and versatile performer, Newcomb occupied a high position in the minstrel profession.

H. S. Rumsey, who was listed among the stars of the Campbell organization, was described as a versatile performer who could make a contribution as a banjoist or interlocutor. "He has attained much proficiency on the banjo, and we doubt there ever having existed a better master of the instrument."[49]

Other instrumental performers in the company were given a high rating by the Nashville critics. For example, C. Kene, the accordionist, was described as "a bright star in the constellation to which he belongs. His solos in every particular are full of pathos, interest and artistic development. As an accordionist he has no superior on this continent, and, we venture a prediction, few equals in the Old World, where we understand the gentleman has performed with marked and decided success."[50] Kene's solos were so arranged that they pleased all types of people.

The Campbells possessed a capable violinist in J. B. Donniker. His style was vigorous yet artistic and upon occasion he ran into "roulades of inspiration which raised the heart to ecstatic appreciation."[51]

In addition to the artists mentioned above the Campbells numbered among their group C. C. Dickinson, a harpist, C. M. Currier, a horn expert, R. E. Ennis, whose instrument was the violoncello, and young T. J. Peel, who was developing into a graceful dancer, "either burlesque, fancy or break-down."[52]

The fact that Nashville critics were opposed to the use of

[47] *Idem;* also March 28, 1857.
[48] *Ibid.,* April 3, 1857.
[49] *Idem.*
[50] *Idem.*
[51] *Idem.*
[52] *Idem.*

Negro themes in the drama has been pointed out in Chapter IV. It seems rather strange that the bitter feeling aroused by the abolitionists was not directed against the minstrels. There is no evidence of it in Nashville before 1858 and, as noted above, the minstrels were never more popular than in the spring of 1857.

However, the Campbells were not so well received when they returned to Nashville in January, 1858. On this occasion the *Republican Banner and Nashville Whig* asserted "the days of the glory of negro-minstrelsy are well nigh passed."[53] The entire sectional controversy could be read into this simple statement. It does not seem logical that a form of entertainment such as the minstrels should lose its appeal in less than a year without some unnatural force being present to bias the public mind. The year 1857 was important in the history of the secession movement. It was a panic year, a panic that started in the North and gradually tied up the economic life of the South. Never before, perhaps, was the South more eager to be freed of Wall Street entanglements. In this respect, the panic was a boom to the movement for Southern Independence and with the intensification of sectional feeling the South was placed more on the defensive with respect to slavery than ever before. Consequently, on first thought, because of the tense situation and strained emotions at the time, one might think that even the innocent minstrels suffered because they tended to exploit an institution that had in part created the bitterness between North and South. But this theory is exploded by the fact that in October of the same year the Campbells were greeted with large audiences and the press carried words of praise.[54] It would seem, therefore, that the ᛫cause for the poor support given the minstrels in January, 1858, was purely economic. It should be remembered that the theater, too, was losing money during the same season.

Throughout the period the minstrels continued to introduce

[53] *Republican Banner and Nashville Whig*, January 3, 1858; Wittke, *Tambo and Bones: A History of the American Minstrel Stage*, 120.
[54] *Nashville Daily Gazette*, October 23, 1858.

and to popularize new songs. In this respect the minstrels in the nineteenth century functioned much as the radio does today. From the pages of the *Republican Banner and Nashville Whig* this graphic description of the popularization of a song is taken:

> The burden of the song is generally about some maiden, who lives near some river, (Sewanee for example), who did or didn't do something, who died somehow, and is supposed to be loved by the singer to the last pitch of distraction . . . the appearance of a new piece of this kind is hailed with great joy by all the young ladies of the Hum-Drum Africanus school, and their name is legion. They steal a couple of hours from their morning slumbers to practice it secretly. They get it first by note, then by ear, then by heart."[55]

The next phase of its history took place in the streets, where it became the property of children and wagoners. Its fame spread. The brass band fell a victim to its sentimental charms and tortured it with French horns, bugles, and bassoons. It was "bleated" and "brayed" from the bridge over the Cumberland and from Capitol Hill. Young men used it for moonlight serenades and almost killed it by repetition. Tailors, drug clerks, gardeners, and draymen sang the melody. Finally it could be heard in every parlor "Done up in civilized style and in every kitchen in raw style."[56] Thereafter the song either died a natural death or lived on to become immortal as was the case with "Old Folks at Home" (1851), "My Old Kentucky Home" (1850), and "Old Black Joe" (1860).[57] In retrospect, both the humor and the sentiment of the minstrel show seem rather rudimentary. Yet the compositions of Stephen Foster must be considered a product of minstrelsy and this alone justifies its creation. "It would be absurd to deny that the vein of feeling which Stephen Foster and the best of his sort worked was of genuine gold, although as thin, perhaps, as the petal of the cotton blossoms, or that the

---

[55] *Republican Banner and Nashville Whig*, June 9, 1858.
[56] *Idem*.
[57] Robert P. Nevin, "Stephen C. Foster and Negro Minstrelsy," in *Atlantic Monthly*, XX (1867), 612.

Negro minstrel drolleries sometimes had a contagious jollity and a rich unction which were all their own."[58]

Foster's genius raised what might easily have been simply transitory popular ditties into the art of folk songs. As one critic has stated, "The art in his hands teemed with a nobler significance. It dealt, in its simplicity, with universal sympathies, and taught us all to feel with the slaves the lowly joys and sorrows it celebrated."[59] Viewed aesthetically, it is of little consequence that Foster had never seen a plantation when he composed "Old Folks at Home."

[58] Clapp, "Reminiscences of a Dramatic Critic," in *Atlantic Monthly*, LXXXVIII (1901), 159.
[59] Nevin, "Stephen C. Foster and Negro Minstrelsy," in *Atlantic Monthly*, XX (1867), 616.

CHAPTER VII

AMATEUR AMUSEMENTS: BENEFITS AND BALLS

AMONG THE citizens of Nashville there were numerous persons who possessed considerable musical talent or dramatic ability. From time to time these gifted amateurs gave concerts, tableaux, or plays, usually for the sake of charity, but occasionally for the aesthetic pleasure such entertainment afforded.

The cause of drama, music, and charity was aided by several organizations, such as the Nashville Dramatic Club, the Robertson Dramatic Club, and the German Harmonia Club. However, it would seem that these organizations were of a transitory nature, or at best only sporadically active.[1] The Robertson Dramatic Club was a division of the charitable organization known as the Robertson Association which was formed in February, 1856.[2] This organization sponsored amateur dramatics and lectures and used the proceeds to aid the poor of the city. During the winter of 1857-1858 alone the Robertson Association spent over $1600 for relief purposes.[3]

Amateur talent in the city expressed itself more frequently and to better advantage musically than it did dramatically. The press encouraged amateur singers and musicians and urged the people to patronize the amateur concerts. It was believed that such performances tended to cultivate and to extend the musical talents of the people and to elevate and refine the moral and intellectual tone of society.[4]

There were various types of amateur concerts. Some were given by the pupils of the various music teachers or music

---

[1] The newspapers of the period offer the most valuable information pertaining to charitable activities.
[2] Randal W. MacGavock, Diary, February 15, 1856.
[3] *Republican Banner and Nashville Whig*, October 12, 1858.
[4] *Ibid.*, October 9, 1858.

schools. For example, the pupils of one teacher gave a concert at Odd Fellows Hall on July 13, 1856,[5] while certain pupils of the Nashville Musical Academy presented some of their own compositions in concert on May 18 of the same year.[6] The school for the blind occasionally allowed its talented students to perform in public,[7] and the young ladies of the Nashville Female Academy gave concerts in the school chapel from time to time.[8]

Many of the amateur concerts were given in order to raise money for the Protestant and Catholic orphans. A series of concerts in the fall of 1855 was sponsored for this purpose.[9] Other concerts were given in order to raise money for the poor and the destitute, as well as for the orphans. This was the chief motive behind a group of concerts presented by amateur musicians in the fall of 1857.[10] There were times when these public-spirited citizens gave concerts for the benefit of the relief organizations. Thus, on December 4, 1858, a group of amateurs gave a concert for the benefit of the Robertson Association, which, it will be remembered, was a social welfare club.[11]

From time to time professional actors and musicians gave concerts or benefit performances for charity. Mrs. William Macready, the dramatic reader and actress, gave a benefit for the Robertson Association during her engagement in Nashville in May, 1856.[12] Mrs. Macready and Camille Urso, a violinist, attracted more attention by giving a free concert in the insane asylum. During the performance one of the inmates rose to his feet and with an excellent voice furnished an accompaniment for one of the violin solos. "His song was the out-pouring of his own crazed brain and melancholy heart, wild, erratic, but full of

[5] *Nashville Union and American*, July 13, 1856.
[6] *Nashville Daily Gazette*, May 18, 1856.
[7] *Nashville Union and American*, March 27, 1857.
[8] *Republican Banner, and Nashville Whig*, October 22, 1858; John Berrien Lindsley, Diary, October 3, 1858.
[9] *Nashville Daily Gazette*, September 23, November 21, 1855.
[10] *Ibid.*, November 24, 1857; Lindsley, Diary, November 26, 1857.
[11] *Republican Banner and Nashville Whig*, December 5, 1858.
[12] *Nashville Daily Gazette*, May 11, 1856.

pathos and melody. Without being at all disconcerted, Miss Urso continued the strain and they both concluded together."[13]

One of the most pretentious amateur concerts was presented in the Hall of Representatives on January 20, 1858.[14] The company consisted of a full chorus and piano, violin, and vocal soloists. It was reported that the large audience was "frantic with admiration and delight. No better evidence of the superior quality of the music and of its pleasing effect upon the audience could be given than the fact that nearly every piece on the programme was encored, and some of them two or three times."[15] The outstanding number of the evening was "Holy Mother" sung by two young ladies who were able to cast a spell over their audience. "Softly as the dews of evening, the melodious notes fell from their lips upon the enraptured ears of the audience."[16]

The concert was a social and aesthetic success. It reflected high credit on all concerned and demonstrated beyond a doubt that Nashville possessed real musical talent. It was also a financial success, as nearly $500 was realized above expenses.[17] This was a considerable sum to be used for charity purposes.

The Germans in Nashville were partly responsible for the great interest shown in music of all types. It is not surprising, therefore, to discover that a Schiller Music Festival was organized in November, 1859, in celebration of the one hundredth anniversary of the birth of the great poet. The main event of the celebration was a concert and dance given in Harmonia Hall on November 10. The Hall was decorated with evergreens, pictures, and German mottoes. The concert consisted of choral music and piano solos. The program was varied with dramatic sketches.[18]

The German influence may be seen also in the presentation for the first time in Nashville of Haydn's oratorio on February 25, 1858[19] and Handel's Messiah on March 4, 1859.[20] The oratorio

---

[13] *Ibid.*, May 4, 1856.   [14] Lindsley, Diary, January 20, 1858.
[15] *Republican Banner and Nashville Whig*, January 22, 1858.
[16] *Idem.*   [17] *Ibid.*, February 3, 1858.
[18] *Nashville Daily Gazette*, November 12, 1859; Lindsley, Diary, November 10, 1859.   [19] *Ibid.*, February 25, 1858.
[20] *Nashville Daily News*, March 5, 1859.

was quite successful and critics compared it favorably with a performance of the same work given in Philadelphia with all the advantages of a large organ.[21]

The most spectacular type of entertainment sponsored by the social workers of Nashville was the tableau, usually given in a series in order to provide entertainment for several hours. Such a performance was given at Odd Fellows Hall on October 23, 1851, for the benefit of the Protestant orphans. The program consisted of eleven tableaux as follows:

1. Cotters' Saturday Night—from Burns.
2. The Brother and Sisters—fancy scene.
3. The Toothache—a sad reality.
4. Scenes from Bluebeard.
5. The Return—from the *Vicar of Wakefield*.
6. Three Graces.
7. Scene from Cinderella.
8. The Lily and the Rose.
9. The Enchantress.
10. The Sultana and Her Slaves.
11. The Dame's School.

Following the tableaux, which began at 7 P.M., supper was served. The price of admission was 50 cents. Children were admitted at half price.[22]

The most successful tableau of the period was presented on January 15, 1858, by the managers of the Protestant Orphans Asylum. The demand for tickets was so great that the entire program was repeated several times.[23] The performance opened with a fairy scene in which there appeared a group of lovely little girls, beautifully dressed, and looking so unearthly in their simplicity and innocence that no one in the audience would have been very much surprised if they had actually spread their imitation wings and flown away to fairyland.

The initial scene was followed by a humorous tableau entitled

---

[21] *Republican Banner and Nashville Whig*, February 27, 1858.
[22] *Nashville Daily Gazette*, October 23, 1851.
[23] *Republican Banner and Nashville Whig*, January 13, 15, 17, 20, 21, 1858; Lindsley, Diary, January 18, 1858.

"Married Life in Two Scenes." The first scene represented a young couple the day after marriage and the second scene pictured them the day after the honeymoon. This was followed by "Zuleika in the Bride of Abydos" and "The Swiss Girl Pining for Home." In the latter, "the very poetry of grief was portrayed in her graceful form, her slightly drooping head and pensive look. The effect was magical."[24] This scene so appealed to the audience that it was repeated as soon as the applause died down.

The next scene represented a fortune-telling gipsy. This was followed by "The Sultana." "The beautiful Sultana and her attendants made a picture of surpassing loveliness."[25] This, too, was repeated and then the first part of the program was brought to a close with a comic feature called "The Old Maids' Tea Party."

The second half of the program opened with two beautiful scenes from *Ivanhoe* featuring Rowena and Rebecca. The tableaux which followed depicted a Wyoming Indian camp, a Negro preacher, the three graces, characters from Byron's *Corsair*, and a stolen kiss. The last scene on the program was entitled "The Slave Market" and consisted of "all the dazzling glories of nearly all the preceding tableaux . . . collected into one grand and glorious group, thus forming a fitting finale to so beautiful an exhibition."[26]

The tableau, staged with such artistry, became a thing of beauty and was indicative of the good taste that was becoming more prevalent in Nashville society as the period drew to a close. As has been shown above, this ability to appreciate the cultural things of life was reflected in the theater, the opera, the concert hall, and the university class room. Also it has been revealed that the people not only appreciated, they produced. This was true with respect to the tableau—an indication not only of appreciation but of creative ability as well.

One of the most popular amusements in Nashville during the

---

[24] *Republican Banner and Nashville Whig*, January 17, 1858.
[25] *Idem.*   [26] *Idem.*

fifties was dancing, and the public ball rooms were frequently given over to dance benefits for fire companies, military clubs, or charity organizations. It has been pointed out in Chapter II and Chapter IV that the clergy were opposed to dancing. The charity ball was not exempt from their ban. Although the enemies of the dance could hardly attack the humane purpose of a dance benefit, they could and did criticize what they termed the vanity and immodesty of the ball room belles whose "charms which nature intended as domestic secrets . . . are publicly exhibited in all their naked loveliness."[27] While it is true that the style of the period called for a low neckline and bare shoulders, it was not so extreme as to cause "profane eyes . . . to revel in unmuslined mysteries sacred to poetic reveries and lovers' dreams."[28] However, there was some truth in the statement that the styles cheated "the imagination of its divinest illusions."

In 1856, the Presbyterians passed a resolution to the effect "that the practice of dancing, and attending upon dancing parties, is eminently and exclusively that of the world which lieth in wickedness."[29] This was typical of the attitude of the conservative and occasionally bitter church element, but in spite of this opposition dancing continued to be regarded as a social grace by Nashville society.

The *Nashville Daily Gazette* expressed another opinion when it stated that "the youth of our cities commence business life so early and frequently devote themselves to it with such fixed intensity, that exhilarating amusement is necessary to their physical and mental health, and, of all amusements, dancing is the most inspiring and the least injurious. It brings our young men under the gentle, softening, humanizing influence of the more beautiful and holier portion of creation and thus profitably occupies the hours which might otherwise be spent in less innocent relaxation."[30]

[27] "Ball Room Belles," in *The Parlor Visitor*, II (1854), 18.
[28] *Idem*.
[29] *Nashville Christian Advocate*, May 8, 1856.
[30] November 6, 1853.

Every holiday of importance, such as Washington's birthday, the Fourth of July, or the anniversary of the Battle of New Orleans, was usually recognized with celebrations such as cotillion parties, fancy balls, and supper dances. At times these affairs had a motive other than simply affording pleasure or recreation. But the fact that the money taken in at the door was to be used for some philanthropic purposes never dampened the spirit of the merrymakers. At times a supper was included in the price of admission which frequently was as high as $5.00 for a gentleman and two ladies.[31]

St. Valentine's Day was another favorite for dances. One of the most elaborate celebrations was arranged under the auspices of the German Dramatic Society to celebrate Valentine's Day in 1858. "There was good music, merry hearts, nimble feet and a mutual understanding on the part of all to trip it on the light fantastic toe."[32] At midnight, the guests removed their masks and took their places at the supper tables which glittered with plate and glassware and reflected the skill of the confectioner.[33]

It was customary for the proprietor of a dancing school to open the season with a *Soirée Dansant*. Such a dance was given in honor of the teacher's most perfect class, and the parents of the students and all others interested in the art of dancing were welcome. A party of this nature appealed to young and old alike and was a dignified but effective method of advertising.[34]

St. Maur Stuart was one of the most popular of Nashville's dancing teachers. A party sponsored by him invariably included a program of fancy and interpretative dances presented by his best students. The entertainment began with a grand march, or a "Grand Entrée Polonaise," which might include the entire school or merely students selected for their grace and talent. Stuart specialized in Spanish and Mexican dances and it was his custom to have the students present on these occasions the cachu-

---

[31] *Ibid.*, December 19, 1850; *Nashville Patriot*, January 2, 5, February 16, 18, 1859.
[32] *Republican Banner and Nashville Whig*, February 17, 1858.
[33] *Idem.*
[34] *Nashville Daily Gazette*, November 6, 1853, October 1, December 3, 1857.

cha, the arragonesa, or perhaps the difficult *pas de rancho*.[35] A dancing exhibition of this nature was always well received by the audience.

Sometimes dances were given on the river boats. Such affairs were attended by the "beauty, fashion and gallantry of the city," and were usually lively and gay and occasionally boisterous. At least on one occasion the faculty of the Medical School of the University of Nashville sponsored a ball and supper. Dancing continued until three o'clock in the morning, which was not unusual. A supper dance in the fifties meant a full night of entertainment followed by a full day of headaches.[36]

One of the favorite places for a grand ball was the County Courthouse. As every floor in the building was made available, a large crowd could be easily accommodated. Couples began to dance on the first floor and as the evening grew old and the crowd grew larger "they kept going up until they got to the roof."[37] The capitol was used for the same purpose. The round of parties, teas, dinners, and dances given in connection with the annual meeting of the American Medical Association (May 5-7, 1857) came to a spectacular close with a grand ball in this building which had been such an inspiration to local architects. About three hundred people attended, although not every one danced. A delicious supper contributed to the success of the occasion, which was probably the most dignified and certainly the most important social event of the decade. One guest considered it "the grandest entertainment that ever came off in the South."[38]

There were several military organizations in Nashville, such as the Nashville Blues and the Rock City Guards, which sponsored a military ball or a soirée whenever money was needed.[39] The Rock City Guards, which was composed of the leading young society men, was organized primarily for social purposes.

[35] *Ibid.*, August 8, 1854.
[36] MacGavock, Diary, February 9, 1855.
[37] *Nashville Patriot*, September 8, 1859.
[38] MacGavock, Diary, May 5, 6, 7, 1857.
[39] *Republican Banner and Nashville Whig*, January 6, March 13, 1853; December 20, 1857.

Some of the parties given by the Guards or to them were highlights of the social season. These entertainments were bright with pretty girls in billowing dresses, fine fellows in richly colored uinforms, candlelight, champagne, and music. Perhaps the most enjoyable parties were the unexpected, informal ones. Whenever the Guards unintentionally, or perhaps intentionally, paraded by a residence where a number of young ladies were being entertained the young men were usually invited to share in the fun and the hospitality. It is inconceivable that the young hostesses were ever denied. In a twinkling of an eye, arms were stacked in the street and the Guards "took possession" of the house. Salutations were exchanged, champagne was served, and then the waltzing began.[40]

The ability to entertain graciously is usually associated with people who have reached a comparatively high cultural level. On this basis Nashville, by 1860, could claim distinction. The citizens of the better classes, when they presented a charity benefit or staged a ball for distinguished guests, showed a high degree of intelligence and hospitality and also an appreciation af aesthetic values. The rainbow brilliance of a grand ball in the capitol was an announcement to the world that Nashville had progressed much further from the frontier than the calendar years might seem to indicate.

[40] *Memoir of Thomas H. Malone* (Nashville, 1928), 98-99.

Chapter VIII

PENS AND PRINTERS' INK, 1850-1860

IT IS IMPOSSIBLE to measure the influence that literature exerts over human minds and over nations. That it is prodigious is an obvious truth. The press of a nation or of a community, turning out books, pamphlets, magazines, and newspapers, is always a determining factor in progress or retrogression, in war or peace, in ignorance or culture.

In the decade before the Civil War the southern press was more powerful, perhaps, as an agent of political philosophy, religious dogmatism, and general propaganda than of pure literature. This, of course, was due to the necessity of defending southern civilization against the attacks of abolitionism.

But not every pen in the South was dipped in the gall of political strife or religious sectarianism. There were poets, novelists, essayists, and textbook writers who wrote spontaneously and without an axe to grind. There were writers imbued with the romanticism of ante-bellum days, and who developed the art of forgetting the bitterness in the world around them.

One keen observer of the times declared that literary men were regarded with greater consideration than formerly, and were not any longer compelled to walk under the high legs of politicians, and peep about to find themselves dishonorable graves. "It is getting to be thought that a man may perhaps accomplish as much for the South by writing a good book as by making a successful stump speech; that he who contributes to the enjoyment of his fellow-citizens by a lofty poem, or shapes their convictions by a powerful essay, is not an idle dreamer merely; and that the pen devoted to the treatment of subjects out of the range of politics and commercial activities is as usefully employed as the tongue which is exercised in the wearisome declamation of legislative halls."[1]

Many of the authors and poets of the period have become literary ghosts, their names forgotten, their works either lost or buried in the pages of old periodicals. This was "the fleeting literature of the press, the forum, the lyceum, or the association which will warble for a moment and then perish forever."[2]

Tennessee and Nashville produced such literature, but much of it has been destroyed along with the periodicals in which it appeared. Of the Nashville literary magazines that have survived the *Parlor Visitor, The Southern Ladies' Companion,* and *The South Western Monthly* are the most valuable and the most interesting. With respect to literary production, the poems of Virginia French and Clara Cole and the editorials of John Leake Marling are the best of the available indexes of Nashville literary talent for the decade under consideration.

But before examining the work of the writers associated with the Nashville scene it will be of interest to glance at the libraries in the city and at the literature that the people were reading.

The best general library was to be found at the University of Nashville. As a matter of fact, the University collection consisted of several libraries: the medical library, the general academic library, and the library of the literary societies. In the combined University library there were about 14,000 volumes in 1860.[3]

The Mechanics Association of Nashville had established a library in 1844,[4] and by 1860 there were about 5,000 volumes in this collection.[5] (It is assumed that many of these books were of a technical nature.) The Y. M. C. A., which was established in Nashville in 1855, had managed to collect about 400 volumes

---

[1] John R. Thompson, in *The Southern Literary Messenger* (Richmond, 1834-1864), XXIX (1857), 315; quoted in Edward Ingle, *Southern Sidelights, A picture of Social and Economic Life in the South a Generation before the War* (New York, 1896), 200.

[2] J. Quitman Moore, "American Letters," in *DeBow's Review* (New Orleans, 1846-1880), XXVIII (1860), 663.

[3] *Nashville City and Business Directory*, V (1860-1861), 29.

[4] *South Western Literary Journal and Monthly Review* (Nashville, 1844—?), I (1845), 339.

[5] *Nashville City and Business Directory*, V (1860-1861), 45.

for its circulating library by 1860.⁶ Included in this collection were many valuable standard works.⁷ The reading room at the Y. M. C. A. library was supplied with the leading newspapers and periodicals of the day. The Tennessee Historical Society, which had grown out of the Tennessee Antiquarian Society (1820) and the Tennessee Society for the Diffusion of Knowledge (1835), possessed about 900 books and possibly 1,000 pamphlets in 1860.⁸ Among the rare books owned by the Society was a copy of *Ovid* printed in Venice in 1482.⁹

One of the finest collections of literary works in the South was to be found in Berry's Book Store in Nashville. "It included the finest bound and best printed books of European writers, ancient and modern, and the current fiction of the time. Mr. Berry was by nature a book man, and had a great liking for rare and quaint productions of authorship and the printers' art and kept them in stock to please southern customers of similar tastes."[10]

Berry's Book Store was more than a place of business. It was a browsing library, and a part of the store was furnished with cushioned chairs for the convenience of customers and visitors. The store at times resembled a literary and political club as it was a favorite meeting place for scholars and statesmen of Tennessee and other states of the South.[11]

The Catholic Church had a small circulating library[12] and no doubt there were numerous private libraries of considerable interest and value.[13] Bishop Miles, for example, possessed 2,300 volumes of sacred literature and theology including Bibles written in seven different languages.[14] Professor James Hamilton of

[6] *Ibid.*, 81.   [7] *Idem.*
[8] *Ibid.*, 43.   [9] *Ibid.*, 42.
[10] Douglas Anderson, "Negro Slavery and the White Man's Genius. A Reply to Northern Criticisms of the South's Place in American Literature and History," in Nashville *American*, October 16, 1904; also in Anderson's Scrapbook, Article No. 10 (Carnegie Library, Nashville).   [11] *Idem.*
[12] *South Western Literary Journal and Monthly Review*, I (1845), 339.
[13] Bond, "Life of Brigadier General Felix Kirk Zollicoffer, C. S. A.," 2, 4, 5; J. H. Ingraham, *Life and Experiences of a Southern Governess in the Sunny South* (New York, 1880), 123, 169-173.
[14] *South Western Literary Journal and Monthly Review*, I (1845), 339.

the University of Nashville had a personal collection of over 400 volumes. The majority of Hamilton's books were scientific, but there was some poetry, philosophy, history, and theology. In his collection were works in French, Greek, and Latin. The ancient classics were represented by Herodotus, Xenophon, Pindar, Sophocles, Euripedes, Florus, and Terence. Among the history books was Voltaire's *History of the Empire of Russia under Peter the Great*.[15] It seems probable that the various fire companies had libraries, as the power to establish libraries was delegated to these organizations when they were incorporated by the state.[16] In 1860 the formation of the Young Men's Mercantile Library Association of Nashville was another indication of the general interest in literature of all types. This organization was created to "promote the moral, intellectual and professional culture of the young men of Nashville."[17]

The most pretentious library was in the state capitol. Between 1854 and 1856 the legislature of the state appropriated $5500 for the purpose of buying books for the new library.[18] In 1858 in order to raise additional funds for the library the legislature levied a small emergency tax on the taxable property of the state. This law was in force for two years and netted $4,000.[19] In 1860 the legislature voted $2,500 for the library and according to the act this amount was to be appropriated annually. Therefore, up to 1860, presumably $12,000 had been spent on books and pamphlets as the librarian's salary was not included in the appropriations mentioned above.[20]

As a result of these grants from the state the library, at the close of the decade, was able to boast of 11,000 volumes and about 4,000 pamphlets.[21] Conspicuous in the collection, of course,

[15] Catalogue of Books Presented to the Library of the University of Nashville by the Late Prof. James Hamilton, 1850 (MS in Peabody College Library).
[16] Tennessee *Acts*, 1849-1850, p. 6.
[17] Tennessee *Acts of a Private Nature*, 1859-1860, p. 407.
[18] Tennessee *Acts*, 1853-1854, p. 773; *ibid.*, 1855-1856, p. 236.
[19] *Third Biennial Report Upon the Library of the State* (Nashville, 1859), 146-149.
[20] Tennessee *Acts of a Private Nature*, 1859-1860, p. 247.
[21] *Nashville City and Business Directory*, V (1860-1861), 40-41.

were law books and government publications such as *The English Parliamentary History and Debates from 1066 to 1840* (157 volumes), *The English State Trials* (22 volumes), *The Annals of Congress* (1789-1824), *The Congressional Debates* (1824-1837), and *The Congressional Globe* (1833-1859). There was a set of *Lemare's Latin Classics* (147 volumes), and *The Library of the Fathers* (39 volumes). The medical science was represented by forty volumes published by the Sydenham Society. The librarian had not overlooked English literature and he was able to display Child's edition of the *British Poets* (105 volumes), and three editions of Shakespeare in eight, twelve and fifteen volume sets. In addition to works published by such institutions as the Massachusetts Historical Society and the Smithsonian Institution there were general works on History, Science, and Politics written in English and French.[22]

Among its periodicals the state library listed *The Edinburgh Review* (112 volumes), *The North American Review* (84 volumes), *Hunt's Merchants Magazine* (40 volumes), *DeBow's Review* (20 volumes), *Niles Register* (67 volumes), and *Blackwood's Magazine* (86 volumes).[23]

It would seem that by 1860 the library facilities in Nashville were appropriate for both general and specialized study. That novel reading was a popular pastime especially for women becomes evident from a perusal of the periodicals and newspapers of the day. And, just as there were voices raised in opposition to the theater and to dancing, so there were voices which denounced the novel.

According to *The Parlor Visitor,* novel reading was becoming more than a diversion. It was an obsession. "Many girls, of really fine intellects," declared this journal, "are throwing away all hope of a vigorous mental culture by an insatiable craving for fictitious works."[24] Another article in the same issue of this magazine (March, 1857) sounded the warning that novel read-

---

[22] *Idem.*
[23] *Idem; Third Biennial Report upon the Library of the State,* 146-149.
[24] *The Parlor Visitor,* VII (1857), 339.

ing would lead to "intellectual imbecility." Furthermore, "the excitement from novel-reading grows by that which it feeds upon, like the appetite for ardent spirits. It seems to debauch the intellect of some almost as obviously as the cup."[25]

A young moralist writing for *The Naturalist* imagined "a city belle seated on her luxurious ottoman, perusing her interesting romance, and asked concerning the mysteries of baking a hoecake or picking a goose, she would stare with unfeigned surprise; yet she can sigh, faint, weep and quote Byron with the most consummate effect."[26]

One contributor to *The Parlor Visitor* went so far as to call the common practice of novel-reading a calamity. "Let us refrain from these engines of Satan as we would a loathsome disease," he wrote, "having for our motto—*Touch not, Taste not, Handle not.* Novel reading may well be considered the most dreadful and most to be feared of any calamity that ever has or ever will oppress our nation."[27]

That such bombastic criticism had any effect on the fiction reading public is very doubtful. Nashville supported at least four book stores,[28] and if their advertisements are any indication of the fiction they sold it appears that they did a good business. Among the English novelists who were widely read in Nashville were Scott, Dickens, Reade, Trollope, Bulwer-Lytton, Thackeray, and Oliphant.[29] Scott's works had long since "passed the ordeal of criticism" in the South.[30] When the Nashville reader turned to English poetry he was apt to pick up a volume of Milton or Cowper, or perhaps Gray's *Elegy*.[31] Byron, too, was popular and probably exerted considerable influence on Nashville and Tennessee poets, as will be noted below. Pollock and Thompson

[25] *Ibid.*, 417.
[26] *The Naturalist and Journal of Natural History, Agriculture, Education, and Literature*, I (1846), 189. [27] *The Parlor Visitor*, II (1854), 15.
[28] *South Western Literary Journal and Monthly Review*, I (1845), 339.
[29] Bond, "Life of Brigadier General Felix Kirk Zollicoffer, C. S. A.," 4; Ingraham, *Life and Experiences of a Southern Governess*, 169-173.
[30] *South Western Literary Journal and Monthly Review*, I (1845), 182.
[31] Catalogue of Books Presented to the University of Nashville by the Late Prof. James Hamilton; see also newspaper advertisements for the period.

were studied in Nashville academies,[32] and there was probably a copy of Shakespeare in every private library.[33] The German element in Nashville, and possibly the general reading public, was interested in the works of Goethe and Schiller.[34]

With respect to American literature, the discriminating taste of the Nashville reading public frequently came into conflict with their loyalty to the South. This was as natural as it was inevitable. And when a choice *was* made the literature of the North was usually sacrificed in the name of the Southern cause. The press took up the question and became increasingly vituperative in its criticism of northern men of letters. While in 1845 the editor of Nashville's *Literary Journal and Monthly Review* might praise Cooper's *Afloat and Ashore* and call it the author's *chef d'œuvre,* ten years later Nashville editors and critics were apt to agree with DeBow when he declared that Cooper was simply an imitator of Scott.[35] DeBow did not confine his remarks to Cooper alone. Irving was unfavorably compared with Addison, and Bancroft and Prescott with Macaulay. Longfellow and Bryant were described as third-rate poets and Emerson was considered "but a paltry copy of Carlyle."[36]

DeBow, it would seem, had been influenced by Poe's criticism of the same writers. But Poe was interested only in literary criticism. DeBow was influenced by sectionalism, and the date of this editorial, 1858, is significant. By this time the attacks of the abolitionists, together with the results of the panic of 1857, had stirred the South into a belligerent mood. Northern writers were not to escape the flames of sectional passion.

In Nashville the *Daily Union and American* was a conspicuous champion of southern literature and southern periodicals. The *Southern Literary Messenger* was given special praise. The literature of the North, and especially the literature in northern

[32] *Nashville Ladies College, First Annual Catalogue* (1853), I.
[33] Ingraham, *Life and Experiences of a Southern Governess,* 123.
[34] *Nashville Union and American,* February 1, 1857; Lindsley, Diary, November 10, 1859.
[35] [J. B. DeBow,] "American Literature—Northern and Southern," in *DeBow's Review,* XXIV (1858), 173. [36] *Idem.*

magazines was described as "trash."[37] The same feeling of antagonism is suggested in the following brief notice of Emerson's *English Traits.* "Mr. Emerson sees only the bright side of English life and manners," said the *Daily Union and American,* "but he has admirers enough to buy his books even were he to praise something worse than the traits of our foreign cousins."[38]

But in spite of the attempt to discredit the literary products of the North, the South continued to subscribe to northern journals. After all, these magazines were better than anything the South had to offer, with the exception of *DeBow's Review,* and *The Southern Literary Messenger.* And so *Harper's Weekly, Frank Leslie's Illustrated News, Godey's Ladies Book, Graham's Magazine,* and other serials published in the North were being read in Nashville on the eve of secession.[39] The same was true with respect to Emerson, Longfellow, Holmes, Cooper, Irving, and other northern writers.

The South had always claimed Poe as its own genius and he was read extensively in Nashville and undoubtedly influenced some of Nashville's writers, as will be pointed out later. Originally, one of the chief reasons for the popularity of *Graham's Magazine* in the South and the West had been Poe's connection with this journal. In the forties the extensive circulation of this magazine in Tennessee was considered amazing and this was partly due to Poe, whose pen often added "to the worth of the columns."[40]

It required no effort for Nashville book lovers to concentrate on Poe. His works were already well known and accepted as a matter of course and by 1860 Kennedy and Simms were also becoming popular. In the field of sociology and philosophy the South produced two important writers in Thomas Dew (1802-1864) and George Fitzhugh (1806-1881) and their works, either

[37] *Nashville Union and American,* January 31, 1857.
[38] *Ibid.,* August 26, 1856.
[39] *Nashville Patriot,* January 2, 1860, and subsequent issues; Bond, "Life of Brigadier General Felix Kirk Zollicoffer," 3.
[40] *South Western Literary Journal and Monthly Review,* I (1845), 52.

in book form or as magazine articles, circulated widely. Fitzhugh's most popular and probably his best work was *Sociology for the South, or the Failure of Free Society,* published in 1854.[41] Dew, influenced by German philosophy, was too deep and too technical to be popular but his works were an important factor in the pro-slavery argument and his name was not unfamiliar in Nashville literary and political circles.

Plantation and slavery fiction was popular in Nashville, as it was throughout the country.[42] The famous book by "Mrs. Uncle Tom Beecher Stowe"[43] eclipsed all other publications but there were other novels based on slavery that had a tremendous sale in the fifties although they are little more than titles today. Among these should be included the plantation stories of Mrs. E. D. E. N. Southworth (1819-1899), which were denounced as untrue by southern critics, and the pro-slavery novels of Caroline Lee Hentz.[44] *Aunt Phillis' Cabin,* by Mrs. M. H. Eastman, was among the first of the novelistic replies to *Uncle Tom's Cabin.*[45]

The campaign for an independent southern literature finally directed attention to the textbooks that were being used in southern schools. It was discovered that in almost every case the text books were written by northern men unfriendly to the South. A contributor to the New Orleans Picayune declared, "It is a fact that almost every other book sent from the North, where it is possible to make it so, is used as a vehicle for misrepresentation or abuse of us; that nearly every school book, especially those used in private establishments, contains some of the poison."[46] Some of the text books on the black list, including Mitchell's

[41] James W. Davidson, *The Living Writers of the South* (New York, 1869), 181.

[42] Francis Pendleton Gaines, *The Southern Plantation: A Study of the Development and Accuracy of a Tradition* (New York, 1924), 36-94.

[43] *DeBow's Review,* XXI (1856), 652.

[44] Caroline Lee Hentz (1800-1856). For an excellent discussion of these novels see Gains, *The Southern Plantation: A Study in the Development and Accuracy of a Tradition,* 49-54; also Jeannette Reid Tandy, "Pro-Slavery Propaganda in American Fiction in the Fifties," in *South Atlantic Quarterly* (Durham, 1902—), XXI (1922), 170-178.

[45] *Ibid.,* 170.

[46] C. R. Marshall, "Southern Authors, School Books, and Presses," in *DeBow's Review,* XXI (1856), 520.

geographies, Parley's histories, and *Webster's Dictionary*, were used in Nashville academies.[47] It was claimed that Peter Parley seized every opportunity "to insult and misrepresent the institutions of the South"[48] while Mitchell ignored its literary and industrial enterprises.[49] *Webster's Dictionary* was criticized because it defined a slave as "a person subject to the will of another, a drudge."[50]

On the eve of the Civil War a number of textbooks were written and published by Nashville scholars. The most interesting and important at the time were the *Orthographical Spelling-Book*, by William Mulkey (1856), *Key to the Geology of the Globe*, by Richard Owen (1857), *Barrington's Elements of the Natural Science*, by Mrs. Frances B. Fogg (1858), *A New System of English Grammar*, by Sidney S. Caldwell (1859), *Philological Readers* (books one to four), by S. A. Poindexter (1860-1861), and the *Principles of English Grammar*, by A. S. Worrell (1861).

These works represent one manifestation of the increased literary activity in the South, but it is possible that they were more truly products of Nashville's stimulating educational circles than of the campaign for southern school books. Worrell's book on grammar, which was not published until after secession took place, was an exception. In the preface, the author declared that "every independent nation must furnish its own literature. . . . The southerners have been content to have their books furnished them by the North. This not only discouraged southern authorship, and cramped genius, but it allowed the North the chief means of shaping national bias—the press. But now that the southern people have separated from the North and established an independent nationality she will, of course, hail with pleasure every industrious effort of her own sons to free her from abolition dependencies."[51] Worrell was a supporter of the southern cause but like all authors he wished his book to sell.

[47] *Nashville Ladies College, First Annual Catalogue* (1853), 11.
[48] Edwin Heriott, "Education at the South," in *DeBow's Review*, XXI (1856), 651.
[49] *Idem.*   [50] *Idem.*
[51] A. S. Worrell, *The Principles of English Grammar* (Nashville, 1861), iii.

Perhaps there were many southern writers and school men whose ideals did not prevent them from exploiting the patriotic hysteria attending secession.

The title of Mrs. Fogg's work, *Barrington's Elements of Natural Science,* is misleading. Naturally the student would expect the book to be the scientific studies of Barrington, edited by Mrs. Fogg. This does not seem to be the case. Barrington is either a family name or one manufactured by Mrs. Fogg for reasons best known to herself.

Perhaps she did not wish to be held directly responsible for the scientific theories presented in the book. This assumption becomes almost a conviction when it is taken into consideration that the book denounces Nott's theories of the origin of the Negro race. Briefly, then, Mrs. Fogg did not accept the scientific phase of the pro-slavery argument, but because she lived in a community that did accept it, it may be assumed that she deliberately invented a title that would be confusing and possibly direct attention away from her if Nashville critics were to attack her theories.

Basing her argument on Prichard's *Natural History of Man* (published in 1854)[52] Mrs. Fogg asserted "that the human race is specifically one: there is no permanent or specific difference between one race and another."[53] She discountenanced the hair and color theory of the Nott school and supported the climatic theory of the abolitionists. "We would ask those who make color a distinction of species, whether the black side of a cow or cat is of a different species from the white."[54]

In addition to a brief discussion of ethnology, the book purported to be an introduction to hydrology, geognosy, geology, mineralogy, paleontology, meteorology, anemography, climatology, botany, zoology, religion, government, and economics.

Richard Owen, author of *Key to the Geology of the Globe,*

---

[52] Mrs. Francis B. Fogg, *Barrington's Elements of Natural Science* (Nashville, 1858), 298 n.
[53] *Ibid.,* 299.   [54] *Ibid.,* 298.

was the son of Robert Owen of New Harmony fame.[55] When his book appeared in 1857 he had been professor of geology and chemistry at the University of Nashville for seven years. His book consisted of the general principles of geographical geology.

Poindexter wrote his *Philological Reader* in order to encourage home study and "to make spelling, pronunciation and enunciation a pleasing study." Furthermore, it was his intention to provide reading matter which should inspire "a love of reading, a love of learning, a love of nature." The selections in the book range from the old favorite *Excelsior* to a brief essay on fire engines. In general the book is didactic as the author was attempting to draw young minds "through nature up to nature's God."[56]

Caldwell's *A New System of English Grammar,* while it would be considered old-fashioned today, was well organized and clearly stated. The author divided his book into four parts. The first section he gave over to a treatment of the parts of speech. The second section contained thirty-seven rules of syntax with numerous examples of false syntax. Part three Caldwell devoted to prosody which he said comprised "all the laws of elocution."[57] In a fourth section, the appendix, the author treated such subjects as rhetoric, composition, and the use of capital letters.

William Mulkey's *Orthographical Spelling-Book* attracted considerable attention. In its issue for January 18, 1857, the *Nashville Daily Union and American* carried a lengthy notice of the book. "That a more correct philography and orthoëpy of the English language is much needed," asserted the journal, "is ... universally admitted ... by all intelligent persons engaged in imparting a knowledge of our language to the youthful mind. ... Of the various plans of systematizing the difficulties

---

[55] Richard Owen, *Key to the Geology of the Globe* (Nashville and Philadelphia, 1857), 10.

[56] S. A. Poindexter, *Philological Reader* (Nashville, Richmond, Atlanta, 1861), v-vi, 8-9, 81, 121, 191 ff., 215, 295, 297.

[57] Sidney S. Caldwell, *A New System of English Grammar by the Study of Which Youths and Adults May Become Accomplished Grammarians in Three or Four Months Without the Aid of a Teacher* (Nashville, 1859), 355.

of the language, none, in our opinion, seems to meet the exigencies of the case more completely or in a more philosophical manner than that of Prof. William Mulkey; and we are glad to know that we are sustained in this opinion by gentlemen of learning and intelligence in this community. . . . His spelling book now in print is the best we have seen."[58]

Mulkey emphasized sounds and he made phonetics as prominent as possible in his book in order to keep them constantly before the mind of the student. He also believed that the student should know how to read before attempting to learn to spell. Mulkey's speller, with its 195 rules, would appear like a Chinese puzzle to the modern teacher.

The Nashville press turned out political, scientific, and literary journals which were important elements in the city's intellectual development.[59] One of these magazines, *The Southern Lady's Companion* was important historically because it was a pioneer, and a comparatively successful one, in its field. It was the first journal designed especially for the entertainment of the women of the South.[60]

The editorial policy of the *Southern Lady's Companion* was expressed briefly by the editor, Rev. M. M. Henkle. "Whenever we can have a supply of good original matter," he announced, "it will be preferred to selections of equal value; but we think a good selection better than an inferior original article, and shall act on that decision."[61] An examination of the surviving numbers of the magazine leaves the impression that Henkle was frequently injudicious in his selection of material. Many of the articles deal with morals and manners, domestic relations, or bad habits such as dipping snuff.[62] One contribution was entitled "On Marriage by a Father." As it is both amusing and typical it is reproduced here in part:

[58] See also Lindsley, Diary, January 27, 1857; Nashville *Christian Advocate*, March 4, 1858.
[59] *Nashville City and Business Directory*, V (1860-1861), 27.
[60] *Southern Lady's Companion* (Nashville, 1847-1854) V (1851), 367.
[61] *Ibid.*, II (1848), 24.
[62] *Ibid.*, V (1851), 313-316.

A conversation between a father and his daughter:

Father: "My daughter, you will in a short time be old enough to marry; and your hand and heart will be sought by young gentlemen having various claims to their possession. And, as I wish you to make a happy choice, I desire to give you some advice on that subject."

Caroline: "I am willing, Pa, to hear anything you may have to say on that subject; but I think it hardly necessary to advise me on the subject of matrimony. I have not yet finished my education; besides I do not think that I shall ever marry."

Father: "Your father thinks differently. He believes that you ought to marry . . ."

Caroline: "I should like to hear the reasons why you think I ought to marry."

Father: "I will give them with pleasure . . . I am certain that a matrimonial union judiciously formed, is the happiest state in which mankind can live."

Caroline: "Do you think, Pa, that I can ever be happier in this life than I am at home with you and Ma?"

At this point the father asked his daughter if she were willing to be an old maid and she replied, "I am certain that I have no desire to be an old maid. The thought is repulsive." The conversation then turned to the governing principles in selecting a husband and the father warned his daughter against the drunkards, the gamblers, the Sabbath-breakers, the profane swearers, and the infidels. "A man should be industrious, economical and firm," said the father. "However, men are not perfect. You will, most likely, have to take one with some defects."[63]

Another contributor, in this case a bishop, described the duties and qualities of an ideal wife. "In the first place," wrote the bishop, "let us say it is essential that you love your husband. It is not enough that you respect him, or that you propose to treat him respectfully because his position as your husband demands it. . . . The good wife loves her husband and is prepared

---

[63] *Ibid.*, IV (1850), 172-177.

to make large allowances for his imperfections."[64] The bishop had little patience with women who wrote poetry and neglected their domestic duties.

A fantasy called "A Dream of Life and Death" illustrates the attempt of an obscure romanticist to create something novel and effective for the *Companion*. In a dream, life appears as a beautiful goddess whose "elastic step was light as the footfall of a fairy." All the world was glad at her approach. Wherever she went "health and beauty met her with smiles, and the desert grew into an oasis of surpassing loveliness. Flowers burst their petals at her approach, and, as they shined in all their variegated colors, they greeted her with a cloud of sweet-scented odor . . . little birds . . . shook their little world of care from their tiny wings, and in transports flew around her . . . the wild untamed beasts of the forests crowded in gladness at her feet and courted a glance of her eyes . . . the young with their ringing laugh, danced around her, while the aged drew near to feel the warm, genial influence of her inspiring breath. This was Life!—vitality personified."

But following life came Death, a dark, passionless river "swallowing up her footsteps" and flowing on to the ocean of eternity. Upon the flood sat a satiated sea bird with raven wings. Everything, even time, fell a victim to the bird. The dreamer of this dream was bewildered by the spectacle and asked Death to explain what it all signified. Whereupon Death, for the first time, slowly lifting his drowsy form, and shaking his sluggish wings in triumph, in hollow tones replied, "It is said that time shall be no more."[65] In all probability the sea bird with raven wings was Poe's famous bird in a new disguise.

It is difficult to become enthusiastic over the poetry that appeared in the *Southern Lady's Companion*. Of all the contributors, Clara Cole, whose verse will be considered below, possessed the most talent. The periodical poetry of the day was melancholy and even morbid, and death was one of the major themes.

---

[64] *Ibid.*, 97-100. [65] *Ibid.*, II (1848), 1-3.

The poems in the *Companion* were no exception. The following is an example of the better type of melancholy verse.

> I know not why, but autumn ever
>   Doth o'er my spirit fling
> A deeper, sweeter spell than all
>   The beauties of the spring.
> Perhaps some pleasant memories
>   These falling leaves renew,
> Or that my own heart hath a tinge
>   Of melancholy hue.[66]

Quite different are the following lines entitled "Dying Charlie":

> Little Charlie's dying, Mother,
>   His breath grows shorter now,
> His eyes have lost their brightness, Mother,
>   And the cold sweat's on his brow.
>
> Little Charlie's dying, Mother,
>   See how quick and soft he breathes;
> His cheeks have lost their bloom, Mother,
>   And look like autumn-faded leaves.
>
> Little Charlie's dead, Mother,
>   His heart has ceased to beat;
> His spirit's gone to heaven, Mother,
>   And is nestling at Jesus' feet.
>
> Let us kneel and pray, Mother,
>   That we may like him, die,
> Gently close our eyes in sleep, Mother,
>   Without a groan or sigh.[67]

In many respects the *Parlor Visitor* resembled the *Southern Lady's Companion*. The editor, B. W. P. Jones, was opposed to dancing, the theater, fiction-reading, and hard liquors. Jones was narrow in his views, but apparently sincere. He thought that his magazine was a moral guide for the people of Tennessee. Perhaps it was, but it might have enjoyed more permanent success had the editor given less attention to what he called morality and more attention to good literature.

[66] Omicron, "Autumn," *ibid.*, 205.
[67] Katrina, "Dying Charlie," in *ibid.*, IV (1850), 162.

The most pretentious journalistic attempt in Nashville was the ill-starred *South-Western Monthly*.[68] This magazine was brought forth in 1852 and it was a beautiful specimen of the printer's art. It was printed with new type cast by Guilford and Jones of Cincinnati, the cover design was an attractive vignette, and the fine steel engravings were the best that money could buy. The purpose of the new magazine was to develop the latent literary talent of the Southwest. "The fact has to be demonstrated, and finally," declared the editor, "that the South either *can*, or *cannot*, *build up a literature of its own*. The fact has to be shown—that the South either *will* or *will not* do its own thinking and its own writing, in preference to letting other sections do it for them!"[69] If it came to a choice between northern and southern literature all true southerners, as a matter of pride, the editor believed "would decide the question overwhelmingly *in favor of home literature*."[70]

This appeal to sectional pride was not very successful. Except for several articles dealing with the early history of Tennessee, no suitable literary contributions were forthcoming. But throughout its brief life of one year the magazine continued to be conducted on a high plane although most of the literature was copied from American and English journals of recognized standing. Occasionally the editor himself supplied some poetry. The following lines, entitled "Memories," are typical.

> My dreams are of thee, in the hush of night,
> My visions of thee, in the noon of day;
> Time is forgotten in his ceaseless flight,
> Whilst I am thinking of thee—far away;
> Since first I gazed upon thy faultless brow,
> Swiftly have sped the moments until now.
>
> The memory of thee, like some wondrous spell,
> Hath clothed with joy and hope each lonely hour;
> And thy soft tones seem still with me to dwell,

---

[68] *The South-Western Monthly, A Journal Devoted to Literature and Science, Education, the Mechanic Arts and Agriculture* (Nashville, 1852). Only two volumes were published.

[69] *Ibid.*, I (1852), 323.   [70] *Idem.*

Like fairy music, in their magic power;
And as I note thine absence, with regret,
I see thy dark eyes beaming on me yet.

I have been with thee in the land of dreams,
And oft with thee have wander'd far and wide,
By moonlit lake, by summer woods and streams,
I've gazed on thee in gladness by my side;
Life, whilst with thee, was one long summer day,
Which blithely fled in blissful hours away.

Though only dreams they were of thee—of thee!
With whom my spirit revels, e'en alone;
Then let me meet once more in ecstasy,
E'en in the land of dreams, thee, lovely one;
Thou art the world to me when thou art nigh,
And thy sweet smile will haunt me till I die.

Then let me look upon thee, meet thee, still,
Heedless of darker hours, with shadows dim,
In thy dear presence still defy each ill,
Which mantles oft life's goblet to the brim;
May joyous Hope still crown thee with her light!
And the bright future know for thee no night.[71]

The South-Western Monthly was a noble attempt to give the Southwest a first class magazine but at the end of the first year came the announcement that it was to be discontinued because of lack of sufficient support. It had been an expensive enterprise and the journal was on the verge of bankruptcy. "To go on with a work like ours," an editorial declared, "requires a warm, earnest, hearty support, such as we are now strongly convinced, will not be given to Southern literary enterprize, whilst habit has made the South look to the North for works of this kind."[72] And so this promising periodical came to an end.

One of the most prolific and certainly the most popular of Nashville's poets was Mrs. Clara Marling Cole (1805-1880?). Very little is known about her except that she was the daughter of John and Sarah Mithel Leake of Virginia, that she lost her

[71] *Ibid.*, I (1852), 261.   [72] *Ibid.*, II (1852), 323.

first husband when he fell off the bridge over the Cumberland, and that she was the mother of John Leake Marling,[73] the Nashville journalist and editor. Her poems appeared again and again in the Nashville papers and periodicals and finally, in response to the entreaties of her friends and admirers, she published a collection of her verse under the title of *Clara's Poems*.[74]

Clara was not a poetic genius but she was a pleasing versifier and possessed poetic instincts and interests. What her contemporaries regarded as the better features of her poems, "morality, and a prevailing tone of religious effect," become tiresome today. But Clara was simply one of many southern writers who wrote "with no intention of publishing, but merely to gratify their instincts."[75]

The best and only authentic description of Clara Cole is to be found in one of her own poems entitled "Who is Clara?"

>She's a queer little woman, that dwells in a cot,
>So lowly and simple, that the world knows her not;
>Where the birds sing all day, and the sweet flowers bloom,
>Filling the air with song and perfume,
>And peace seems to brood on her halcyon wings,
>O'er the dear little nest where unnoticed she sings.
>
>She's a sad little woman, though appearing as gay
>As the lark, soaring high at the dawning of day.
>Far up the blue heavens, to gaze on the sun,
>Yet folding her wings ere his bright course is run;
>All drooping and weary she sinks to her nest,
>To hide the keen arrow still deep in her breast.
>
>Yet she's lonely and sad, for death has bereft
>Her home of its jewels—not one now is left
>To wake its lone echoes with music and mirth;
>Like sunbeams they've passed from the beautiful earth,
>Shrouding her spirit in darkness and gloom,
>That the sunlight of heaven alone can illume.

[73] By her first husband.
[74] [Mrs. Clara M. Cole], *Clara's Poems* (Philadelphia, 1861), Preface and Introduction; *Nashville Patriot*, February 11, 1860; Mary Tardy (ed.), *Southland Writers*, 2 vols. (Philadelphia, 1870), II, 718-721; James W. Davidson, *The Living Writers of the South*, 99-100. [75] Edward Ingle, *Southern Sidelights*, 198.

And she sits in her bower, and dreams of the past;
When Twilight's pale shadows around her are cast,
And Zephyrs kiss softly the whispering leaves,
Sweet visions of beauty and gladness she weaves,
In low thrilling numbers, that flow from a heart
Where the world and its follies have never a part.[76]

When Clara Cole first began to write is unknown. Probably her first published poem was "Farewell to Nashville" which was written in St. Louis and printed in the *Nashville Whig* on February 10, 1842. As this early effort is not included in *Clara's Poems* it is reproduced here in its entirety.

FAREWELL TO NASHVILLE

Fair city of the hill, adieu,
    With feeling of regret
Thy fast receding shade I view,
    For how can I forget
The scenes of youthful hope and joy,
    When all seem'd bright and gay,
When not a grief or care arose
    To cloud my life's young day.

Sweet Cumberland! by thee I've stray'd
    And cull'd Spring's earliest flowers,
And on thy verdant banks I've played
    In childhood's happiest hours;
But, ah, no more I'll pensive view
    Thy crystal waters glide;
I go where Mississippi rolls
    Her broad majestic tide

Yet, tho' I wander far from thee
    There is a hallow'd spot
Within my bounds, which ne'er can be
    While Life remains, forgot;
For there in death's dark slumbers rest
    The friends so kind and dear,
Whose memory's shrin'd within my breast,
    With fond religious care.

---

[76] [Cole], *Clara's Poems*, 279.

> But now, when gentle Spring returns,
>   With all her vernal showers,
> Some other hand than mine shall strew
>   Their lowly graves with flowers.
>
> And dear lov'd ones in grief I leave
>   Whose hearts are warm and true,
> And deep the anguish of my soul
>   As I bid them adieu.
> And yet, to soothe each aching heart,
>   A hope divine is given,
> Tho' friends so dear on earth must part,
>   We all can meet in heaven.
>
> And now the last embrace is o'er.
>   The boat hath left the strand,
> And I perhaps shall see no more
>   One of the dear loved band,
> And as I gaze the winding stream
>   Conceals them from my view.
> Ye friends so dear, a long farewell,
>   Home of my youth, adieu.[77]

Dreams have always been considered legitimate foundations on which to build poetic phantasies. Clara Cole used this device and produced a poem which she called "Thanks for the Unfinished Serenade." In addition to the conventional romantic atmosphere the poem contains an attempt at humor, unusual with Mrs. Cole.

> 'Twas midnight—lonely, witching hour!
>   Deep silence reigned profound,
> When o'er my sleeping spirit stole
>   A soft, delicious sound.
>
> 'Twas low and sweet as summer winds
>   Amid the dewey flowers;
> Or like the tinkling melody
>   Of gentle April showers.
>
> Entranced I listened. Fairy forms
>   Seemed floating through my room,
> Diffusing from their starry wings
>   A radiance and perfume.

[77] *Nashville Whig*, February 10, 1842.

> Dissolved in ecstasy, my soul
>   From that sweet dream awoke,
> Just as, alas, with mournful twang,
>   *The fiddle-strings all broke!*[78]

It is often possible, in reading between the lines of her poetry, to reconstruct certain intimate scenes in the life of Clara Cole. Among her souveniers was a lock of brown hair that belonged to a youthful lover who may have been her first husband, Samuel Marling. This tuft of hair was the inspiration for a poem that reflects the pleasure she found in life before tragedy saddened her. She pictures the man she loved—his blue eyes which were as placid as a mountain lake until fired by Clara's emotional embraces. She describes her lover's awakening passion in the following lines.

> But love will mar that quiet sleep,
>   All quivering with delight, where'er
> Soul meets its kindred soul, and wakes
>   The deep volcano slumbering there,
> And leaves with passion-throes the lake,
>   Till all its waves in dimples break.[79]

In smoother verse, Clara expressed a similar reminiscent thought in a poem she composed for the consolation of a man who lost his wife, "Reflection of a Husband on the Miniature of His Wife."

> Oft in my lonely hours, when sadly musing
>   O'er by-gone days of happiness with thee,
> I fondly gaze on this, thy faint resemblance,
>   That, true to life, still seems to smile on me.
>
> But thou art gone, whose love made life so precious,
>   And earth to me a paradise of bliss—
> Thy soft dark eyes no more can beam upon me,
>   Nor thy sweet lips return me kiss for kiss.[80]

[78] [Cole], *Clara's Poems*, 190.
[79] "That Soft Brown Curl," in *ibid.*, 57.
[80] [Cole], *Clara's Poems*, 168. The idea for this poem might have been suggested by Byron's "Lines Written Beneath a Picture."

Occasionally Clara deserts her retrospective mood in order to describe scenes of everyday life. "The Stage Horn" is an example. The opening lines are given below.

> I love to hear the merry stage-horn
> As it comes with its soft mellow tones,
> Borne on the gentle breeze along,
> While mountain and valley re-echo its song
> Of tra-la-lira-lee—
> Oh, the merry stage-horn is dear to me. ·
> What though at a sluggard's pace we creep,
> Our pulses anew will throb and leap,
> And each gallant steed will prick up his ears
> Whenever the merry stage-horn he hears
> Playing tra-la-lira-lira-lee—
> The jolly old stage-horn, wild and free.[81]

The thought and the expression in the following lines leaves the impression that Clara Cole might have become an important figure in southern literature had she developed her poetic instinct.

> Fair queen of night . . .
> With all thy glittering hosts of starry planets,
>   Forever singing one great hymn of love,
> I gaze with wonder on thy glorious beauty,
>   Undimmed by age, still rolling changeless on;
> While countless millions 'neath thy sight have perished,
> Thou art the same as at creation's dawn.[82]

In the twilight of the summer evenings, Clara watched the crimson rays of the sunset fade into the softer light of moonbeams. On such an occasion she received the inspiration for a poem which may be considered as her swan song.

> I know my life is waning—
>   Oh! may it gently close,
> Without murmur or complaining,
>   Like the last sigh of the rose.
> When the silvery cord is loos'ning
>   That bonds my being here,

[81] Ibid., 210-211.   [82] Ibid., 169-170.

> Be thou, my loved and lost one,
>   The white-robed messenger,
> To waft my ransomed spirit
>   Where life's wild storms are past,
> That my song, like the swan's when dying,
>   May be sweetest at the last.[83]

As a poet, Lucy Virginia Smith French (1825-1881), was ranked above Clara Cole by contemporary critics and their judgment in this respect was sound. Lucy Virginia Smith was born in Accomac County, Virginia, in 1825. Her parents, Mease W. and Elizabeth Smith were wealthy and cultured, and Virginia always retained the refinement that she acquired at home in the days of her girlhood. Mease Smith, who was trained in the law, was at one time chancellor of Virginia and eventually became president of Washington College in Virginia.[84]

After the death of her mother, Virginia and her younger sister attended a private school in Washington, Pennsylvania, and graduated there. In the meantime, their father remarried and as the two girls were not happy at home with their step-mother they went to Memphis to teach (1848). Here Virginia's literary career began. Under the pen-name of "L'Inconnue" she began to write for the *Louisville Journal* and in 1852 became the associate editor of the *Southern Ladies Book,* which was published at New Orleans.[85]

The story of her courtship and marriage to Col. Johns Hopkins French of McMinnville, Tennessee, is colored with the romance so often attributed to the South in song and fiction. French, it is claimed, was attracted to Virginia by one of her poems entitled "One or Two." According to the tradition, after reading the poem, French fell in love with Virginia and resolved to ask her to marry him. This seems unlikely as even a romantic gentleman of the Old South would scarcely determine to marry

---

[83] *Ibid.,* 131.
[84] L. Virginia French, *One or Two* (St. Louis, 1883), 11; Sarah G. Bowman, "Lucy Virginia Smith French," in *Dictionary of American Biography,* VII, 25.
[85] French, *One or Two,* 11; Mary Tardy (ed.), *Southland Writers,* II, 688.

a woman he had never seen. It is more logical to believe that they were brought together by a mutual interest in poetry and having once met, soon fell in love and were married.

The marriage, which occurred in 1853, did not put an end to the poet's career. Encouraged by her husband and inspired by the beautiful surroundings of her home near McMinnville, Mrs. French continued to write and from time to time was literary editor of various Atlanta and Nashville journals and was a contributor to *The Parlor Visitor*.[86]

But it would seem that her marriage, while it did not stop her from writing, did tend to limit her production and to prevent the full development of the talent she possessed. "Had she never married," declared Mary Tardy in her *Southland Writers*, "but devoted herself to literature and art, she would assuredly have been eminently successful. But her life is too full of other attractions—home, and home happiness. . . . Her weakness . . . lies not in any lack of power but in a lamentable want of exertion."[87]

An examination of her poems discloses the fact that Virginia French was influenced by Poe, by Byron, and possibly by Bryant. The poem "Leonore," which was included in the 1856 edition of her poems, suggests Poe from the title to the last line. The poem is ragged and inartistic and might have been an expression of Virginia's wit. But whether she intended it to be serious or humorous is of no real consequence as in either case the poem remains a literary curiosity.

> Deeply the midnight knelleth
>   O'er the wold;
> Hoarsely its echo swelleth,
>   Dull and cold,
> Down where a dead heart dwelleth
>   In the mold:
> They wail o'er woes unspoken,
>   And implore

---

[86] French, *One or Two*, 12.
[87] Tardy (ed.), *Southland Writers*, II, 688-689.

> Peace for the lost, heart-broken
>   Leonore!
> Darkly the night-cloud scowleth,
>   Hid from sight—
> Through it the old moon prowleth,
>   Wan and white;
> And the far tempest howleth
>   Round the night.
> Owls high up in the haunted
>   Sycamore
> Echo a name wind-chanted—
>   "Leonore!"
> There folds of darkness rustle
>   Like a pall—
> There, 'mid the reed and thistle,
>   Shadows fall;
> And the rude night-winds whistle
>   Over all,
> Laughing to scorn the faded
>   Days of yore
> They saw thee die degraded,
>   "Leonore!"
> Dread as the fires unholy
>   That scathe and stain,
> The plague-spot sin burned slowly
>   In heart and brain;
> Till the soul's light sank lowly
>   As the stars that wane.
> Ah! Shalt thou be forgiven
>   Nevermore,
> Nor find thy rest in heaven,
>   "Leonore?"[88]

It has been suggested that in "The Iron Horse" Virginia French exhibited her knowledge of Byron. In form it is almost identical with Byron's "The Destruction of Sennacherib" and there is a similarity in phraseology. However, there is no need to press the comparison too far especially since "The Iron Horse" is interesting in itself.

[88] L. Virginia French, *Wind-Whispers* (Philadelphia, 1856), 77-79.

The Iron Horse

From the caverns of art, in the hills of the North,
Sprang a proud-crested charger exultingly forth,
By the spirit of steam was his breathing up-born;
From the strong forest-giants his sinews were torn;
And the gnomes of the mine shouted loud in their ire
O're his iron bound bosom and pulses of fire!

Away! on his mission of power and pride,
As springs the bold eagle the tempest to ride;
Or swift as the bolts of the far-flashing levin,
When the storm is abroad on the dark-rolling heaven;
Down, down on the nations the thunderer came,
With his cold-breathing nostrils and frontlet of flame!

Through the deep-crowded life of the populous mart,
The thick throbbing pulse of the great city's heart,
Where a swarming humanity wavers and reels,
All weary with urging life's fate-driven wheels;
Like a black-bannered monarch from victory won,
The fierce plunging charger dashed haughtily on.

As a spirit of doom by the solitude lone,
Where death sits aloft on his grave-girtled throne;
Where slumbers a silent and shadowy throng,
The dark-bosomed steed came careening along;
And his neigh to the midnight was chillingly dread,
Like the wild-swelling trumpet that rouses the dead.

Where the foam-crested waves in magnificence toss,
The blue ocean armies came sweeping across,
With their banner of darkness abroad on the breeze,
And their war-drum arousing the slumbering seas;
Then, white-winged courser, thy sinews of might
Must be braced for the battle, and strong for the fight.

Hoarse howls the night trumpet; and gathering fast
From their rock-bounded caverns, the king of the blast
Has marshalled his cohorts; yet pale with affright
Are the wild mountain-genii, and feeble their might;
For the horse and his rider—a long gleaming mass—
Through the heart of the mountain triumphantly pass.

> Alone in the desert! Its denizens came—
> Red riders of ruin on whirlwinds of flame,
> The blasting sirocco,[89] the deadly simoom,
> With sand-serried spectres deep-shrouded in gloom;—
> To him they are naught; for his limbs never tire,
> Whose form is of iron, whose spirit is fire![90]

Virginia French's "Great River" indicates that she was familiar with Bryant's works and especially "The Prairies." However, "Great River" is interesting because it represents more exertion than usual on the part of its creator and because it illustrates her ability to handle blank verse.

In considering Clara Cole and Virginia French as creative writers, it is necessary to remember the pleasure their poems gave to their contemporaries. In this respect they made worth-while contributions. Like so many writers of the Old South, neither Mrs. Cole nor Mrs. French sought fame from a literary career but simply wrote spontaneously and with little thought of publication.[91]

Of the two poets, Virginia French reflects more of the life of the time. Her poems are more tangible, and less morbid than Clara Cole's. Neither Mrs. French nor Mrs. Cole mastered the technique of verse writing. Both, as a matter of fact, were more or less indifferent to form technicalities. Clara had only a few themes, and her longing for heaven dominated her work. Virginia French had a wider range, was closer to life, but was influenced by her romantic soul. The shadow of the inevitable conflict did not touch Clara Cole at all but it did influence the later work of Virginia French.

Clara Cole remains somewhat enigmatical. Her poems are tantalizing in the sense that they are suggestive and yet reveal so little. Whether she read Longfellow or Poe or Byron or Simms is unknown. Certainly, there is little in her poetry that suggests the student of literature. Her work is more suggestive of prayer

---

[89] This word suggests Byron. See "Farewell to Malta," second verse. E. H. Coleridge (ed.), *The Works of Lord Byron*, 7 vols. (London, 1904), *Poetry*, III, 24.
[90] French, *Wind-Whispers*, 188-189.   [91] Ingle, *Southern Sidelights*, 197-198.

and meditation, of lavender and old lace, than it is of scholarship. Perhaps, aside from her poetry and her God, Clara's life was but an empty dream.

Clara Cole's son, John Leake Marling (1825-1856), inherited his mother's literary talent and put it to a more practical use. Marling started his journalistic career at the bottom of the ladder as a printer's devil. Owing to unusual talent and ability he rose to be part owner and editor of the *Nashville Daily Gazette* when he was only twenty-five years old.[92]

The new editor made the *Gazette* an independent paper. Consequently during the State Rights Convention held in Nashville in 1850 he felt free to follow his personal convictions and so he denounced the idea of secession voiced by numerous delegates at the convention. His vehement editorials in turn caused the delegates to denounce him and an attempt was made to exclude him from the convention.[93]

In September, 1851, Marling left the *Gazette* to become editor and part owner of the Nashville *Daily Union*. The *Daily Union* was a Democratic paper and so during the presidential campaign of 1852 Marling gave Pierce warm support. But this time his talent for political writing nearly cost him his life. In an attempt to refute certain statements made by Felix Kirk Zollicoffer, the Whig editor of the Nashville *Republican Banner,* Marling wrote an editorial in which he made no attempt to soften his words with subtle innuendoes. Marling called a spade a spade and he virtually called Zollicoffer a liar.

The dramatic climax was inevitable. Before the day was out Zollicoffer met Marling in the street and challenged him to a duel. Both men had been prepared for weeks and there was no necessity for delay. As a result of the shooting Marling received a painful wound in the face and neck but Zollicoffer was only scratched.[94] In 1854, as an anti-climax to the affair, and as a

[92] *Nashville Daily Gazette,* July 30, 1850; Cole, *Clara's Poems,* 301.
[93] *Nashville Daily Gazette,* October 8, November 19, 1850.
[94] *Ibid.,* August 21, 1852; Bond, "Life of Brigadier General Felix Kirk Zollicoffer, C. S. A.," 15. Mrs. Bond, Zollicoffer's Daughter, asserts that her mother knelt at her hearthstone and moulded the bullets that Zollicoffer used in this duel.

reward for his loyalty, President Pierce appointed Marling United States Minister to Guatemala. After two years in the tropics Marling returned to Nashville and died of tuberculosis on October 16, 1856.[95]

As a journalist and editorial writer, Marling deserves to be ranked among the best of his day. His style was clear and forceful and he avoided the flowery phraseology used by so many of his contemporaries. It was unfortunate that he died so young.

In conclusion, one fact above all others is obvious—there was considerable literary activity in Nashville and the city was a part of the world of letters. In domestic and foreign markets Nashville book dealers purchased standard and de luxe editions of classical and popular literature to meet the demands of their customers. On the other hand, journals and books published in Nashville had a wide, if not lucrative, circulation in the Southwest. By 1850 Nashville was recognized as one of the important publishing centers of the nation.

It is difficult to estimate the importance of the literary work created by the writers associated with the Nashville scene. On what basis should this literature be judged? Perhaps it should not be judged as literature at all but simply as historical source material that reflects certain aspects of the Nashville mind and the Southern mind. In any case, its sentimental characteristics need not be considered condemnatory as it is this very feature which definitely places it close to southern life and not aloof from it.

[95] *Nashville Union and American*, July 1, October 17, 1856.

CHAPTER IX

NASHVILLE STREET SCENES, 1850-1860

By 1850 THE Nashville river front section had developed an undesirable quarter called "The Jungle." This district contained cheap saloons, brothels, and hideouts for criminals. However, these "institutions of ill repute" did not receive all their patronage from the lower levels of society. There were times when the gloved hand of the aristocrat held the key to the prostitute's door and there were times when his well-shod feet were caught in the trap of the professional gambler. According to newspaper accounts there were quite a few young men from the better families who sowed wild oats in the jungle. "There are young men in this city," declared the *Republican Banner and Nashville Whig*, "who are in the habit of visiting drinking saloons, gambling houses and houses of prostitution at night, while their parents imagine that they are as far from such places as possible."[1]

The jungle was always a dangerous section for the uninitiated. Not only did it house the painted ladies of the street but it was also the headquarters for card sharks, pickpockets, petty thieves, and confidence men. It was almost impossible for a man to walk through the jungle without being accosted by a woman. One of the newspapers reported the adventure of a man who "was making his humble and unostentatious marks upon the thoroughfare, as he wended his way through the jungle, innocent and unsuspecting. Suddenly his surprised ear was accosted by a female voice, and he saw that the serpent which had tempted his unfortunate relative in the ancestral potato patch, was after him with a sharp stick." He decided, however, to throw himself back on his constitutional rights and resist the siren song of the woman "with a volley of lingual small shot." The entire neigh-

[1] *Republican Banner and Nashville Whig*, November 18, 1858.

borhood was aroused and for this display of his constitutional rights the man was fined thirteen dollars in police court.[2]

Scarcely a night went by that the jungle did not produce some disturbance in the streets. Usually disorderly conduct in public was traced to over-indulgence in hard liquor but there were times when it was due to inherent vulgarity. Sometimes brothel proprietors wrangled with their professional debauchers and it was not uncommon for the latter to drive their employer into the street with a great deal of screaming, scratching, and hair-pulling.[3] After disposing of their employer, the outraged females were apt to return to the house, lock the doors, and spend the night quarreling among themselves.

Not all disturbers of the peace were in the jungle. By 1860 there was a well defined Irish quarter in Nashville, and it did not take much coaxing to involve the sons and daughters of the Emerald Isle in a brawl. This was particularly true with respect to the O'Learys, the Kellers, and the Dwyers who demonstrated more than once that they understood all the fine points of an old-fashioned row as well as the more spectacular street fight. When they were not fighting among themselves the Irish made good citizens, and even organized clubs for social and patriotic purposes. "No people in the world," said the *Republican Banner and Nashville Whig*, "are fuller of the spirit of poetry, song, sentiment, humor and oratory, than the Irish. . . ."[4] But the lyric spirit disappeared like magic when one Irishman called another an English horse.

Impudent free blacks and slaves without passes were a common source of trouble and there were occasions when blacks and whites were involved in a general riot.[5] It was not unknown for legislators to fall off the capitol terrace in the dark and break a leg, or for a nocturnal inebriate to call out a fire company to

[2] *Ibid.*, January 30, 1858.
[3] *Ibid.*, January 2, 1858; *Nashville Daily Gazette*, April 3, 1856.
[4] *Republican Banner and Nashville Whig*, November 9, 1858.
[5] *Ibid.*, June 14, July 7, 1857; October 8, 12, 19, 1858.

extinguish the rising moon.[6] Occasionally a man walked through a plate glass window and sometimes stray cattle did the same thing.[7] The Germans were usually orderly citizens but when they had mixed too many tanglefoot toddies with their beer they could not resist the temptation to stage "a nixcomarouse in the streets."[8] Sometimes the peace was disturbed when some irate person threw stones at the neighbors' children or some children threw sticks at old men sitting unostentatiously in their own front yard. Street fights with knives and pistols were not uncommon and occasionally cold-blooded murder was committed. Duels, especially among men of political and social prominence, were common.

Strangers who visited Nashville in the fifties were impressed by the show of fashion and luxury. On summer evenings the street scenes were especially colorful, for at such times the thoroughfares were crowded with people, some on horseback, some in expensive carriages, some in plain buggies, but all were well dressed. One observer announced: "There is as much fashion here as in New York; and the ladies dress far more than anywhere else I have been."[9]

Horseback riding was considered very fashionable by the ladies and school girls, especially if they were able to dress in a *costume à cheval*.[10] Picnics, old-fashioned barbecues, and excursions into the country were all included in the social whirl of the younger set. Frequently strangers in town saw groups of young people on their way to popular Belle Meade Park to spend the afternoon. The park was described as "a beautiful spot with old forest trees and green grass."[11] At that time the park contained some deer, a buffalo, an elk, and a water-ox.[12]

[6] *Nashville Patriot*, February 10, 23, 1860.
[7] *Nashville Daily Gazette*, November 6, 1858; *Republican Banner and Nashville Whig*, August 11, 1857.   [8] *Ibid.*, January 5, 1858.
[9] Ingraham, *Life and Experiences of a Southern Governess in the Sunny South*, 73.
[10] *Idem.*
[11] *Republican Banner and Nashville Whig*, July 10, 1858.
[12] *Idem.*

The picnic parties usually provided music for their own entertainment. Sometimes there was a complete band, but more frequently a violin or a banjo. The typical picnic supper consisted of ham, sandwiches of various kinds and shapes, pickles, cold chicken, cold broiled pigeons, salad, crackers, and usually a bottle of claret or Scotch ale.[13]

Strawberry festivals were always popular in May and June at the height of the strawberry season. At these parties, frequently given in a garden or on a lawn, gathered the quintessence of Nashville feminine society. And here "in the midst of a great profusion of elegant crinoline, choice blossoms of a thousand hues and the sweet cadence of woman's musical voice, without reference to lavish supplies of strawberries and cream, iced cakes, jellies, and the substantial viands of the epicurean order" gathered the young men representative of Nashville's best families.

One of the favorite pastimes of the young blades was the moonlight or starlight serenade usually dedicated to sweethearts or friends. The serenaders did not always depend on their voices which were likely to become fogged by the night air, but frequently carried with them violin, flute, or banjo. The possibilities of a street serenade were never exhausted. On one occasion, an enterprising group of young gallants not being content with a flute, violin, and clarinet, hired a wagon and added a piano to their open air orchestra. The musical result of this combination of instruments was "soft and sweet enough to have been an angel's whisper."[14] The piano made quite an impression and was taken as an indication of the progressiveness of the age.[15]

It was not only the young ladies who were entertained by street singers and musicians. Prominent business men and newspaper editors were forced to open their eyes in the middle of the night and to listen to a concert in the street or in the back alley. Horn's Brass Band advertised itself in this way. On sev-

---

[13] Ingraham, *Life and Experiences of a Southern Governess in the Sunny South*, 160, 167.
[14] *Republican Banner and Nashville Whig*, July 6, 1858.
[15] *Idem.*

eral occasions, after the city had settled down into its customary midnight calm "the mellow strains of the Band swelled out upon the quiet air unmingled with a ruder sound."[16]

In the winter time the streets were deep in mud and there were days when the city appeared almost deserted except for a few children who braved the inclement weather in order to play hop scotch and roll hoops.[17] Quite frequently in December and January snow fell to a depth of several inches and all those who possessed cutters brought them into use. The musical tinkle of sleigh bells tended to break the monotony of the drab winter days.[18]

The capers of the young social set served the same purpose, and a sleighing party usually terminated at a hotel where warm punch and red wine soon brought a healthy glow to frosted faces. In case the wine failed, more vigorous methods were used to stir up the circulation. It was considered great sport to have the young men climb up the front of the hotel to the second-story porch, there to be rewarded with kisses from the ladies.[19] The popularity of porch-climbing under such conditions can be readily understood when it is remembered that Nashville was famous for its beautiful women. Even Rosenberg, Jenny Lind's husband, who disliked the town, had to admit that its only virtue was to be found, "in the rare beauty of its women. There is, in fact, far more female loveliness in Nashville than you will find in any other city in the union."[20] Other travelers made similar comments.

Styles varied slightly during the decade but a fashionable street dress for winter was usually made of heavy brocaded silk with three-quarter full sleeves trimmed with lace that fell to the wrist. The collar consisted of embroidered muslin and ruffles. A long outer garment called a pelisse was worn over the dress.

[16] *Nashville Patriot,* March 1, 1860.
[17] Bond, "Life of Brigadier General Felix Kirk Zollicoffer, C. S. A.," 12.
[18] *Nashville Daily Gazette,* December 9, 1859.
[19] MacGavock, Diary, February 19, 1858.
[20] Rosenberg, *Jenny Lind in America,* 190.

This outer garment was made of velvet and was generally lined with silk although cheaper garments were made of cheaper materials. The pelisse was trimmed around the bottom with long, heavy fringe. By 1852 a short jacket, or gilet, had been generally accepted. This was worn over the dress and added color as well as comfort. Silk and velvet bonnets of various shapes were popular.[21]

Summer dresses were as light and cool as possible so that a lady might appear as "gauze-like as a dragon-fly."[22] Summer hats were made of imitation lace, straw, and other light-weight materials. Decorations on summer hats were made of straw cleverly woven into imitation leaves, lilacs, roses, hawthorn, lilies of the valley, grasses, and even feathers.[23]

In winter and summer there was considerable visiting and running back and forth between houses. The young women in particular liked to visit their neighbors informally and talk about flowers or household duties. While it is true that they spent many hours indoors reading aloud to a select group of friends, or perhaps sewing or dressing each other's hair, there were many times when they sauntered aimlessly around their neighborhood looking for excitement. Sometimes they visited Old Mack, the Negro cobbler, who taught them how to make shoes. On bright Sunday mornings they went to church pretending not to notice the young men standing under the trees in the church yard. Occasionally there was almost unbearable excitement for a few trusted friends who helped a girl elope. Sometimes the elopements ended in tragedy, but such an unforeseen aftermath had nothing to do with the thrills, the swoonings, the mad dashes to the railroad station or to a secret meeting place in the country.[24]

Christmas eve was always a busy time and the streets and stores were stages for various activities as everyone made preparations for the holiday. Slaves, masters, and housewives were

---

[21] *The South-Western Monthly*, I (1852), 63-64.
[22] *Ibid.*, 125-126.   [23] *Ibid.*, 256-259.
[24] MacGavock, Diary, January 16, 1856; *Memoir of Thomas H. Malone*, 99-100; The Mary E. Hunt Diary, quoted in *Christ Church, Nashville*, 92, 96, 97.

hurrying home with baskets of fruits and confections, oysters, whiskey for eggnogs, fowls, and premium beef. The fireworks shops were scenes of activity, as Christmas without skyrockets was considered a failure by the younger generation.[25] The book stores, too, were well patronized as gift books, joke books, game books, and novels were much in demand. The fashionable barber shops did a fine business as the meticulous gentlemen attempted to glorify themselves for the great day. The shop in the St. Cloud Hotel was favored because it was equipped to give hot and cold baths and "as scientific a shave as can be had on earth."[26]

The erection of the state capitol in Nashville created an interest in architecture and gave the impulse to a building boom that began about 1850. "Within the last two or three years," said the *Nashville Union and American,* "there has been erected a larger number and a better class of buildings both public and private, than within a long series of years previous. The original impulse was most certainly given by the erection of our state capitol."[27] In 1854 the *Republican Banner and Nashville Whig* noticed over a dozen new business blocks which were superior to the buildings of former years "as well in architectural point of view, as in convenience and size."[28]

But in spite of this building boom there were many sections of the city that presented a very plain picture. The river front varied in appearance from a park-like landscape to the gas works and the jungle already mentioned. Certain sections of Front Street (now First Avenue) were given over to wholesale houses, warehouses, and coal and wood yards. Some of the humble laborers such as cart drivers and bar keepers lived on this street and some of the river pilots and boat captains did too. Back from the river and away from the "heart" of the town to the north, south and west were the homes of the middle-class

---

[25] MacGavock, Diary, December 24, 1857.
[26] *Tennessee State Farmer and Mechanic* (Nashville, 1856-?), I (1856), 191.
[27] *Nashville Union and American,* September 16, 1856.
[28] *Republican Banner and Nashville Whig,* January 7, 1854.

citizens. Salesmen, carpenters, tinners, saddle makers, and slave dealers had homes on North Cherry (now Fourth Avenue), North Market (now Second Avenue), and North Summer (now Fifth Avenue). In the opposite direction on South Cherry, South College (now Third Avenue), South Market, and South Summer were the unpretentious homes of clerks, foundry workers, shoemakers, paper hangers, bakers, and some of the bookkeepers who worked at the Southern Methodist Publishing House. Some of the better boarding houses were on South Summer Street and there were respectable rooming houses on Cedar Street not far from Capitol Hill. Westward from Spruce Street (now Eighth Avenue) there were many modest homes, although farther out towards the country, especially on Spring Street (now Church Street), there were some dwellings of more pretentious size.[29]

Many of these middle-class houses were utterly lacking in originality, but some of them reflected the artistic spirit of the owners.[30] Not all the flower gardens were to be found on the premises of the wealthy, as many less pretentious places were made attractive with shrubs, flowers, and vines. One of the most inviting little homes in Nashville was Clara Cole's cottage which had a profusion of flowers in the front yard and vines growing around the doorway.[31]

Most of the "handsome private residences" were either close to the business district or out in what was then the country. In town the best residential section included Summer, High, Vine, and Spruce streets north to Cedar and south to Broad. In this section lived the Foggs, the Zollicoffers, the Polks, the Bowlings, the Walkers, the Kirkmans, the Hills, and other prominent families. Some of these dwellings were typical examples of southern colonial or Greek Revival architecture. Spaciousness and simplicity of line was the chief characteristic. Fluted columns created an impression of dignity and mass, while iron

---

[29] This paragraph is based on information gleaned from Nashville Newspapers and the *Nashville City and Business Directory*, V (1860-1861).
[30] *Nashville Union and American*, September 16, 1856.
[31] *Nashville American*, May 1, 1906.

balconies, covered with honeysuckle, added a touch of the romantic.[32]

Dominating this section of town was the new capitol building on Capitol Hill. In 1844, when the legislature decided to build a new and permanent capitol in Nashville, a committee was appointed to superintend the project. Among other things, this committee, or, to use its official title, Board of Commissioners to Superintend the Construction of the State House, had the task of selecting an architect who could be relied on to produce a structure worthy of Tennessee.[33] As a matter of fact, the selection of the architect was considered the "first and most important step."[34]

After considerable correspondence with reliable persons in northern and eastern cities, the Board of Commissioners decided to offer the position to William Strickland (1787-1854) of Philadelphia at $2,500 a year.[35] Since boyhood, Strickland had liked curves, ornaments, and cupolas, no doubt inheriting his interests and skill from his father, who was a master carpenter. But it takes more than the fundamentals of carpentry to make an architect and Strickland secured the necessary training and inspiration from Benjamin H. Latrobe, the eminent pioneer of the Greek revival in the United States.[36]

By 1844, Strickland was the outstanding architect and engineer in the country. He had designed eighteen famous buildings in Philadelphia, he had placed the distinctive steeple on Independence Hall, he had worked with Latrobe on the capitol building in Washington, he had designed George Washington's

---

[32] *Tennessee State Farmer and Mechanic*, II (1857), 21.
[33] Minutes of the Board of Commissioners to Superintend the Construction of the State House, June 16, 1844 (MS in the archives of the Tennessee Historical Society; typed copy in Tennessee State Library).
[34] Tennessee *Senate Journal*, 26th. Assembly, 1st. Session (1845), Appendix, 52.
[35] Minutes of the Board of Commissioners to Superintend the Construction of the State House, June 16, 1844.
[36] Joseph Jackson, *Early Philadelphia Architects and Engineers* (Philadelphia, 1923), 5 ff.; Thomas E. Tallmadge, *The Story of Architecture in America* (New York, 1927), 113; William Dunlap, *A History of the Rise and Progress of the Arts of Design in the United States*, 3 vols. (Boston, 1918), III, 173, 173 n.

tomb, he had constructed hospitals, canals, gas works, and the Delaware breakwater, and he had visited and studied the outstanding public buildings and many private houses in Europe.[37] The building committee in Nashville was duly impressed with his record. "On all occasions," the committee reported, "he [Strickland] had displayed the utmost good taste."[38]

Strickland arrived in Nashville in May, 1845, and by the twentieth of that month his plans for the capitol were complete. The structure was to consist of a Doric basement, four Ionic porticos, and a Corinthian tower rising from the center of the roof. The tower was a reproduction of the Choragic monument of Lysicrates in Athens and it was considered a unique substitute for the inevitable dome. With respect to the interior, perhaps the most notable feature was the wrought iron spiral stairway in the library, although the heavy bronze and brass chandeliers and the massive, unplastered stone walls attracted attention. With respect to his creation, Strickland made an interesting and diplomatic observation. "There is nothing about the building," he declared, "to offend the taste of a plain and republican but enlightened people."[39]

In view of the final cost of the building, Strickland's estimate seems ridiculously low. According to his figures, based on prices of materials in Nashville in 1845 and on prison labor, the cost should have been about $260,000 plus $20,000 for contingent expenses.[40] Actually the building cost over three times this amount. Up to October 1, 1857, $802,567.59 had been spent. Perhaps the explanation is to be found in delays, labor trouble and strikes, the inefficiency of prison labor, disastrous fires, a tornado, and graft.[41]

Strickland never saw the completed project, as he died on

---

[37] Tennessee *Senate Journal*, 26th. Assembly, 1st. Session (1845), Appendix, 52; Jackson, *Early Philadelphia Architects and Engineers*, 11 ff.
[38] Tennessee *Senate Journal*, 26th. Assembly, 1st. Session (1845), Appendix, 52-53.
[39] *Ibid.*, 53.   [40] *Ibid.*, 56.
[41] Minutes of the Board of Commissioners to Superintend the Construction of the State House, *passim*.

April 1, 1854.[42] He was buried in the walls of the capitol building which he had created. The Board of Commissioners expressed its sympathy by granting Mrs. Strickland the $266 back salary due her husband and by paying the funeral expenses.[43]

The impressive State House on its wind-swept hill was not the only monument Strickland left behind him in Nashville. His influence was felt throughout the city and a number of homes and several churches[44] and public buildings came into existence under the magic touch of his architectural wand. He designed the Acklen house, now a part of Ward-Belmont Junior College, the Elliston home called Burlington which was on the site of the modern Father Ryan High School, and the Kirkman house which was just below the State House on the corner of Summer and Cedar streets. The Acklen house (called Belmont) and Burlington showed an Italian influence. Indeed, it has been claimed that Belmont was a reproduction of an Italian villa. This large house, with its impressive Corinthian columns, was set off by a beautiful formal garden, beds of flowers, marble statues, fountains, and even a small lake to reflect the surrounding loveliness.[45]

The Kirkman house was one of the show places of Nashville and contained many features similar to those in the capitol. White marble mantels, shining wall mirrors, spacious double doors, and paneled high-ceilinged rooms made this home almost regal. Strickland is also credited with the Harry Hill house which was located on a large estate near Vine Street. The most unusual architectural feature of this house was its semi-circular front. The large formal garden was as interesting as the house. It was nearly a city block in size and was marked off with borders of small boxwood trees. The walks were made of white shells which had been brought from New Orleans.[46]

[42] *Republican Banner and Nashville Whig*, April 8, 1854.
[43] Minutes of the Board of Commissioners to Superintend the Construction of the State House, April 20, 1854.   [44] As mentioned in Chapter IV.
[45] Mrs. James E. Caldwell, *Historical and Beautiful Country Homes near Nashville, Tennessee* (Nashville, 1911). The pages are not numbered.
[46] *Nashville Tennessean*, June 15, 1930.

And so the new capitol was more than a building—it was an inspiration. "Who that looks upon it can doubt," asserted the *South-Western Monthly,* "but that it must have the effect of elevating public taste, of begetting, even in crude natures, a love for the beautiful, and thus exerting a silent but powerful influence over the whole region around."[47] Men came and looked upon it and found, perhaps for the first time in their lives, that there are such things as lines of beauty, that strength can be found in pillar and arch, that poetry can be expressed in stone. These men went away thoughtfully, perhaps to carry out in various communities of Tennessee the principles which they had discovered in the shadow of William Strickland's last great public building.

The capitol was symbolic of Nashville's maturing culture. Social processes that had been in evidence since frontier days had at last developed to fruition, and the state house, which was the product of allied arts and sciences and which represented directly or indirectly many forms of human endeavor, became a synthesis of Nashville life. By 1850 Nashville, recognized as an educational center possessing many of the attributes of a cultured society, had been given the title "Athens of the South." By 1860 it was evident that the city deserved the title because its citizens had given proof of their ability to appreciate the cultural things of life and to support essential social institutions. Some of its outstanding citizens made contributions valuable not only to the local community, but to the state and even the nation.

The tragic years of civil war seriously disturbed the threads of Nashville's cultural pattern but the warp and the woof had been woven too firmly to permit destruction. In time, with the coming of more halcyon days, and with the fading of the war psychosis, Nashville became a powerful factor in the renaissance of the New South.

[47] *The South-Western Monthly,* II (1852), 134.

BIBLIOGRAPHY

I. Manuscripts

Bond, Mrs. O. Z. "Life of Brigadier General Felix Kirk Zollicoffer, C. S. A." (MS in Tennessee State Library).

Catalogue of Books Presented to the Library of the University of Nashville by the Late Prof. James Hamilton (MS in Peabody College Library).

Inaugural Dissertations Submitted to the University of Nashville for the Degree of Doctor of Medicine (MSS in Peabody College Library). There are 477 of these essays.

Lindsley, John Berrien. Diary (MS in possession of Miss Louise G. Lindsley, Nashville. Typed copy in Peabody College Library). Portions of the diary are quoted in John Edwin Windrow, *John Berrien Lindsley,* Chapel Hill, 1938.

Lindsley, Philip to Rev. William B. Sprague, February 2, 1848 (MS in Peabody College Library).

MacGavock, Randall W. Diary, October, 1852-January, 1858 (MS in Peabody College Library. Typed copy in Tennessee State Library).

Minutes of the Board of Commissioners to Superintend the Construction of the State House (MS in Tennessee Historical Society Library. Typed copy in Tennessee State Library).

Minutes of the Board of Trustees of Transylvania University, 1817 (MS in Transylvania College Library).

Minutes of the University of Nashville, 1844, 1850, 1855 (MSS in Peabody College Library).

Records of the First Presbyterian Church of Nashville, 1833-1860 (film copies in Vanderbilt University Library. The original manuscripts are preserved in a Nashville bank vault).

Manuscript Describing Nashville in 1823 (in Tennessee Historical Society Library).

II. Government Publications

Annals of Congress, 9th Congress, 1st Sess. (1805-1806), XV, Washington, Gales and Seaton, 1852.

Census Reports of the United States: *Seventh Census of the United States,* Washington, Robert Armstrong, 1853; *Eighth Census of the United States,* Washington, Government Printing Office, 1864.

Safford, James M. *A Geological Reconnoissance of the State of Tennessee,* Nashville, G. C. Torbett and Company, 1856.
———. *Geology of Tennessee,* Nashville, S. C. Mercer, 1869.
Tennessee *Acts,* 1824-1860, Nashville, Publisher varies.
Tennessee Senate Journal, 26th. Assembly, 1st. Session, 1845.
Third Biennial Report upon the Library of the State, Nashville (pamphlet published by the state), 1859.
Troost, Gerard. *Geological Reports* (3 to 9 inclusive), Nashville, Publisher varies, 1835-1848.
Wood, Elvira. *A Critical Summary of Troost's Unpublished Manuscript on the Crinoids of Tennessee,* Washington, Government Printing Office, 1909.

III. Biographies and Memoirs

Barnum, P. T. *Struggles and Triumphs, or Forty Years Recollections,* Buffalo, Warren, Johnson and Company, 1873.
Boles, H. Leo. *Biographical Sketches of Gospel Preachers,* Nashville, Gospel Advocate Company, 1932.
Burnett, J. J. *Sketches of Tennessee's Pioneer Baptist Preachers,* Nashville, Marshall and Bruce Company, 1919.
Coulter, E. Merton. *William G. Brownlow, The Fighting Parson of the Southern Highlands,* Chapel Hill, University of North Carolina Press, 1938.
Davidson, James W. *The Living Writers of the South,* New York, Carlton, 1869.
Drew, John. *My Years on the Stage,* New York, E. P. Dutton and Company, 1922.
Drew, Mrs. John. *Autobiographical Sketch, with an Introduction by Her Son, John Drew, and Biographical Notes by Douglas Taylor,* New York, Charles Scribner's Sons, 1899.
Driver, Leota S. *Fanny Kemble,* Chapel Hill, University of North Carolina Press, 1933.
Fitzgerald, O. F. *John B. McFerrin, A Biography,* Nashville, Publishing House of the Methodist Episcopal Church, South, 1888.
Franklin, Joseph and Headington, J. A. *The Life and Times of Benjamin Franklin,* St. Louis, John Burns, 1879.
Garland, Hamlin. *Roadside Meetings,* New York, The Macmillan Company, 1930.
Green, William Mercer. *Memoir of the Rt. Rev. James Hervey Otey, D.D., LL.D., The First Bishop of Tennessee,* New York, J. Pott and Co., 1885.

Guild, Josephus C. *Old Times in Tennessee, with Historical, Personal, and Political Scraps and Sketches,* Nashville, Tavel, Eastman, and Howell, 1878.
Halsey, L. J. (ed.). *The Works of Philip Lindsley, D.D.,* 3 vols., Philadelphia, J. B. Lippincott and Co., 1866.
Hutton, Lawrence. *Curiosities of the American Stage,* New York, Harpers, 1891.
Ingle, Edward. *Southern Sidelights, a Picture of Social and Economic Life in the South a Generation Before the War,* New York, Thomas Crowell and Co., 1896.
Ingraham, J. H. *Life and Experiences of a Southern Governess in the Sunny South,* New York, G. W. Carlton and Co., 1880.
Jackson, Joseph. *Early Philadelphia Architects and Engineers,* Philadelphia, privately printed by the author, 1923.
Jefferson, Joseph. *Autobiography,* New York, Century Co., 1889.
Ludlow, N. M. *Dramatic Life as I found It,* St. Louis, C. I. Jones and Co., 1875.
Macready, William Charles. *Reminiscences,* New York, Macmillan Co., 1875.
Malone, Thomas H., Memoir of. Nashville, Baud-Ward, 1928.
Matthews, Brander and Hutton, Lawrence. *The Life and Art of Edwin Booth and His Contemporaries,* Boston, L. C. Page and Co., 1886.
Mayhew, Carroll C. *The Life and Times of Rev. Carroll C. Mayhew,* Nashville, S. Stevenson and F. A. Owen, 1857.
Morris, Clara. *Life on the stage, My Personal Experiences and Recollections,* New York, McClure, Phillips Co., 1901.
Nichols, Thomas Lou. *Forty Years of American Life, 1821-1861,* New York, Stackpole Sons, 1937.
O'Daniel, V. F. *The Father of the Church in Tennessee, or the Life, Times, and Character of the Right Reverend Richard Pius Miles, O.P., the First Bishop of Nashville,* Washington, The Dominicana, 1926.
Richardson, Robert (ed.). *Memoirs of Alexander Campbell,* 2 vols., Philadelphia, J. B. Lippincott, 1870.
Rosenberg, C. G. *Jenny Lind in America,* New York, Stringer and Townsend, 1851.
———. *You Have Heard of Them,* New York, Redfield, 1854.
Russell, W. Clark. *Representative Actors,* London, Frederick Warne and Co., n.d.

Russell, William Howard. *My Diary North and South*, Boston, Burnham, 1863.

Scott, Clement. *Drama of Yesterday and Today*, 2 vols., London, Macmillan and Co., Limited, 1899.

Smith, Sol. *Theatrical Management in the West and South*, New York, Harper and Bros., 1868.

Srygley, F. D. (ed.). *Seventy Years in Dixie, Recollections, Sermons, and Sayings of T. W. Caskey and Others*, Nashville, Gospel Advocate Publishing Co., 1891.

Strickland, W. P. (ed.). *Autobiography of Peter Cartwright, the Backwoods Preacher*, Cincinnati and New York, Carlton and Porter, 1856.

Tardy, Mary (ed.). *Southland Writers*, 2 vols., Philadelphia, Claxton, Remsen, and Haffelfinger, 1870.

Thomas, Jane. *Old Days in Nashville*, Nashville, Publishing House of the Methodist Episcopal Church, South, 1897.

Upton, George P. *Musical Memories, My Recollections of Celebrities of the Half Century, 1850-1900*, Chicago, A. C. McClurg and Co., 1908.

Windrow, John Edwin. *John Berrien Lindsley, Educator, Physician, Social Philosopher*, Chapel Hill, University of North Carolina Press, 1938.

Winter, William. *Life and Art of Edwin Booth*, New York, Macmillan Co., 1896.

———. *Shadows of the Stage*, New York, Macmillan Co., 1900.

———. *The Wallet of Time*, 2 vols., New York, Moffat, Yard and Co., 1913.

Wood, William B. *Personal Recollections of the Stage*, Philadelphia, Henry Carey Baird, 1855.

IV. Church Histories and Controversial Literature

Both Sides: A full Investigation of the Charges Preferred Against Elder J. R. Graves by R. B. C. Howell and Others, Nashville, The Spring Street Baptist Church, 1859.

Brown, John T. *Churches of Christ, an Historical, Biographical, and Pictorial History of the Churches of Christ in the United States, Australia, England, and Canada*, Louisville, John P. Norton and Co., 1904.

Brownlow, William G. *The Great Iron Wheel Examined; or its False Spokes Extracted and an Exhibition of Elder Graves, Its Builder*, Nashville, Published for the author, 1856.

Chapman, James L. *Americanism Versus Romanism; or the Cis-Atlantic Battle Between Sam and the Pope,* Nashville, Published for the author, 1856.

Christ Church, Nashville, 1829-1929, Nashville, Marshall and Bruce, 1929.

Constitution of the Young Men's Christian Association, Nashville, by the association, 1857.

Directory of the First Lutheran Church, Nashville, J. W. Patterson, 1926.

Ferguson, J. B. *Spirit Communion: a Record of Communications from the Spirit-Spheres,* Nashville, Union and American Steam Press, 1854.

First Presbyterian Church, Nashville; the Addresses Delivered in Connection with the Observance of the One Hundredth Anniversary, November 8-15, 1914, Nashville, Foster and Parks Co., 1915.

Graves, J. R. *The Great Iron Wheel,* Nashville, Southwestern Publishing House, 1856.

——. *The Watchman's Reply,* Nashville, Graves and Shankland, 1853.

History and True Position of the Church of Christ in Nashville, with an examination of the speculative Theology Recently Introduced from Neologists, Universalists, etc., (a pamphlet), Nashville, Cameron and Fall, 1854.

Jacobs, William S. *Presbyterianism in Nashville,* (a pamphlet), Nashville, n.p., 1904.

McFerrin, John B. *History of Methodism in Tennessee,* 3 vols., Nashville, Southern Methodist Publishing House, 1875.

Noll, Arthur Howard. *History of the Church in the Diocese of Tennessee,* New York, James Pott and Co., 1900. "The church" in the title refers to the Episcopal Church.

Pendleton, J. M. *An Old Landmark Reset,* Nashville, Southwestern Publishing House, 1854.

Spencer, J. H. *A History of Kentucky Baptists from 1769 to 1885,* 2 vols., Cincinnati, J. R. Baumes, [1885].

Sweet, William Warren. *Methodism in American History,* New York, Methodist Book Concern, 1933.

——. *Religion on the American Frontier,* I, *The Baptists, 1783-1830,* New York, Henry Holt and Co., 1931.

——. *Religion on the American Frontier,* II, *The Presbyterians, 1783-1840,* New York and London, Harper and Bros., 1936.

Tewksbury, Donald George. *The Founding of American Colleges and Universities before the Civil War, with Particular Reference to the Religious Influences Bearing upon the College Movement,* New York, Columbia University Press, 1932.

Tomes, Reverend Charles. *An Unfinished Sermon* (a pamphlet), Nashville, Bang, Walker and Co., 1857.

V. DIRECTORIES AND TRAVEL BOOKS

Caldwell, Mrs. James E. *Historical and Beautiful Homes near Nashville, Tennessee,* Nashville, n.p., 1911.

Featherstonhaugh, G. W. *Excursion Through the Slave States, from Washington on the Potomac to the frontier of Mexico,* London, John Murray, 1844.

Foster, Lillian. *Way-Side Glimpses, North and South,* New York, Rudd and Carleton, 1860.

Hall, Frederick. *Letters from the East and from the West,* Washington, F. Taylor and W. M. Morrison, 1840.

[Hoffman, Charles Fenno]. *A Winter in the West,* 2 vols., New York, Harper and Bros., 1835.

Nashville City and Business Directory, (title varies), vols. I-VIII (1853-1872). Publisher varies.

Southern Business Directory and General Commercial Advertiser, vol. I, Charleston, Walker and James, 1854.

VI. LOCAL HISTORIES, ADDRESSES, CATALOGS, AND OTHER SOURCES OF A LOCAL NATURE

Addresses Delivered Before the Medical Classes of the University of Nashville, 1851-1872, Nashville, publisher varies, 1851-1872. Originally published separately, these addresses have been collected and bound together.

Annual Announcement of the University of Nashville, 1851-1910, (title varies), Nashville, published by the university, 1851-1910.

Bell, John. *An Address Delivered at Nashville, October 5, 1830, Being the first Anniversary of the Alumni Society of the University of Nashville,* Nashville, Hunt, Tardiff and Co., 1830.

Caldwell, Sidney S. *A New System of English Grammar, by the Study of Which Youths and Adults May Become Accomplished Grammarians in Three or Four Months Without the Aid of a Teacher,* Nashville, Southern Methodist Publishing House, 1859.

Clayton, W. W. *History of Davidson County, Tennessee, with Illustrations and Biographical Sketches of its Prominent Men and Pioneers,* Philadelphia, J. W. Lewis and Co., 1880.

[Cole, Mrs. Clara Marling]. *Clara's Poems,* Philadelphia, Lippincott and Co., 1861.

Tardis, George. *Description of the Plan, Structure, and Apartments of the State Capitol of Tennessee,* Nashville, G. C. Torbett and Co., 1855.

Eve, Paul F. *A Collection of Remarkable Cases of Surgery,* Philadelphia, Lippincott and Co., 1857.

Ewing, Edwin H. *An Address of the Honorable Edwin H. Ewing at the Celebration of the Centennial Anniversary of the University of Nashville, December 10, 1885,* Nashville, Albert B. Tavel, 1885.

Fogg, Mrs. Francis B. *Barrington's Elements of Natural Science,* Nashville, Graves, Marks and Co., 1858.

French, L. Virginia. *One or Two,* St. Louis, Meriwether Bros., 1883.

———. *Wind-Whispers,* Philadelphia, Lippincott and Co., 1856.

General Laws of the City of Nashville, 1806-1860, 3 vols., Nashville, published by the city, 1860.

Hamer, Philip M. (ed.). *The Centennial History of the Tennessee State Medical Association, 1830-1930,* Nashville, Tennessee State Medical Association, 1930.

Hume, Alfred. *Report on the Subject of Public Schools in the City of Nashville,* Nashville, W. F. Bang and Co., 1852.

Laws of Cumberland College, Nashville, Bang and Co., 1825.

Mulkey, William. *The Orthographical Spelling-Book,* Nashville, Southern Methodist Publishing House, 1856.

Nashville Female Academy, July, 1852 (pamphlet in Tennessee State Library, Nashville).

Nashville Female Academy—Dancing, October 16, 1857 (circular in Tennessee State Library).

Nashville Female Academy, April 2, 1858 (circular in Tennessee State Library).

Nashville Ladies College, First Annual Catalogue (1853).

Owen, Richard. *Key to the Geology of the Globe,* Nashville, Stevensen and Owen, 1857; Philadelphia, Lippincott and Co., 1857.

Poindexter, S. A. *Philological Reader,* Nashville, Richmond, Atlanta, South Western Publishing House, 1861.

Revised Laws of the City of Nashville, 1806-1855, Nashville, Union and American Steam Press, 1854 [sic].

Worrell, A. S. *The Principles of English Grammar,* Nashville, Graves, Marks and Co., 1861.

Wooldridge, John (ed.). *History of Nashville, Tennessee,* Nashville, Publishing House of the Methodist Episcopal Church South, 1890.

VII. Newspapers

(Dates indicate files consulted and do not necessarily indicate complete or unbroken files).

Nashville Whig, 1825-1826; 1838-1849.
Nashville Whig and Banner, 1826.
National Banner and Nashville Whig, 1826-1837.
National Banner and Nashville Daily Advertiser, 1833-1835.
Daily Union (Nashville), 1837-1853.
Republican Banner (Nashville), 1837-1849.
Catholic Advocate, 1840, 1841.
Nashville Christian Advocate (title varies), 1846-1860; also the issue of May 21, 1887.
Tri-Weekly Nashville Union, 1848.
Nashville Daily Gazette (title varies), 1849-1860.
Republican Banner and Nashville Whig, 1849-1860.
Evening Post (New York), August 14, 1851.
Nashville Union and American, 1856-1857.
Nashville Daily News, 1857-1859.
Nashville Patriot, 1856-1860.
The Gospel Advocate (Nashville), September 22, 1870.
Daily American (Nashville), March 20, May 17, 1887.
Nashville American, October 16, 1904; May 1, 1906.
Nashville Tennessean, April 1, 1928; June 15, 1930.
Nashville Banner, September 6, 1931; September 13, 1931.

VIII. Periodicals

American Geologist (Minneapolis, 1888-1905), especially vol. XXXV (1905).
American Journal of Medical Sciences, old series (Philadelphia, 1827-1832), new series (Philadelphia, 1832-1853).
Atlantic Monthly (Boston, 1857—), especially vols. 17 (1866), 20 (1867), 88 (1901).
Barnard's *Journal of Education* (Hartford, 1856-1881), especially vols. XXVII (1877) and XXVIII (1878).
Boston Medical and Surgical Journal (Boston, 1828—), especially vols. XLVI-LIII (1852-1860).
Christian Age (Cincinnati, 1849-1856).
Christian Magazine (Nashville, 1848-1853).
Columbian, The (Nashville, 1918—), especially vol. 8 (1926).
Confederate Veteran (Nashville, 1893-1932), especially vol. XXXII (1924).

BIBLIOGRAPHY

DeBow's Review (New Orleans, 1846-1880).
Ecclesiastic Reformer (Frankfort, Kentucky, 1848-1853?). There is some doubt about the date of the last issue of this periodical.
Guardian; A Family Magazine (Columbia, Tennessee, 1841-1849?). There is some doubt about the date of the last issue of this magazine.
Harpers Magazine (New York, 1850—), especially vol. LXXIX (1889).
Heretic Detector (Middleburg, Ohio, 1837-1841).
Journal of the Academy of Natural Science of Philadelphia (Philadelphia, 1817-1842), especially vols. II-V (1821-1825).
Millennial Harbinger (Bethany, 1830-1870).
Nashville Journal of Medicine and Surgery (Nashville, 1851-1861).
Naturalist, The, and Journal of Natural History, Agriculture, Education, and Literature (Nashville, 1846-1850?). There is some doubt about the date of the final number of this journal.
Parlor Visitor, The (Nashville and Murfreesboro, 1854-1857).
Proceedings of the American Association for the Advancement of Science (Philadelphia, 1848—), especially vol. II (1849).
Science (New York, 1883—), especially vol. LXXVI (1932).
Scribners (New York, 1887—), especially vol. LVII (1915).
Silliman's *American Journal of Science and Arts* (New Haven, 1818—), *passim* and especially vols. XII-XXX (1829-1836).
South Atlantic Quarterly (Durham, 1902—), especially vol. XXI (1922).
Southern Baptist Review and Eclectic (Nashville, 1855-1861?). There is some doubt about the date of the last issue. It should be noted, too, that there is a slight variation in the title.
Southern Lady's Companion (Nashville, 1847-1854).
Southern Literary Messenger (Richmond, 1834-1864), especially vol. XXIX (1857).
South Western Literary Journal and Monthly Review (Nashville, 1844-?). It is difficult to determine the span of dates for this rare periodical. Volume I seems to have consisted of six numbers that appeared during 1844 and 1845.
South-Western Monthly, The, A Journal Devoted to Literature and Science, Education, the Mechanic Arts and Agriculture (Nashville, 1852). Only two volumes were issued, both in 1852.
Tennessee State Farmer and Mechanic (Nashville, 1856-?).
Tennessee Historical Magazine (Nashville, 1915—).

Transactions of the American Ethnological Society (New York, 1845-1853).
Transactions of the American Medical Association (Philadelphia, 1848-1882).
Transactions of the Geology Society of Pennsylvania (Philadelphia, 1834-1835).
Western Journal of Medicine and Surgery (Louisville, 1840-1855).

IX. Periodical Literature and Newspaper Articles of Special Interest

Anderson, Douglas. "Negro Slavery and the White Man's Genius. A Reply to Northern Criticisms of the South's Place in American Literature and History," in *Nashville American*, October 16, 1904. See also Anderson's scrapbook, Nashville Carnegie Library.
"Assumption, Pioneer Parish of North Nashville," in *The Columbian* (Nashville, 1918—), VIII (1926), 1.
"Ball Room Belles," in *The Parlor Visitor* (Nashville and Murfreesboro, 1854-1857), II (1854), 18.
Bell, Mrs. Bennett D. "Female Schools in Tennessee Prior to 1861," in *Confederate Veteran* (Nashville, 1893-1932), XXXII (1924), 171.
Clapp, Henry Austin. "Reminiscences of a Dramatic Critic," in *Atlantic Monthly* (Boston, 1857—), LXXXVIII (1901), 155-165, 344-354, 490-501, 622-634.
Cooke, J. C. "Memories of Days of Long Ago Recalled," in *Nashville Banner*, September 6, 1931; September 13, 1931.
[DeBow, J. B. D.]. "American Literature—Northern and Southern," in *DeBow's Review* (New Orleans, 1846-1880), XXIV (1858), 173-177.
Dow, Chalmers T. "Paul Fitzsimmons Eve, M.D.," in *Transactions of the American Medical Association* (Philadelphia, 1848-1882), XXIX (1878), 641-646.
"Dr. Cartwright on the Caucasians and the Africans," in *DeBow's Review*, XXV (1858), 45-56.
"Dr. Cottrell's Letter," in *Nashville Christian Advocate*, May 21, 1887.
Eve, Paul F. "An Introductory Lecture, Delivered in the Medical College of Georgia, November 5, 1849," partly quoted in *American Journal of the Medical Sciences*, new series (Philadelphia, 1832-1853) XIX (1850), 471-474.
———. "On Asiatic Cholera Morbus," in *American Journal of the Medical Sciences*, old series (Philadelphia, 1827-1832), X (1832), 524-526.

———. "Report of the Surgical Clinic for the First Week of the Preliminary Lectures in the Nashville University," in Nashville Journal of Medicine and Surgery (Nashville, 1851-1861), VII (1854), 449-552.

———. "Report of Twenty-Five Cases of Urinary Calculus," in *American Journal of Medical Sciences,* new series, XXIV (1852), 41-53.

Fairchild, Herman L. "Earth Rotation and River Erosion," in *Science* (New York, 1883—), LXXVI (1932), 423-424.

Fitzgerald, O. P. "Dr. McFerrin as a Man," in Nashville *Daily American,* May 17, 1887.

Glen, L. C. "Gerard Troost," in *American Geologist* (Minneapolis, 1888-1905), XXXV (1905), 35-89.

Heriott, Edwin. "Education at the South," in *DeBow's Review,* XXI (1856), 650-659.

Hopkins, B. S. "Cold Water in Surgery," in *Nashville Journal of Medicine and Surgery,* VIII (1855), 270-272.

Hunt, Douglas L. "The Nashville Theatre, 1830-1840," in Birmingham-Southern College Bulletin (Birmingham), XXVIII (1935).

Hutton, Lawrence. "The Negro on the Stage," in *Harpers* Magazine (New York, 1850—), LXXIX (1889), 131-145.

Jones, B. W. P. "The Theatre and the Dance," in the *Parlor Visitor* (Nashville and Murfreesboro, 1854-1857), VI (1856), 45.

McFerrin, John B. "Valedictory," in *Nashville Christian Advocate,* July 1, 1858.

McTyeire, Bishop. "Sermon at the Funeral of Dr. McFerrin," in *Nashville Christian Advocate,* May 21, 1887.

Marshall, C. R. "Southern Authors—School Books and Presses," quoted in *DeBow's Review,* XXL (1856), 520.

Matthews, Brander. "The Rise and Fall of Negro Minstrelsy," in *Scribners* (New York, 1887—), LVII (1915), 754-759.

Moore, J. Quitman. "American Letters," in *DeBow's Review,* XXVIII (1860), 657-667.

Nevin, Robert T. "Stephen C. Foster and Negro Minstrelsy," in *Atlantic Monthly,* XX (1867), 608-616.

Pendleton, J. M. "A Plea for Thorough Female Education," in *The Southern Baptist Review and Eclectic* (Nashville, 1855-1861?), II (1856), 369-384.

"Report of the General Conference of 1858," in *Nashville Christian Advocate,* June 10, 1858.

Rooker, Henry Grady. "A Sketch of the Life and Work of Dr. Gerard Troost," in *Tennessee Historical Magazine* (Nashville, 1915—), series II, vol. III (1932), 3-19.

Stedman, E. C. "Edwin Booth," in *Atlantic Monthly,* XVII (1866), 585-595.

Tandy, Jeannette Reid. "Pro-Slavery Propaganda in American Fiction of the Fifties," in *South Atlantic Quarterly* (Durham, 1902—), XXI (1922), 170-178.

Troost, Gerard. "Account of the Pyroxene of the United States and Descriptions of Some New Varieties of the Yessite of Rhode Island, and Several Other American Minerals," in *Journal of the Academy of Natural Science of Philadelphia* (Philadelphia, 1817-1842), II (1821), 222-224.

———. "An Account of Some Ancient Remains in Tennessee," in *Transactions of the American Ethnological Society* (New York, 1845-1853), I (1845), 355-365.

———. "Description of a New Crystalline Form of Apophyllite, Laummite, and Amphibole, and a Variety of Pearlstone," in *Journal of the Academy of Natural Science of Philadelphia,* V (1825), 51-56.

———. "Description of a New Crystalline Form of Quartz," in *Journal of the Academy of Natural Science of Philadelphia,* II (1821), 212-214.

———. "Description of a New Form of the Andalusite," in *Journal of the Academy of Natural Science of Philadelphia,* IV (1824), 122-123.

———. "Description of a New Species of Fossil Asterias," in *Transactions of the Geological Society of Pennsylvania* (Philadelphia, 1834-1835), I (1834), 224-231.

———. "Description of Some New Crystalline Forms of Minerals of the United States," in *Journal of the Academy of Natural Science of Philadelphia,* II (1821), 55-58.

———. "Observations on the Zinc Ores of Franklin and Sterling, Sussex County, New Jersey," in *Journal of the Academy of Natural Science of Philadelphia,* IV (1824), 220-231.

——— and Lessieur, "On Calamine, Cobalt and the Lead Ores of Missouri," in Silliman's *American Journal of Science and Arts* (New Haven, 1818—), XII (1829), 376-378.

———. "On the Localities in Tennessee in Which Bones of the Gigantic Mastodon and Megalonyx Jeffersonii are Found," in *Transactions of the Geological Society of Pennsylvania,* I (1834), 139-146; 236-243.

———. "On the Pentremites Reinwardtii, a New Fossil," in *Transactions of the Geological Society of Pennsylvania,* I (1834), 224-231.

Windrow, J. E. "Collins D. Elliott and the Nashville Female Academy," in *Tennessee Historical Magazine,* ser. II, vol. III (1932), 74-106.

X. Reference Books and Special Works of a Miscellaneous Nature

Appleton's Cyclopedia of American Biography, 8 vols., New York, D. Appleton and Co., 1887-1889.

Coleridge, E. H. (ed.). *The Works of Lord Byron,* 7 vols. (London, 1904), *Poetry,* vol. III.

Dictionary of American Biography, 20 vols., New York, 1928-1938.

Dunlap, William. *A History of the American Theatre,* New York, J. and J. Harper, 1832.

———. *A History of the Rise and Progress of the Arts of Design in the United States,* 3 vols., Boston, Goodspeed's Book Shop, 1918.

Faust, Albert Bernhardt. *The German Element in the United States,* 2 vols., Boston and New York, Houghton Mifflin and Co., 1909.

Flint, Timothy. *The History and Geology of the Mississippi Valley,* Cincinnati, E. H. Flint and L. R. Lincoln, 1832.

Gaines, Francis Pendleton. *The Southern Plantation, A Study in the Development and Accuracy of a Tradition,* New York, Columbia University Press, 1924.

Grove's Dictionary of Music and Musicians, 6 vols., New York, The Macmillan Co., 1927-1928.

Harlow, Alvin F. *Old Towpaths, The Story of the American Canal Era,* New York and London, D. Appleton and Co., 1926.

Hornblow, Arthur. *A History of the Theatre in America from Its Beginnings to the Present Time,* 2 vols., Philadelphia and London, Lippincott and Co., 1919.

Martens, Frederick H. *A Thousand and One Nights of the Opera,* New York and London, D. Appleton and Co., 1926.

Murdock, James E. *Analytic Elocution,* New York, Van Antwerp, Bragg and Co., 1884.

———. *A Plea for the Spoken Language,* Cincinnati and New York, Van Antwerp, Bragg and Co., 1883.

Nelson's Perpetual Loose-Leaf Encyclopaedia, New York, Thomas Nelson and Sons, 1921.

Nott, Josiah Clark and Gliddon, George R. *Types of Mankind,* Philadelphia, Lippincott and Co., 1857.

Quinn, A. H. *A History of the American Drama from the Beginning to the Civil War,* New York, Harper and Brothers, 1923.

Rous, Samuel H. *The Victrola Book of the Opera,* Camden, 1917.

Sprague, William B. (ed.). *Annals of the American Pulpit; or Commemorative Notices of Distinguished American Clergymen of Various Denominations,* 8 vols., New York, C. Carter and Brothers, 1857-1869.

Tallmadge, Thomas E. *The Story of Architecture in America,* New York, W. W. Norton and Co., 1927.

Wittke, Carl. *Tambo and Bones; A History of the American Minstrel Stage,* Durham, Duke University Press, 1930.

INDEX

Academies, Nashville Female Academy, mentioned, 1; students at, 9; prosperity of, in 1850, 41; buildings, 42; curriculum, 42-44; dancing controversy, 44-45; amusements at, 46; Nashville Male Academy, curriculum, 50; Nashville Female Institute, founded, 50; Miss Coleman's School, 50; Miss Nichols' School, 50; Alfred Hume's School, 50; Bishop Miles' School, 50, 110, 111; Academy of St. Cecelia, 50; William Ferrel's School, 50, 51, 52; students at Female Academy give concerts, 161. *See also* Schools.

Adrienne the Actress, popular play, Eliza Logan fails in, 128-129; Jean Davenport stars in, 128-129; original translator of, 131

Alabama, Methodist circuits in, 86

Alarmo, Carolina, opera singer, 142

American Medical Association, Paul Eve, President of, 58; convention in Nashville, 167

Amsterdam, Troost teaches pharmacy in, 21. *See also* Troost, Gerard.

Amusements, at Female Academy, 46; horseback riding, 201; picnics, 201-202; barbecues, 201; strawberry festivals, 202; serenades, 202-203; sleighing parties, 203; fireworks, 205. *See also* Music, Nashville, Opera, Tableaux, Theater, Variety shows.

Architecture, new buildings, mentioned, 1; Cathedral of Seven Dolors, 110-111; influence of Capitol, 205, 210; building boom, 205-206; middle class homes, 206; Greek Revival, 206-207; William Strickland, designs Capitol, 207-209; designs homes, 209; Capitol a symbol of Nashville culture, 210

Arditi, Signor Luigi, opera conductor, 139-142

Aunt Phillis' Cabin, reply to *Uncle Tom's Cabin*, 177

Baptists, mentioned, 84; gentleman's agreement with Presbyterians, 89; first Nashville church, 92; early schism, 92; R. B. C. Howell saves first church, 92; Howell-Graves controversy, 92, 99-100; Pedobaptists criticised, 96. *See also* Graves, J. R., and Howell, R. B. C.

Barnum, P. T., manages Jenny Lind, 145-146, 148; sells concert tickets, 146; donation to orphans, 146; members of party in row, 147; visits Hermitage, 149; mentioned, 154, 155. *See also* Lind, Jenny.

Barrymores, mentioned, 135

Basking Ridge, New Jersey, Philip Lindsley attends school at, 3

Beggars. *See* Nashville.

Bell, John, criticises frontier characteristics, 13; promotes education, 13-14

Belle Meade Park, mentioned, 201

Bennett, James Gordon, as character in play *Victoria*, 124

Bernard, William Boyle, playwright, 120

Berrys Book Store, 171

Bitting, C. C., director of Nashville Female Institute, 50

Blackburn, Gideon, establishes first Presbyterian church, 90

Bleeding. *See* Medical therapy.

Booth, Edwin, mentioned, 118; depends on local stock companies, 120-121, 137; sketch of, 135; opens in Nashville, 135; becomes famous Hamlet, 136-137; presents Hamlet in Nashville, 137; approved minstrels, 154. *See also* Hamlet, Theater.

Booth, J. B., mentioned, 125

Boucicault, Dion, playwright, influence of on American drama, 125

Bowling, Dr. W. K., praises Lindsley and Troost, 2-3; mentioned, 56; as editor of *Nashville Journal of Medicine*, 57; early career, 57; against quacks, 59-61; on consumption, 67; on bleeding, 68; helps found medical school, 83

Briggs, W. T., mentioned, 56

Brothels, 199-200

Bryant, W. C., mentioned, 193, 196

Buchanan, Dr. A. H., mentioned, 56

[225]

INDEX

Burke, Charles, comedian, 123-124; introduces *Rip Van Winkle* and *People's Lawyer*, 124; praised by press, 125

Byron, Lord, his play *Werner* produced, 126; influence in Nashville, 174; mentioned, 194, 196

Caldwell, Sidney, writes grammar, 178, 180

Campbell, Alexander, mentioned, 92; describes Ferguson's doctrine as revolutionary, 103; appeals for support, 104; aided by Benjamin Franklin, 106; goes to Nashville, 106; weakens Ferguson's position, 107

Cartwright, Peter, describes educated ministers, 17 n.

Catholics, criticised by Protestant press, 108; embarrassed by Know Nothings, 108; schools condemned, 108; Chapman's *Americanism Versus Romanism*, 108-109; Bishop Miles, 109-112. See also Miles, Richard.

Channing, W. E., sends spirit message, 106

Chapman, James L., writes anti-Catholic propaganda, 108

Charities, 36, 111, 160, 161, 162, 163, 165

Cherokees, taught Methodism, 86

Chestnut Street Theatre, Philadelphia, mentioned, 132

Christmas Eve, busy time in Nashville, 204-205

Church, Samuel, opposes J. B. Ferguson, 104

Circus, competition with theater, 27-28; with minstrels, 154

Clarke, Conrad, mentioned, 126

Clay, Henry, interested in John Todd Edgar, 91

Clothes. See Dress.

Cole, Clara, Nashville poet, 186; writes "Who is Clara," 187; "Farewell to Nashville," 188-189; "Thanks for the Unfinished Serenade," 189-190; describes lover's passion, 190; writes "Reflection of a Husband on the Miniature of His Wife," 190; "The Stage Horn," 191; "Fair Queen of Night," 191; swan song, 191-192; compared to Virginia French, 192, 196-197; John L. Marling, her son, 197; lives in vine-covered cottage, 206

Colleges, Nashville Ladies College, founded, 47; Shelby Medical College, founded, 48; faculty, 48; buildings and equipment, 48; care of paupers, 49; Carney's Nashville Commercial College, founded, 49; Southern Commercial College, founded, 49; Nashville Commercial College, founded, 50; courses at, 50

Commercial colleges. See Colleges.

Cooper, J. F., mentioned, 176

Cowel, Joe, comedian, 128

Cowper, William, mentioned, 174

Crichfield, Arthur, editor, 101

Criminals, 199, 201

Crisp, Mrs. William, mentioned, 138

Crisp, William, manages Gaiety Theater, 134; opens theater club room, 134; remodels Gaiety, 137-138; abolished theater saloon, 144

Cross, Nathaniel, mentioned, 50

Cross, N. D., mentioned, 50

Cumberland College. See University of Nashville; Lindsley, Philip.

Currier, C. M., mentioned, 156

Cushman, Charlotte, mentioned, 118; described, 121-122; influenced by William Macready, 122; as Lady Macbeth, 122-123; as Romeo and as Rosalind, 123; appears at Gaiety, 123; described as genius, 123; mentioned, 134

Cushman, Robert, mentioned, 122

Dancing, bran dance, 28; ballroom dances of forties, 28-29; church opposition to, 28, 44, 165, 173; holiday balls, 29, 166; as popular amusement, 164-165; dance benefits, 165; dancing school parties, 166; grand ball in court house, 167; in capitol for American Medical Association, 167; sponsored by military clubs, 167-168

Darwin, Charles, mentioned, 75, 82

D'Augri, Elena, concert singer, 150

Davenport, Jean, in *Adrienne the Actress*, 128-129, 131; as translator, 131; supreme in role of Julia, 132; introduces *Camille*, 139. See also Logan, Eliza; Rachelle; Theater.

Davis, Joel, theater manager, 130; becomes unpopular, 130, 132, 133-134; mentioned, 138

Dean, Julia, appears in Nashville, 121; as Juliet, 125; in *The Duke's Wages*, 125; mentioned, 134

INDEX

DeBow, J. D. B., and *DeBow's Review*, 173, 175, 176
DeVries, Rosa, prima donna, 141, 142
Dew, Thomas, social philosopher, 176-177
DeWilhorst, Madame, star of Strakosch's Concert Company, 152
Dickenson, G. K., harpist, 156
Dickinson, C. C., heads stock company, 128
Disciples of Christ, split from Baptists, 92; Church of Christ of Nashville, progress of, 100-102; factional strife in, 102-107
Disease. *See* Doctors, Medical therapy.
Doctors, in Nashville at early date, 8; create medical school, 33; competition with quacks, 59; knew little about disease, 66-67, 70; judged in light of times, 82
Donniker, J. B., with minstrels, 156
Dress, at costume balls, 29; at theater, 143; hoops, 143; street dress, 203-204; summer dress, 204
Drew, John, mentioned, 118; biographical sketch, 132; in Nashville, 132-133; mentioned, 135
Drew, Louisa Lane, actress, theatrical manager, 132-133
Dumas, Alexander, his *Mademoiselle de Belle-Isle* adapted by Fanny Kemble, 125

Eastman, Mrs. M. H., writes *Aunt Phillis' Cabin*, 177
Edgar, John Todd, early career, 90; takes Nashville church, 90; reasons for success, 90; his theology, 91-92
Education. *See* Academies, Colleges, Schools.
Eggers, Herman, Lutheran pastor, 114
Elliott, C. D., principal of Nashville Female Academy, 44-45; in dancing controversy, 44; mentioned, 46
Emerson, R. W., his *English Traits* mentioned, 176
Ennis, R. E., with minstrels, 156
Episcopalians, organize congregation, 112; James Tomes, pastor, 112
Eve, Paul F., prominent surgeon, goes abroad for equipment, 35; medical education, 57; and Medical College of Georgia, 57; teaches at Louisville, 57; reputation, 58; president American Medical Association, 58; character, 58-59; against quacks, 59-61; removes uterus, 61; as lithotomist, 61; operates before students, 61; tumor operation described, 62-64; on cholera, 67; on hygiene, 74; place in medical history, 82-83

Fairchild, Herman L., comments on Ferrel's Law, 32
Family Ties, a play, 123
Ferguson, Hannah, mentioned, 100
Ferguson, Jesse B., writes for *Heretic Detector*, 100-101; called to Church of Christ, Nashville, 101; personality, 101-102; builds new church, 101-102; doctrinal views, 102-103; controversy with Campbell, 102, 103-107; a spiritualist, 107; as wandering preacher, 107; criticises circus and theater, 144
Ferguson, Robert, mentioned, 100
Ferrel, William, early career, 50-51; writes "On the Hypothesis of the Internal Fluidity of the Earth," 51; creates Ferrel's Law, 51; becomes editor, 51; invents tide machine, 52; Ferrel's work evaluated, 52
Field, J. M., actor, dramatist, 123-124; writes *Victoria*, literary curiosity, 124
Field, Mrs. J. M., mentioned, 123
Finley, Robert, influences Philip Lindsley, 3
Fitzhugh, George, social philosopher, 176-177
Flint, Timothy, quoted, 8
Fogg, Mrs. Frances B., writes science text, 178, 179
Forrest, Edwin, mentioned, 127
Foster, Lillian, comments on schools, 54
Foster, Stephen, and minstrels, 158-159
Franklin, Benjamin, edits *Christian Age*, 106; in Ferguson controversy, 106
French, John, mentioned, 192
French, Virginia, early life, 192; courtship, 192-193; influenced by Poe, 193-194; writes "Iron Horse," 194-196; "Great River," 196; compared to Clara Cole, 192, 196-197
Frontier, spirit of, hindrance to education, 2; restless nature of, 6; frontier tradition defined, 9-10; frontier and Philip Lindsley, 12-20; religion on, 16-19; frontier mind, 30; disappearing in Nashville, 84

Gamblers, 199-200
Games. *See* Amusements.
Georgia, Anti-Mission Baptists in, 18

INDEX

Germans, build church, 111-112; Lutherans establish Tennessee Synod, 114; and music festivals, 162-163; and St. Valentine's Day, 166; disturb the peace, 201
Gliddon, George B., co-author of *Types of Mankind*, 75 ff. *See also* Medical therapy.
Gougenheim, Joey, in *Hidden Hand*, 138-139
Graham, Richard, actor, mentioned, 123
Graham's Magazine, and Poe, 176; circulation in Tennessee, 176
Graves, James Robertson, early career, 92-93; pastor of Central Baptist Church, 93; as editor, 93; his theology, 93-97; writes *Great Iron Wheeel*, 95; describes Methodist revival, 95-96; controversy with R. B. C. Howell, 97 ff.; church trial, 99-100. *See also* Howell, R. B. C., Baptists.
Graves, Lois, mentioned, 92
Graves, Zuinglius, mentioned, 92
Gray, Thomas, mentioned, 174
Griffin, James L., on pneumonia, 69. *See also* Medical therapy.
Guthrie, Samuel, discovers chloroform, 64

Hamlet, Murdock production of, 130; Booth production of, 136-137. *See also* Booth, Edwin; Murdock, James.
Hampden, Walter, mentioned, 136
Hany, René Just, mentioned, 21
Henkle, M. M., as editor, 181
Holmes, Oliver W., mentioned, 176
Hospitals, 36, 48
Hotels, mentioned, 1; Jackson Hotel, 8; increase prices for Jenny Lind's troupe, 147, 199; serve wine for sleighing parties, 203; St. Cloud's barber shop, 205
Houses. *See* Architecture.
Howard, G. C., mentioned, 123
Howard, Mrs. G. C., mentioned, 123
Howard, Robert, character in *People's Lawyer*, 124
Howell, Robert B. C., saves Baptist church, 92; controversy with J. R. Graves, 92; career of, 98; summons Graves to trial, 98. *See also* Baptists, Graves, J. R.
Hume, Alfred, studies schools of East, 52; his report, 52-53; "Father of Nashville Schools," 54
Hume, William, 89
Hunchback, popular comedy, stars Eliza Logan, 127; role of Julia in, 131-132.
See also Davenport, Jean; Kemble, Fanny; Logan, Eliza.
Hunt, William G., on cultural processes, 13-14
Hutton, Lawrence, evaluates minstrels, 153
Hygiene. *See* Eve, Paul; Medical therapy.

Ince, Annett, actress, mentioned, 128
Irish, disturb peace, 200; and lyric spirit, 200
Irving, Washington, mentioned, 176
Iser, Alexander, Rabbi, 114

Jackson, Andrew, mentioned, 85
Jameson, George, actor, mentioned, 128
Jefferson, Joseph, mentioned, 135; and minstrels, 154
Jenkins, W., Lutheran pastor, 114
Jennings, Dr. T. R., 56
Jews, organize church in Nashville, 114-115
Jones, B. W. P., denounces theater, 144, 184
Jones, Robert, writes *Hidden Hand*, 138
Journals. *See* Magazines.
"Jungle," on river front, 199-200

Kemble, Fanny, writes *Duke's Wages*, 125
Kene, C., with minstrels, 156
Kennedy, J. P., mentioned, 176
Kentucky, Anti-Mission Baptists in, 18; mentioned, 97
Kimpel, George, directs comic opera, 150
Knowles, J. Sheridan, writes *Hunchback*, 127
Know Nothings, stage riot, 108
Knoxville, population, 1850, 2n.

Lady of Lyons, popular melodrama, 124, 125
Lapsley, R. A., and female education, 47
Latrobe, Benjamin, 207
Leake, John, mentioned, 186
Libraries, 170-173; in Capitol, 172-173
Lind, Jenny, mentioned, 135; in Nashville, 145-149; "Jenny Lind Fever," 145; managed by Barnum, 145-146, 148; personal appearance, 147. *See also* Barnum, P. T.
Lindsley, Isaac, 3
Lindsley, John Berrien, inherits interest in education, 21, 33; influenced by Gerard Troost, 21, 27; reorganizes literary de-

partment, 32; dean of medical school, 33, 83; trip abroad, 35; at Ladies College, 47; mentioned, 56, 57
Lindsley, Phebe, 3
Lindsley, Philip, mentioned, 2; praised by Dr. Bowling, 3; early life, 3-4; president Cumberland College (University of Nashville), 4 ff.; arrives in Nashville, 5; his description of Tennessee, 5-6; and frontier tradition, 9-10, 12-20; plans great university, 10-12; and student regulations, 11-12; reasons for resignation, 19-20, 32; influence of, 20-21, 31, 32, 54
Literature, influence of, 169; southern press before Civil War, 169; in libraries, 170-173; novel reading, 173-174; northern literature, 175-176; plantation fiction, 177; text books, 178-181; magazine contributions, 181-184; southern literature, 185; Nashville poetry, 186-187; value of, in Nashville, 198
Litton, E. L., actor, mentioned, 128
Logan, Eliza, receives ovation, 121; described, 121-122; in *London Assurance*, 125; mentioned, 126; in *Hunchback*, 127; fails in *Adrienne the Actress*, 128-129, 131; mentioned, 134. See also Davenport, Jean; Rachelle.
London Assurance, successful play, 125
Long, Crawford W., and ether, 64
Longfellow, H. W., mentioned, 176
Lucia di Lammermoor, puzzles Nashville audience, 140-141. See also Opera.
Lutherans, establish church, 114

McFerrin, James, mentioned, 85
McFerrin, John B., opposes dancing, 44; born on frontier, 85; joins Methodists, 85; early career, 85-86; as editor, 86-87; as director of publishing house, 87-88; as preacher, 88; as controversialist, 88; as author, 89; criticises Catholic schools, 108
M'Gavock, Felix Grundy, on anaesthesia, 65
Macready, Mrs. William, dramatic reader, 161
Macready, William, and Charlotte Cushman, 122
Magazines, in Nashville, mentioned, 1-2; *Nashville Journal of Medicine and Surgery*, 57, 59-61; *Tennessee Baptist*, 93; *Southern Baptist Review and Eclectic*, 93; *Christian Magazine*, 101, 144; *Parlor Visitor*, 144, 170, 173-174, 184; listed in state library, 173; *Southern Literary Messenger*, 175; *De Bow's Review*, 176; *Southern Lady's Companion*, 181-184; *South-Western Monthly*, 185-186
Manners, in church, 7; in theater, 143-144; drunkenness, 144, 200-201; at dances, 167-168; in streets, 203, 204
Marling, John L., as editor, 122; dramatic critic, 122-123, 125, 128, 148; as journalist, 197-198; duel with Felix Zollicoffer, 197-198
Martineau, Harriett, and "water cure," 74
Mathews, John Charles, on theology in medicine, 65-66
Matthews, Brander, evaluates minstrels, 153
May, Dr. John Frederick, at Shelby Medical College, 48
Medical School of the University of Nashville, Lindsley's prophecy of, 10, 32; founded, 33-35; equipment, 35-36; faculty, 56; dissertations of students at, 69 ff.; aware of race differences, 75 ff.; sponsors ball, 167
Medical therapy, study of, at University of Nashville, 37; therapeutics behind surgery, 61; anaesthetics, 64-65; place of God in medicine, 65-66; bleeding, 67-68; pneumonia, 68-70; typhoid, 70-73; cold water cure, 73-74; hygiene, 74-75; medicine and racial differences, 75-82
Meigs, Dr. Charles D., teaches Paul Eve, 57
Memphis, population of, in 1859, 2 n.
Methodists, early activity in Nashville, 84-85; and John B. McFerrin, 85-89; controversy with Baptists, 95-96. See also McFerrin, John B.
Miles, Nicholas, 109
Miles, Richard, early career, 109; becomes Bishop of Nashville, 109; organizes diocese, 110-111; builds cathedral, 110; builds church for Germans, 111-112
Military organizations, for social purposes, 167-168
Milton, John, mentioned, 174
Minstrels, various troupes in Nashville, 154; Mat Peel's Campbell Minstrels, 154-156; and sectionalism, 157; and panic of 1857, 157; introduce Foster's songs, 158-159
Mobile Theatre Company, mentioned, 123
Morton, W. G. T., and ether, 64
Mulkey, William, writes spelling book, 178, 180-181

INDEX

Murdock, James, mentioned, 118; depends on local stock companies, 120-121; as Hamlet, 130; mentioned, 134; as Othello, 138

Murfreesboro, population of, in 1850, 2 n.

Music, interest in, 29-30, 117; Jenny Lind's concerts, 145-149; Ole Bull and Patti, 149-150; comic opera, 150; instrumentalists, 150-151; Strakosch's Concert Company, 151-152; Swiss Bell Ringers, 152; Variety shows, 152-153; minstrels, draw material from slaves, 153-154; at peak of popularity, 155-157; Stephen Foster's songs, 158-159; amateur concerts, 160-163; benefits, 161; Schiller Music Festival, 162-163

Nashville, in 1850, 1-2; influence of Philip Lindsley and Gerard Troost, 2-3; beggars in, 6-7; early institutions, 7-9; social life in, 27-31, 143-144, 160-168, 201 ff.; negative force of frontier mind in, 30; fame as educational center, 32; public schools, 52-55; religious denominations in, 84 ff.; interest of people in theater, 117-139; opera in, 139-143; concerts in, 145-152; variety shows, 152-153; minstrels, 153-159; German influence in, 162-163; military clubs in, 167-168; libraries in, 170-173; publications in, 174-198; slum district in, 199-200; beautiful women in, 203; homes, public buildings, 206 ff.; effect of Civil War on, 210

Nashville and Northwestern Railroad, buys Bishop Miles' property, 111

Nashville Blues, military club, 167-168

Nashville Female Academy. *See* Academies.

Nashville Horticultural Society, maintains botanical garden, 1

Neafie, J. A., actor, appears in *Mahommed;* disliked, 127

Negroes, racial features of, discussed by medical students, 75 ff.; in drama, 129, 138; in theater, 143; in minstrels, 153-154; in literature, 177, 179; as criminals, 200-201. *See also* Medical therapy, Minstrels, Theater.

Newcomb, W. W., with minstrels, 156

Newspapers, in Nashville, mentioned, 1; John L. Marling and *Nashville Daily Gazette, Daily Union,* 197

Norma, musical score of, appeals to Nashville audience, 141. *See also* Opera.

Nott, Josiah Clark, co-author of *Types of Mankind,* 75 ff.; mentioned, 179. *See also* Medical therapy.

Novels, an obsession, 173; criticised by press, 174; English novels in Nashville, 174

Ohio University, mentioned, 4

Old Mark, Negro cobbler, 204

Ole Bull, violin virtuoso, 149-150

Opera, relation to drama, 139; Arditi's Opera first in Nashville, 139-142; *Lucia di Lammermoor,* 139-141; *Norma,* 141; Norma's prayer to moon, 141-142; New Orleans Opera Troupe, 142; Parodi's Opera Company, 142-143

Oregon, a play, 123

O'Reilly, Mrs. Mary, mentioned, 21

Otey, James, 112

Otis, Charles, hero in *People's Lawyer,* 124

Owen, Richard, writes geology textbook, 178, 179-180

Owens, Robert, mentioned, 22, 180

Parley, Peter, textbook writer, 178

Parlor Visitor, 144, 170, 173-174, 184

Parodi, Teresa, prima donna, 142, 151

Patti, Adelina, child prodigy, 149-150

Peacock, L. H., on hygiene, 74

Peel, Mat. *See* Minstrels.

Peel, T. J., mentioned, 156

Pendleton, J. M., editor, 93; and J. R. Graves, 97; publishes *Old Landmark Reset,* 97, 97 n.

People's Lawyer, popular play, 124

Plantation fiction, 177-178

Pneumonia. *See* Medical therapy.

Poe, Edgar Allan, works read in Nashville, 176; mentioned, 183, 193

Poetry, in *Southern Lady's Companion,* 184; in *South-Western Monthly,* 185-186. *See also* Cole, Clara; French, Virginia.

Poindexter, S. A., publishes textbook, 178, 180

Pope, Mrs. Coleman, heads stock company, 126-127

Porter, Robert M., dies of blood poisoning, 56

Presbyterians, mentioned, 84; gentleman's agreement with Baptists, 89; organize church, 89-90; influence of John Todd

INDEX

Edgar, 90-92; condemn dancing, 165. See also Edgar, John Todd.
Princeton (College of New Jersey), influence on Philip Lindsley, 3-4
Prostitutes, 199-200

Quacks. See Eve, Paul; Doctors.

Rachelle (Elizabeth Felix), French actress, 128, 128 n. See also Davenport, Jean; Logan, Eliza.
Recreation. See Amusements.
Religion, on frontier, 16-19, 84; Presbyterians support education, 16-17; early Methodists, Baptists, not interested in education, 17-18, 17 n.; Anti-Mission Baptists unprogressive, 18; role in American life, 84; denominations in Nashville, 84; Baptists and Presbyterians agree on activity, 89; Baptist controversies, 93-100; Disciples of Christ, 92, 100-107; Catholics, 107-112; Episcopalians, 112-114; Lutherans, 114; Jews, 114-115; religious leaders evaluated, 116; conflicts with dancing, 44, 144, 165, 173
Richardson, Dr. John W., and difficulties of physicians, 67
Rip Van Winkle. See Burke, Charles.
Roberts, J. B., actor, 125, 126, 127; as Richard the Third, 127
Robertson Association, welfare club, 160-161
Rock City Guards, military club, 167-168
Rumsey, H. S., with minstrels, 156
Rush, Benjamin, mentioned, 41

Schools, private, mentioned, 1, 50; public, mentioned, 1; Alfred Hume and Nashville system, 52-54; dancing schools, 166-167. See also Academies.
Science. See Eve, Paul; Ferrel, William; Medical therapy; Troost, Gerard.
Sectionalism, in twenties, 19; in connection with medical school, 34; effects medical students, 75 ff.; in dramatics, 129; in minstrels, 157; in literature, 169, 175-178, 179, 185-186, 196, 197
Shelby Medical College, 48-49
Shingle, Solon, character in *People's Lawyer,* 124
Simms, W. G., mentioned, 176
Simpson, Sir, James Y., and chloroform, 64

Sisters of Charity, arrive in Nashville, 36; establish school, 50, 110
Smith, Le Grand, mentioned, 146 n., 147
Smith, Samuel Stanhope, mentioned, 4
Southern Lady's Companion, 181-184
Southern Literary Messenger, 175, 176
South-Western Monthly, 185-186
Southworth, Emma, novelist, 138, 138 n., 177
Sports. See Amusements.
Stevenson, James, mentioned, 4
Stowe, Harriet Beecher, as "Dame Stowe,' 129, 177
Strakosch Concert Company, program of, 152
Street scenes, in summer, 201; fashion in, 201; serenades, 202-203; street dress, 203-204; houses and buildings, 205 ff.
Strickland, Mrs. William, mentioned, 209
Strickland, William, mentioned, 91, 111; builds Capitol, 207-209; designs homes, 209
Stuart, St. Maur, dancing teacher, 166-167
Students. See Academies, Medical therapy, Schools.
Swiss Bell Ringers, 152

Tableaux, 163-164
Talbot, J. Boyde, on typhoid fever, 71. See also Medical therapy.
Tardy, Mary, quoted, 193
Telegraph, mentioned, 1
Tennesseans, and cock fights, 9; prejudiced against colleges, 15; majority Baptists, Methodists, 17; objected to Philip Lindsley, 19; become geology conscious, 27; *Parlor Visitor,* moral guide for, 184
Tennessee, frontier condition in 1825, 10; pioneer leaders in, 12; undesirables in, 12-13; public lands and education, 14-15; pneumonia in, 69; typhoid in, 70; Methodist circuit in, 84, 86; Catholics in minority, 107; Lutherans in, 114; literature in, 169; poets in, mentioned, 174; *Graham's Magazine* in, 176; State Capitol, 207 ff.
Thalberg, Sigismund, pianist, 150-151
Theater, new theater, mentioned, 1; before 1820, 8; precarious existence before 1850, 27-28, 118; index to cultural level, 117; in nineteenth century, 117-118; Adelphi Company chartered, 118; Adelphi described, 119; initial season, 119-121; Shakespearean plays presented, 120-

123, 125-127, 130, 135-137; Eliza Logan compared to Charlotte Cushman, 121-122; extravaganzas, 126; improved stock company, 127-128; *Old Plantation, or the Real Uncle Tom,* 129; Adelphi becomes Nashville Theatre, 130; Joel Davis regime, 130-134; Jean Davenport and the Drews, 131-133; William Crisp changes name of theater to Gaiety, 134; panic of 1857 and box office, 134; Edwin Booth, 135-137; burlesque, 138-139; *Camille* introduced, 139; audiences of 1850, 1860, 143; Jenny Lind, 147; minstrels, 154-159; amateur dramatics, 160; tableaux, 163-164
Tomes, James, early career, 112; becomes Episcopalian minister, 112; contributions in Nashville, 112-114
Torriani, Angelo, opera conductor, 142
Transylvania University, mentioned, 4, 4 n.
Troost, Anna, mentioned, 21
Troost, Everhard, mentioned, 21
Troost, Gerard, mentioned, 2; praised by Dr. Bowling, 3; well known in Europe and America, 21; early scientific work in America, 21-22; teaches at University of Nashville, 22; as state geologist, 23 ff.; his hobbies, 26; work evaluated, 26-27, 31; zoological collection, 35
Typhoid. *See* Medical therapy.

Uncle Tom's Cabin, 129, 177
University of Nashville, mentioned, 1; Philip Lindsley as president, 4 ff.; as Cumberland College made little progress, 9; reorganized under Philip Lindsley, 9-12; students at, 11-12; Cumberland College becomes University of Nashville, 12; importance of, 20, 32; reorganized by John B. Lindsley, 32 ff. *See also* Lindsley, John Berrien; Lindsley, Philip.
Urso, Camille, violinist, 161-162

Variety shows, 152-153
Vieutemps, Henry, violinist, 150-151

Waller, John L., leader of Kentucky Baptists, 97
Washington, George, birthday of, 166
Watson, Dr. J. M., mentioned, 56; on chloroform, 64; on Darwin, 82
Webster, Noah, defines "slave," 178
Werner, Abraham Gottlob, mentioned, 21
Whitman, Walt, quoted, 148
Wilhorst, Madame de, 152
Wilson, Samuel T., influences Richard Miles, 109
Winston, Dr. C. K., on materials for hospitals, 35; mentioned, 56
Wood, Elvira, writes critical summary of Troost's unpublished manuscript, 25
Woodworth, Samuel, playwright, 125
Worrell, A. S., writes textbook, 178

Yandell, L. P., mentioned, 8 n.
Y. M. C. A. organized, 115-116

Zollicoffer, Felix, in duel with John Marling, 197-198

www.ingramcontent.com/pod-product-compliance
Lightning Source LLC
Chambersburg PA
CBHW021401290426
44108CB00010B/328